Chomsky's Universal Grammar

Second Edition

Chomsky's Universal Grammar
An Introduction

SECOND EDITION

Vivian Cook and Mark Newson

BLACKWELL
Publishers

Copyright © Vivian J. Cook, 1996

The right of Vivian J. Cook to be identified as author of this work has been asserted in accordance with the Copyright, Designs and Patents Act 1988.

First published 1988
Reprinted 1989 (twice), 1991, 1992, 1993, 1994, 1995
Second edition 1996
2 4 6 8 10 9 7 5 3 1

Blackwell Publishers Ltd
108 Cowley Road
Oxford OX4 1JF
UK

Blackwell Publishers Inc.
238 Main Street
Cambridge, Massachusetts 02142
USA

British Library Cataloguing in Publication Data

A CIP catalogue record for this book is available from the British Library.

Library of Congress Cataloging-in-Publication Data
Cook, V. J. (Vivian James), 1940–
    Chomsky's universal grammar / Vivian J. Cook and Mark Newson. — 2nd [updated] ed.
        p.   cm.
    Includes bibliographical references (p.) and index.
    ISBN 0–631–19796–6. — ISBN 0–631–19556–4 (pbk.)
    1. Chomsky, Noam.   2. Grammar, Comparative and general.
3. Generative grammar.   4. Principles and parameters (Linguistics)
5. Government-binding theory (Linguistics)   6. Language acquisition.
7. Minimalist theory (Linguistics)   I. Newson, Mark.   II. Title.
P85.C47C66 1996
415—dc20   95–30630
                                                                              CIP

Typeset in 10 on 12 pt Palatino
by Graphicraft Typesetters Ltd, Hong Kong
Printed in Great Britain by T.J. Press Ltd, Padstow, Cornwall

This book is printed on acid-free paper

Contents

Preface to the Second Edition

The first edition of this book essentially covered the mid-1980s version of Chomsky's Universal Grammar theory. The second edition bases itself on the work of the later 1980s from *Barriers* (Chomsky, 1986) onwards and includes some of the later developments in the Minimalist Programme (Chomsky, 1993, 1995b). Hence it was necessary to bring in a co-author who could speak with authority on this later work.

As usual the writing would not have been possible but for the background inspiration of Keith Jarrett, Sidney Bechet and Ornette Coleman, and for the e-mail bridge between authors living in Budapest and Colchester. We would also particularly like to thank Michael Hegarty and Huba Bartos for comments on drafts of chapter 9.

1

The Nature of Universal Grammar

This chapter will discuss the following topics:

— Structure-dependency
— The head parameter
— The Projection Principle
— General ideas of language
— Types of universals
— The language faculty
— Principles and rules.

The aim of this book is to convey why Chomsky's theory of language is stimulating and adventurous and why it has important consequences for all those working with language. The goals of the theory are to describe language as a property of the human mind and to explain how it is acquired. To achieve these goals, it establishes an apparatus of considerable complexity. Though the specific proposals put forward are not necessarily correct, the theory provides a unified framework within which they may be tested.

This book is intended chiefly as an introduction for those who want to have a broad overview of the theory with sufficient detail to see how its main concepts work, rather than for those who are specialist students of syntax, for whom technical introductions such as Haegeman (1994) and Ouhalla (1994) are more appropriate. Nor does it cover Chomsky's political views, an account of which can be found in Salkie (1990).

The central concept is **Universal Grammar (UG)**: 'the system of principles, conditions, and rules that are elements or properties of all human languages . . . the essence of human language' (Chomsky, 1976, p. 29). All human beings share part of their knowledge of language;

UG is their common possession regardless of which language they speak. While within the tradition of Chomsky's thinking since the 1950s, the current theory couches UG in terms of the specific proposals advanced in Chomsky's writings of the 1980s and 1990s. This was first known as **Government/Binding (GB)** theory after *Lectures on Government and Binding* (Chomsky, 1981a); it was developed further in publications such as *Knowledge of Language* (Chomsky, 1986a) and *Barriers* (Chomsky, 1986b).

The term **principles and parameters theory** has, however, become more popular in recent years as it conveys the unique central claim of the theory that language knowledge consists of principles universal to all languages and parameters that vary from one language to another; this term will therefore be used here, with some modification in chapter 9. The combination of Universal Grammar with principles and parameters theory inevitably leads to a complex overall theory involving several sub-theories, but at the same time it creates a new simplicity: knowledge of language comes down to variations in a small number of properties.

UG is a theory of knowledge, not of behaviour; its concern is with the internal structure of the human mind. The nature of this knowledge is inseparable from the problem of how it is acquired; a proposal for the nature of language knowledge necessitates an explanation of how such knowledge came into being. UG theory holds that the speaker knows a set of principles that apply to all languages, and parameters that vary within clearly defined limits from one language to another. Acquiring language means learning how these principles apply to a particular language and which value is appropriate for each parameter. Each principle or parameter of language that is proposed is a substantive claim about the mind of the speaker and about the nature of language acquisition. UG theory is not making vague or unverifiable suggestions about properties of the mind but precise statements based on specific evidence. The general concepts of the theory are inextricably connected with the specific details; the importance of UG theory is its attempt to integrate grammar, mind and language at every moment.

The aims of linguistics are often summarized by Chomsky in the form of three questions, for example in Chomsky (1991a):

1 *What constitutes knowledge of language?* The linguist's prime duty is to describe what people know about language – whatever it is that they have in their minds when they know English or French or any language, or, as we see later more precisely, a grammar.

2   *How is such knowledge acquired?* A second aim is to discover how people acquire this knowledge. Studying acquisition of language knowledge means first establishing what the knowledge that is acquired actually consists of, i.e. on first answering question (1).

3   *How is such knowledge put to use?* A third aim is to see how people use this acquired language knowledge. Again, investigating how knowledge is used depends on first establishing what knowledge *is*.

Sometimes a fourth question is added, as in Chomsky (1988, p. 3):

4   *What are the physical mechanisms that serve as the material basis for this system of knowledge and for the use of this knowledge?* There must be some physical correlate to this mental knowledge, in other words some link between mind and brain. Though our understanding of the physical basis for memory is now advancing, for example Rose (1992), Chomsky (1988, p. 6) calls this question 'a relatively new one, in fact one that is still on the horizon'. It will not be tackled in this book.

One or two conventions followed in this book need briefly stating. As usual in linguistics books, an asterisk indicates an ungrammatical sentence; example sentences and phrases are numbered for ease of reference, i.e.:

1.   *That John left early seemed.

While much of the discussion is based around English for convenience, the UG theory gains its power by being applied to many languages. Indeed, since the early 1980s there has been a vast proliferation in the languages studied, in particular the Romance languages and Japanese, which will be drawn on when possible. However, sentences are used in this book as examples of particular syntactic issues rather than necessarily being based on complete analyses of the languages in question. A quick reference list of principles and parameters mentioned in the book is provided on pages 345–9.

Structure-dependency

To give an immediate idea of UG, let us look at the specific principle of **structure-dependency**. Since at least Chomsky (1971) this principle has been used to introduce the idea of principles; in later chapters it will be subsumed under more complex ideas. Structure-dependency asserts that knowledge of language relies on the structural relationships in the sentence rather than on the sequence of words. To understand it, we need first to establish the concept of phrase structure within which these structural relationships take place.

A major assumption in linguistics since the 1930s has been that sentences consist of phrases – structural groupings of words: sentences have **phrase structure.** Thus the **sentence (S)**:

2.   The child drew an elephant.

breaks up into a **Noun Phrase (NP)** *the child*, and a **Verb Phrase (VP)** *drew an elephant*; the VP in turn breaks up into a **Verb (V)** *drew* and a further Noun Phrase *an elephant*.

3.

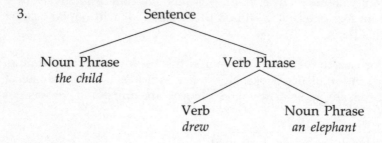

These phrases also break up into smaller constituents; the NP *the child* consists of a **Determiner (Det** or **D)** *the* and a **Noun (N)** *child*, while the NP *an elephant* consists of a Determiner *an* and a Noun *elephant*.

4.

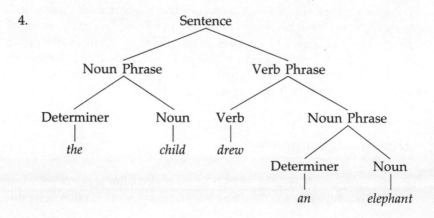

The phrase structure analysis of the sentence breaks it up into smaller and smaller constituents. A sentence is not just a string of words in a linear sequence but is structured into phrases, all of which connect together to make up the whole.

Phrase structure can be represented in several ways. One form of representation that will be frequently used here is the **tree diagram**. As we have just seen, this lays out the structure of the sentence in a graphic way, similar to family trees. Alternatively, phrase structure may be represented by putting pairs of square brackets around each constituent (**labelled bracketting**) as in:

5. [s [NP The child] [VP drew [NP an elephant]]]

This represents the same analysis as the tree; it is less cumbersome for some purposes than tree diagrams and will be used from time to time here.

One of Chomsky's first influential innovations in linguistics was a third form of representation called a **rewrite rule** (Chomsky, 1957), seen in:

S ⟶ NP VP
VP ⟶ V NP

In this the 'rewrite' arrow '⟶' can be taken to mean 'consists of'. The rules mean exactly the same as the tree or as the bracketted form of the sentence, namely that the Sentence (S) 'consists of' a Noun Phrase (NP) and a Verb Phrase (VP), and the VP 'consists of' a V and an NP. Once more this form of representation in no way changes the analysis. It is less often used today, for reasons we shall see later in this chapter.

The principle of structure-dependency can now be introduced through the relationship of active and passive sentences in English. The traditional analysis of the passive used in language teaching, for example Bosewitz (1987, p. 193), sees passive sentences as formed from active sentences by moving various elements of the sentence around. The passive sentence:

6. Barnes was fired by the manager.

is taken to be related to the active sentence:

7. The manager fired Barnes.

through movement of various elements. The object *Barnes* in the active sentence moves to be the subject of the passive; the active subject *the manager* moves after the Verb in the passive and gains a Preposition *by* (thus becoming a **Prepositional Phrase (PP)**); and the Verb changes from the active form *fired* to the passive form *was fired*. The passive auxiliary *be* is also inserted.

The manager fired Barnes.

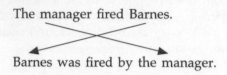

Barnes was fired by the manager.

The principles and parameters analysis proper of passives, to be developed in chapter 6, resembles this traditional account in describing certain aspects of the passive in terms of movement. Restricting the discussion to the movement of the subject, the analysis sees *Barnes* as moving from an underlying object position in the VP after the Verb *fire* to a subject position at the beginning of the sentence:

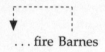

. . . fire Barnes

Passives are formed by movement of the object to subject position – and of course by other factors we shall not go into for the moment.

But what is actually moved? One possibility is that it is the word that occurs in a particular place in the sentence, say the fourth word:

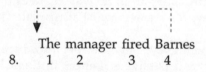

    The manager fired Barnes
8.   1   2   3   4

But this would not work for other passive sentences. For example, if the Prepositional Phrase *on Tuesday* came in the sentence:

9.   On Tuesday the manager fired Barnes.
     1   2   3   4   5   6

moving the fourth word (and changing the Verb form) yields a nonsense passive:

10.   *Manager on Tuesday the was fired Barnes.

English passives do not depend on moving the fourth word, or the fifth word, or indeed any word in a particular numbered place in the sequence of the sentence. The rule that states how to make passives is not just a matter of counting words in a linear sequence.

Nor is it accurate to say that what is moved is a *word*. Let us expand the active sentence slightly to get:

11. The manager fired the player.

Moving a single word (and assuming the other relevant changes) will not yield a passive sentence, whether moving the Determiner:

12. *The was fired player by the manager.

or the Noun:

13. *Player was fired the by the manager.

It is not the word that moves but the *phrase*; forming a passive means moving the object Noun Phrase to the beginning of the sentence, whether the phrase consists of a single word such as *Barnes*, or two words such as *the player*, or as many words as you like, as in, say:

14. The player who once played for England and used to appear in TV commercials for soft drinks was fired by the manager.

We now need to take in other types of English sentence. Take a question like:

15. Will the manager fire Barnes?

This can be seen as derived by movement from another structure, i.e.:

The manager will fire Barnes

It is not simply the third word that moves, otherwise:

16. On Tuesday the manager will fire Barnes.

would become:

17.   *The on Tuesday manager will fire Barnes?

But it is still not enough to specify the kind of word or phrase that moves, whether the auxiliary or something else. Let us illustrate this by combining questions with relative clauses. The sentence:

18.   The manager who will fire Barnes will succeed.

gives us a choice of two auxiliaries *will*. But only one of these can move to get a question. Every English speaker knows that the correct question is:

19.   Will the manager who will fire Barnes succeed?

not:

20.   *Will the manager who fire Barnes will succeed?

The only auxiliary that can be moved is the *will* in the main clause *the manager will succeed*, not the one in the relative clause *who will fire*, that is to say, the auxiliary *will* occurring in a particular place in the structure of the sentence.

This introduces the major aspect of the principle of structure-dependency: movement in the sentence is not just a matter of recognizing phrases and then of moving them around but of moving the *right* element in the *right* phrase: movement depends on the structure of the sentence. The *will* which moves is the one directly within the main clause, not the one within the relative clause; it plays a particular role in the structure of the sentence. The movement involved in the formation of English questions is the central example of structure-dependency used in Chomsky's writings. Chomsky, for example, contrasts:

21.   Is the man who is here tall?

with:

22.   *Is the man who here is tall?

as evidence for the claim that 'the rules of language do not consider simple linear order but are structure-dependent . . .' (Chomsky, 1988, p. 45).

Similarly in:

23. The manager fired Barnes.

it is the object NP within the VP that moves to get the passive:

24. Barnes was fired by the manager.

as we see by the impossibility of making the passive:

25. *President was elected John.

out of the active:

26. They elected John President.

by choosing another NP to move instead of the direct object as in:

27. John was elected President.

In order to know which element of the sentence to move, one has to know its underlying structure. The element that can be moved to subject position in the passive is the object NP from the VP in its entirety; what may be moved in the question is the auxiliary verb *is* from the main clause VP. Only if the speaker knows the structure of the sentence can the right part of the sentence be moved. English passive sentences and questions cannot be formed without knowing something about phrase structure. Simple counting of the first, second, or nth word does not work. It is the structure that matters. In other words, the rules for English passives and questions are structure-dependent, not based on the linear order of elements.

Structure-dependency also affects the interpretation of sentences. Take the sentence:

28. John says that the manager will fire him.

An English speaker knows that *him* can refer to the same person as *John* – the manager is firing John – but cannot refer to the manager. But in the sentence:

29. John says that the manager will fire himself.

a native speaker is equally sure that the reflexive *himself* refers to the manager, odd as the meaning may be. The knowledge that accounts for this is highly complex, as we shall see in chapter 2. But, simply put, the reflexive *himself* must refer to someone mentioned within the same part of the sentence *the manager will fire himself*; the pronoun *him* on the other hand must refer to someone who is *not* mentioned in the same part of the sentence but who may either be mentioned in the other clause *John says that* . . . or may not be mentioned directly at all (i.e. it might refer to somebody already established from the context, such as *Barnes*). In other words, interpreting who *him* and *himself* refer to depends on our knowledge of the clause structure of the sentence – knowing which is the relevant part of the clause and which is not: the rule is structure-dependent.

Since structure-dependency seems to apply to several types of rule, the generalization can be advanced that English itself is a structure-dependent language: the principle of structure-dependency applies to all the types of structure found in English. Any speaker of English knows structure-dependency.

But the same seems to apply to other languages. Equivalent sentences in German also demonstrate structure-dependency. In the passive sentence:

30. Hans wurde von Marie gesehen.
     (Hans was   by Mary seen)
     Hans was seen by Mary.

it is the object NP *Hans* that moves to the subject position, not the fifth word or any other numbered word or any other NP that might be in the sentence: the German passive rules are structure-dependent. In the question:

31. Wurde Hans von Marie gesehen?
     (was   Hans by Mary seen?)
     Was Hans seen by Mary?

the auxiliary *wurde* has moved from the Verb Phrase to precede the subject: German question rules are structure-dependent. In the French sentence:

32. Pierre dit que Jean se   regarde dans la glace.
     (Peter says that John himself looks at in   the mirror)
     Peter says John looks at himself in the mirror.

the interpretation that *se* refers to *Jean*, not to *Pierre*, depends on the knowledge that *Jean se regarde dans la glace* is a main clause. Not only English but also French and German have structure-dependent rules.

Or indeed Greek, as in the passive:

33.   o   giatros didachtike Aglika apo ton Peter.
(the doctor was taught English by   Peter)
The doctor was taught English by Peter.

where *o giatros* has moved from later in the sentence. Or Spanish questions, as in Chomsky (1988, p. 42):

34.   Está el   hombre, que está contento, en la casa?
(Is   the man,   who is   happy,   at home?)
Is the man who is happy at home?

where *esta* (is) has moved from the main clause VP, not the relative clause VP. Or Arabic:

35.   qala Ahmed ?anna zaydun qatala nafsahu
(said Ahmed that   Zaid   killed himself)
Ahmed said that Zaid killed himself.

where the pronoun *nafsahu* must refer to the same person as *Zaid* within the same clause. None of these languages permits movement or interpretation to rely on the linear order of words alone; all require a knowledge of the sentence structure. When describing passives, questions and reflexives in English, French, Greek, German or Arabic, it is not necessary to state that every instance is structure-dependent. Instead the generalization can be made that the rules in each of these languages are structure-dependent. Of course, like any scientific hypothesis, later evidence from other languages may tell us that this is wrong.

Structure-dependency can therefore be put forward as a universal principle of language: whenever elements of the sentence are moved to form passives, questions, or whatever, such movement takes account of the structural relationships of the sentence rather than the linear order of words; 'all known formal operations in the grammar of English, or of any other language, are structure-dependent' (Chomsky, 1971, p. 30). An important insight into the nature of human language will be missed if structure-dependency is treated as a feature of a particular language. Instead it seems that the principle of structure-dependency is used in *all* languages. Any human being who knows any language therefore includes the principle of structure-dependency within their knowledge of language.

Why should this be the case? As human beings it seems perfectly obvious to us that this is what language is like; how could it be any other way? But there is no logical necessity for a language to be structure-dependent. Computers find no particular problems in dealing with structure-independent movement, for instance, by reversing the order of the sentence to get a question so that, say, 123 order becomes 321 order. The sentence:

36.   John is tall.
          1   2   3

could become:

37.   *Tall is John?
          3   2   1

Yet no human language works like this; it is never the linear order alone that is changed but the order of structural elements. Structure-dependency is a discovery about the nature of human language; it is a property of human language in general, a principle of Universal Grammar.

The important aspects of language knowledge are not those that are true of one individual language alone but those that are true of *all* languages; to show the internal structure of the mind, the grammar must reflect properties of all minds, rather than just those that happen to know English or French. Chomsky has always seen linguistics as developing by making deeper accounts of human language in general rather than accounts of particular languages; 'Real progress in linguistics consists in the discovery that certain features of given languages can be reduced to universal properties of language, and explained in terms of these deeper aspects of linguistic form' (Chomsky, 1965, p. 35). Diverse phenomena in English can be reduced to a single principle of structure-dependency; similar phenomena in other languages can be linked to the same principle. Many other principles, and hence aspects of mind, can be discovered by the same process.

Why should this principle occur in all languages and why should we find it so obvious? It is unlikely that people ever encounter rules that contravene structure-dependency outside the pages of linguistics books; how do they instantly know that:

38. *Is John is the man who tall?

is wrong? Children learning English probably never hear any sentences of this type; how do they learn structure-dependency? A theory of language acquisition has to explain how 'children unerringly
use computationally complex structure-dependent rules rather than
computationally simple rules that involve only the predicate "leftmost"
in a linear sequence of words' (Chomsky, 1986a, pp. 7–8). The UG
theory claims that such principles are inherently impossible to learn;
if they are not learnt, they must be part of the human mind.

Structure-dependency

Nature: a principle common to the syntax of all languages

Definition: operations on sentences such as movement require a knowledge of the structural relationships of the words rather than their
 linear sequence

Example (Chomsky, 1980a):

 (1) *Is the man who is tall John?*
 (2) *Is the man who tall is John?*

Gloss: question formation in English involves moving the auxiliary from
 the main clause to the front; thus making (1) grammatical and (2)
 ungrammatical

Extension: Chapter 6 deals with movement in detail

Source: Used by Chomsky in many places, e.g. Chomsky (1971; 1980a;
 1986a; 1988)

The Head Parameter

Structure-dependency seems common to all languages. Yet languages
obviously differ in many ways; if knowledge of language consisted
solely of unvarying principles, all human languages would be identical. To see how the theory captures variation between languages,
let us take the example of the head parameter, which specifies the

order of certain elements in a language. The simple version of the head parameter to be presented in this chapter will need to be greatly extended later.

Principles and parameters theory incorporates a particular theory of phrase structure called X-bar syntax, which is developed in chapter 4. Its aim, as always, is to express generalizations about the phrase structure of all human languages rather than features that are idiosyncratic to one part of language or to a single language. One distinctive claim is that the essential element in each phrase is its **head**. Thus the VP *drew an elephant* has a head Verb *drew*; the NP *the child* has a head Noun *child*; a PP such as *by the manager* has a head Preposition *by*; and so on for all phrases.

An important way in which languages vary concerns where the head occurs in relationship to other elements of the phrase, called **complements**. The head of the phrase can occur on the left of the complements or on their right. So in the NP:

39. education for life

the head Noun *education* appears on the left of the complement *for life*. In the VP:

40. showed her the way

the head Verb *showed* appears on the left of the complements *her* and *the way*. Similarly in the PP:

41. in the car

the head Preposition *in* appears on the left of the complement *the car*.
Japanese is very different. In the sentence:

42. E wa   kabe ni kakatte imasu
     (picture wall on is hanging)
     The picture is hanging on the wall

the head Verb *kakatte imasu* occurs on the right of the Verb complement *kabe ni*, and the *post*position *ni* (on) comes on the right of the PP complement *kabe*. There are thus two possibilities for the structure of phrases in human languages: head-left or head-right.

Chomsky (1970) suggested that the relative position of heads and complements needs to be specified only once for all the phrases in a given language. Rather than a long list of individual rules specifying the position of the head in each phrase type, a single generalization suffices: 'heads are last in the phrase' or 'heads are first in the phrase'. If English has heads first in the phrase, it is unnecessary to specify that Verbs come on the left in Verb Phrases, as in:

43. liked him

or Prepositions on the left in Prepositional Phrases, as in:

44. to the bank

Instead, a single head-first generalization captures the order of elements in English phrases.

Japanese can be treated in the same way; specifying that Japanese is a 'head-last' language means that the Verb is on the right:

45. Nihonjin desu.
     (Japanese am)
     (I) am Japanese

and that it has postpositions:

46. Nihon ni.
     (Japan in)
     In Japan

And the same for other languages. Human beings know that phrases can be either head-first or head-last; an English speaker has learnt that English is head-first; a speaker of Japanese that Japanese is head-last, and so on. The variation between languages can now be expressed in terms of whether heads occur first or last in the phrase. This is the **head parameter**; the variation in order of elements between languages amounts to a single choice between head-first or head-last. Universal Grammar captures the variations between languages in terms of a limited choice between two or so possibilities, known as a **parameter**. The effects of the parameter yield languages as different as English and Japanese. 'Ideally, we hope to find that complexes of properties differentiating otherwise similar languages are reducible to a single parameter, fixed in one or another way' (Chomsky, 1981a, p. 6).

The discussion has first shown that the speaker of a particular language knows a single fact that applies to different parts of the syntax

– the phrases of the language have heads to the left. Then it postulated a parameter that all languages have heads consistently either to the left or to the right of complements. Unlike the universal necessity for structure-dependency, the head parameter admits a limited range of alternatives: 'head-first' or 'head-last'. Alongside the unvarying principles that apply to all languages, UG incorporates 'parameters' of variation; a language 'sets' or 'fixes' the parameters according to the limited choice available. English sets the head parameter in a particular way – the heads of phrases come on the left; to acquire Japanese, evidence is needed that they come on the right. This account of the head parameter simplifies a complex issue; alternative approaches to the word order within the phrase are discussed in more detail in chapter 4. In particular it should be noted that there are some exceptions to the notion that all phrases have the same head setting in a particular language, notably in the case of German.

The Head Parameter

Nature: a parameter of syntax concerning the position of heads within phrases, for example Nouns in NPs, Verbs in VPs, etc.

Definition: a particular language consistently has the heads on the same side of the complements in all its phrases, whether head-first or head-last

Examples:

English is head-first:
  in the bank: Preposition head-first before the complement NP in a PP
  amused the man: Verb head-first before the complement NP in a VP
Japanese is head-last:
  Watashi wa nihonjin desu (I Japanese am): V (*desu*) head-last in a VP
  Nihon ni (Japan in): P (*ni*) head-last in a PP

Extensions: X-bar syntax in chapter 4

The Projection Principle

As well as the syntactic principles discussed so far, principles and parameters theory emphasizes the words of the language, that is to say, the lexical items of the mental lexicon; speakers know what the words in their language mean and how they sound; they also know how they may be used in sentences. The theory integrates the syntactic description of the sentence with the properties of lexical items via the **Projection Principle**, which requires the syntax to accommodate the characteristics of each lexical item. It has always been recognized that there are restrictions on which words can occur in which constructions. For instance, some Verbs are followed by object Noun Phrases:

47. Helen prefers Scotch whisky.

but not:

48. *Helen prefers.

Other Verbs are not followed by NPs, for instance:

49. Peter fainted.

not:

50. *Peter fainted the cat.

The linguistic description expresses this through the **lexical entry** that each item has in the lexicon. The lexical entry for each Verb in the dictionary has to show *inter alia* whether or not it is followed by an NP, i.e. whether it is transitive or intransitive. The context for the Verb is here given in square brackets, with an underlined gap for the location of the item itself; this is known as a **subcategorization frame**. The entry:

prefer Verb, [__ NP]

therefore means that the Verb *prefer* must be followed by an NP. A particular Verb has its own combination of possibilities. The Verb *want*, for example, can be followed by an object NP:

51. I want some money.

or by a phrase starting with *to*:

52.   I want to leave.

but it may not be followed by a phrase starting with *that*:

53.   *I want that Bill leaves.

Unlike, for instance, *believe*:

54.   I believe that Bill left.

Hence the entry for *want* is something like:

want Verb, [__ NP/*to*-phrase]

and the entry for *believe*:

believe Verb, [__ NP/*that*-phrase]

where the slash '/' shows either/or. The properties of each lexical item in the language are recorded in its lexical entry. The speaker's knowledge of the occurrence restrictions for all the words in the language is incorporated in such entries in their mental lexicon, potentially a vast amount of information about many thousands of words.

The grammar of English contains what appears to be the rather similar information that some sentences have a Verb Phrase consisting of a Verb and a Noun Phrase, i.e. are transitive:

55.   Jim drinks lager.

while others have a V without an NP, i.e. are intransitive:

56.   Sarah fainted.

This can be formulated as the syntactic rule:

A Verb Phrase consists of a Verb and an optional Noun Phrase.

Alternatively this can be expressed as the rewriting rule:

VP $\longrightarrow$ V (NP)

meaning that the Verb Phrase 'consists of' a Verb and an optional Noun Phrase; round brackets (also known as parentheses) enclose elements that do not necessarily occur. But this rule seems just to repeat the same information given in the lexical entries. On the one hand there are lexical entries indicating that Verbs are transitive [__ NP] or intransitive; on the other a rule of syntax VP → V (NP) that indicates that VPs may have optional NPs.

The distinctive claim of principles and parameters theory is that such duplication is unnecessary. If there are verbs with entries such as:

like Verb, [__ NP]

there is no need for a rule that some VPs include NPs because this is taken care of by the lexical entry; it follows from the entry for *like* that it must be followed by an NP and that sentences in which it has no following NP are excluded, as in:

57.   *Sam likes.

This information need not be stated again in the syntax. The lexical entry is said to 'project' onto the syntax; the lexical specifications of the word ensure that the syntax has a particular form. This is summed up in a central principle known as the **Projection Principle:**

The properties of lexical entries project onto the syntax of the sentence.

Much of the information that could be expressed as syntactic rules is handled as projections from lexical entries. Rules such as:

VP ⟶ V (NP)

provide redundant information since the element NP is no longer optional but predictable from the behaviour of particular lexical items: *like* can have an NP, *go* cannot. In other words, there is no need to say that sentences may be transitive or intransitive if the information available for every Verb specifies whether it can have a following NP or not. The lexicon is not a separate issue, a list of words and meanings; it plays a dynamic and necessary part in the syntax. The knowledge of how the Verb *like* behaves is inseparable from the knowledge of syntax. Consequently many aspects of language that earlier models dealt with as 'syntax' are now handled as idiosyncrasies of lexical items; the syntax itself is considerably simplified by the omission of many rules, at the cost of greatly increased lexical information.

The Projection Principle is a further universal of human language; all languages integrate their syntactic rules with their lexical entries in this fashion. Since, again, there is no logical necessity for language to be this way and no obvious means by which a child could acquire it, the Projection Principle also seems a built-in feature of the mind.

The Projection Principle

Definition: the properties of lexical items project onto the syntax of the sentence
'lexical structure must be represented categorially at every syntactic level' (Chomsky, 1986a, p. 84)

Gloss: syntax is based on the lexicon in the sense that the specifications of lexical items project onto the syntax rather than having to be specified in rules

Example:

Sue likes Picasso
*Sue likes

The properties of the lexical item *like* Verb, [__ NP] ensure that the Verb is followed by an NP in the sentence

Extension: Chapter 5

So far a fragment of Universal Grammar has been presented to represent the type of material with which it deals. The principle of structure-dependency demonstrated both the overall syntactic orientation of the theory and the abstract level at which such principles operate. The central area of syntax takes the form of principles and parameters that are utilized in all languages: structure-dependency applies equally to French, English and Arabic, in combination with the other principles of UG. The head parameter suggested that a single abstract property of syntax could account for a wide variation between languages. Languages only differ within circumscribed limits; several apparent surface differences between them may be reduced to a single parameter of variation. Finally the Projection Principle demonstrated the integration of syntax and the lexicon. Language knowledge on the one hand consists of a few powerful principles and parameters; on the other of information about the idiosyncratic properties of numerous words.

As we will continue to see, UG theory emphasizes not only the importance of syntax but also the crucial role of vocabulary in knowledge of language.

General Ideas of Language

Let us now put this within the context of different approaches to linguistics. Chomsky's work distinguishes **Externalized (E-) language** from **Internalized (I-) language** (Chomsky, 1986a; Chomsky, 1991a). E-language linguistics, chiefly familiar from the American structuralist tradition such as Bloomfield (1933), aims to collect samples of language and then to describe their properties. E-language linguistics collects sentences 'understood independently of the properties of the mind' (Chomsky, 1986a, p. 20); E-language research constructs a grammar to describe the regularities found in such a sample; 'a grammar is a collection of descriptive statements concerning the E-language' (p. 20). The linguist's task is to bring order to the set of external facts that make up the language. The resulting grammar is described in terms of properties of such data through 'structures' or 'patterns'. I-language linguistics, however, is concerned with what a speaker *knows* about language and where this knowledge comes from; it treats language as an internal property of the human mind rather than something external: language is 'a system represented in the mind/brain of a particular individual' (Chomsky, 1988, p. 36). Chomsky's first goal for linguistics – discovering what constitutes language knowledge – is an I-language aim.

Chomsky claims that the history of linguistics shows a move from an E-language to an I-language approach; 'the shift of focus from the dubious concept of E-language to the significant notion of I-language was a crucial step in early generative grammar' (Chomsky, 1991a, p. 10). I-language research aims to represent this mental state; a grammar describes the speaker's knowledge of the language, not the sentences they have produced. Success is measured by how well the grammar captures and explains language knowledge in terms of properties of the human mind. Chomsky's theories thus fall within the I-language tradition; they aim at exploring the mind rather than the environment. 'Linguistics is the study of I-languages, and the basis for attaining this knowledge' (Chomsky, 1987). Indeed, Chomsky is extremely dismissive of the E-language approaches: 'E-language, if it exists at all, is derivative, remote from mechanisms and of no particular empirical significance, perhaps none at all' (Chomsky, 1991a, p. 10).

The E-language approach includes not only theories that emphasize the physical manifestations of language but also those that treat language as a social phenomenon, 'as a collection (or system) of actions or behaviors of some sort' (Chomsky, 1986a, p. 20). The study of E-language relates a sentence to the language that preceded it, to the situation at the moment of speaking, and to the social relationship between the speaker and the listener. It concentrates on social behaviour between people rather than on the inner psychological world. Much work within the fields of sociolinguistics, or discourse analysis, comes within an E-language approach in that it concerns social rather than mental phenomena.

The opposition between these two approaches in linguistics has been long and acrimonious; neither side concedes the other's reality. It has also affected the other disciplines related to linguistics. The study of language acquisition is divided between those who look at external interaction and communicative function and those who look for internal rules and principles; computational linguists roughly divide into those who analyse large stretches of text and those who write rules. An E-linguist collects samples of actual speech or actual behaviour; evidence is concrete physical manifestation. An I-linguist invents possible and impossible sentences; evidence is whether speakers know if they are grammatical. The E-linguist despises the I-linguist for not looking at 'real' facts; the I-linguist derides the E-linguist for looking at trivia. The I-language versus E-language distinction is as much a difference of research methods and of admissible evidence as it is of long-term goals.

The distinction between **competence** and **performance**, first drawn in Chomsky (1965), partly corresponds to the I- versus E-language split. Competence is 'the speaker/hearer's knowledge of his language', performance 'the actual use of language in concrete situations' (Chomsky, 1965, p. 4). Since it was first proposed, this distinction has been the subject of controversy between those who see it as a necessary idealization for linguistics and those who believe it abandons the central data of linguistics. Let us start with a definition of competence: 'By "grammatical competence" I mean the cognitive state that encompasses all those aspects of form and meaning and their relation, including underlying structures that enter into that relation, which are properly assigned to the specific subsystem of the human mind that relates representations of form and meaning' (Chomsky, 1980a, p. 59). The grammar of competence describes I-language in the mind, distinct from the use of language, which depends upon the context of situation, the intentions of the participants and other factors. Competence is independent of situation. It represents what the speaker knows in the abstract, just as people may know the Highway Code or the rules of arithmetic independently of whether they can drive a car or add up a column of figures. Thus it is part of the competence of all speakers of English that rules must be structure-dependent, that heads come first in phrases, and that the Verb *faint* cannot have an object. The description of linguistic competence then provides the answer to the question of what constitutes knowledge of language.

Chomsky's notion of competence has sometimes been attacked for failing to deal with how language is used, and the concept of communicative competence has been proposed to remedy this lack (Hymes, 1972). The current model does not deny that a theory of use complements a theory of knowledge; I-language linguistics happens to be more interested in the theory of what people know; it claims that establishing knowledge itself logically precedes studying how people acquire and use that knowledge. Chomsky accepts that language is used purposefully; indeed in later writings he introduced the term **pragmatic competence** – knowledge of how language is related to the situation in which it is used. Pragmatic competence 'places language in the institutional setting of its use, relating intentions and purposes to the linguistic meas at hand' (Chomsky, 1980a, p. 225). As well as knowing the structure of language, we have to know how to use it. There is little point in knowing the structure of:

58. Can you lift that box?

if you can't decide whether the speaker wants to discover how strong you are (a question) or wants you to move the box (a request).

It may be possible to have grammatical competence without pragmatic competence. A schoolboy in a Tom Sharpe novel *Vintage Stuff* (Sharpe, 1982) takes everything that is said literally; when asked to turn over a new leaf, he digs up the headmaster's camellias. But knowledge of language use is different from knowledge of language itself; pragmatic competence is not linguistic competence. The description of grammatical competence explains how the speaker knows that:

59. Why are you making such a noise?

is a possible sentence of English, and that:

60. *Why you are making such a noise?

is not. It is the province of pragmatic competence to explain whether the speaker who says:

61.   Why are you making such a noise?

is requesting someone to stop, or is asking a genuine question out of curiosity, or is muttering a *sotto voce* comment. The sentence has a structure and a form that is known by the native speaker independently of the various ways in which it can be used: this is the responsibility of grammatical competence.

However, Chomsky's acceptance of a notion of pragmatic competence does not mean that he agrees that the sole purpose of language is communication:

> Language can be used to transmit information but it also serves many other purposes: to establish relations among people, to express or clarify thought, for creative mental activity, to gain understanding, and so on. In my opinion there is no reason to accord privileged status to one or the other of these modes. Forced to choose, I would say something quite classical and rather empty: language serves essentially for the expression of thought. (Chomsky, 1979, p. 88)

The claim for the priority of communication devalues the importance of other uses: 'Either we must deprive the notion "communication" of all significance, or else we must reject the view that the purpose of language is communication' (Chomsky, 1980a, p. 230). Though approached from a very different tradition, this echoes the sentiments of the 'British' school of linguistics from Malinowski (1923) onward that language has many functions, only one of which is communication.

In all Chomskyan models a characteristic of competence is its creative aspect; the speaker's knowledge of language must be able to cope with sentences that it has never heard or produced before. E-language depends on history – pieces of language that happen to have been said in the past. I-language competence must deal with the speaker's ability to utter or comprehend sentences that have never been said before – to understand:

62.   Ornette Coleman's playing was quite sensational.

even if they are quite unaware who Ornette Coleman is or what is being talked about. It must also reflect the native speakers' ability to judge that:

63.   *Is John is the man who tall?

is an impossible sentence, even if they are aware who is being referred to, and are able to understand what the question is about; 'having mastered a language, one is able to understand an indefinite number of expressions that are new to one's experience, that bear no simple physical resemblance to the expressions that constitute one's linguistic experience' (Chomsky, 1972a, p. 100). Creativity in the Chomskyan sense is the mundane everyday ability to create and understand novel sentences according to the established knowledge in the mind – novelty within the constraints of the grammar. 'Creativity is predicated on a system of rules and forms, in part determined by intrinsic human capacities. Without such constraints, we have arbitrary and random behavior, not creative acts' (Chomsky, 1976, p. 133). It is not creativity in an artistic sense, which might well break the rules or create new rules, even if ultimately there may be some connection between them. The sentence:

64.   There's a book on the table.

is as creative as:

65.   There is grey in your hair.

in this sense, regardless of whether one comes from a poem and one does not.

Let us now come back to performance, the other side of the coin from competence. One sense of performance corresponds to the E-language collection of sentences; in this sense performance means any data collected from speakers of the language – today's newspaper, yesterday's diary, the improvisations of a rap singer, the works of William Shakespeare, everything anybody said on TV yesterday. Whether it is W. B. Yeats writing:

66.   There is grey in your hair.

or a radio disc jockey saying:

67.   If you have been, thank you for listening.

it is all performance. An E-language grammar would have to be faithful to a large sample of such language. But an I-language grammar does not rely on the regularities in a collection of data; it reflects the knowledge in the speaker's mind, not their performance.

However, a second use of the term 'performance' should be noted, namely that which contrasts language knowledge with the psychological processes through which the speaker understands or produces language. Knowing the Highway Code is not the same as being able to drive along a street; while the Code in a sense informs everything the driver does, driving involves a particular set of processes and skills that are indirectly related to knowledge of the Code. Language performance has a similar relationship to competence. Speakers have to use a variety of psychological and physical processes in actually speaking or understanding that are not part of grammatical competence, even if they have some link to it; memory capacity affects the length of sentence that can be uttered but is nothing to do with knowledge of language itself. Samples of language may include many phenomena caused by these performance processes; speakers produce accidental spoonerisms – *you have hissed my mystery lectures* – and hesitations and fillers such as *er* and *you know*; they get distracted and produce ungrammatical sentences; they lose track and start the sentence all over again. One reason for the I-linguist's doubts about using samples of language as evidence is that they reflect many other psychological processes that obscure the speaker's actual knowledge of the language.

Types of Universals

Can a principle that is not found in all languages still be called a universal and related to UG? The concept of **movement** plays an important role in the theory and is employed to describe a number of constructions ranging from passives to questions, as we have already seen. But some languages do not appear to move elements of the syntactic structure of the sentence around. In Japanese, for example, the statement:

68. Niwa wa soko desu
    (garden   there is)
    The garden is there.

differs from the question:

69. Niwa wa doko desu ka?
    (garden   where is)
    Where is the garden?

by adding the element *ka* at the end and having the question-word *doko* in the place of *soko*. The question-word *doko* is not moved to the start, as must happen in English (except for echo questions such as *You said what?*). Japanese does not use syntactic movement for questions, though it may need other types of movement, in particular LF movement, as we shall see later.

Other languages also share this property; questions in Bahasa Melayu, for example, can be formed by adding the question element *kah* to the word that is being asked about (King, 1980):

70. Dia nak pergi ke Kuala Lumpurkah?
    (he is   going to Kuala Lumpur?)
    Is he going to Kuala Lumpur?

without moving it to the front. Some languages do not then require movement. The presence or absence of syntactic movement is a parameter of variation between languages; English requires movement, Malay and Japanese do not. The setting of this parameter has a chain of consequences in the grammar. A language with movement requires a complex theory to relate the moved and unmoved forms; it assumes an original level at which the elements are unmoved. Languages like Japanese can dispense with this. In particular, though structure-dependency has widespread effects on the language, it has been presented here primarily as a restriction on syntactic movement; questions in English are structure-dependent in that they involve structural constituents, not the linear order of words. The question:

71. Which video shall we watch?

is based on movement of the constituent *which video*, not on moving the second or fourth or nth word. Since Japanese does not move syntactic elements in questions, it does not need structure-dependency for syntactic movement.

In what sense can a universal that does not occur in a particular language be a universal? Japanese does not, however, *break* any of the requirements of syntactic movement; it does not need structure-dependency for question movement because it does not use movement. Its absence from some aspect of a given language does not prove it is not universal. The disproof would be a language that had syntactic movement that was *not* structure-dependent. Provided that the universal is found in some human language, it does not have to be present in all languages. UG does not insist all languages are the same; the variation introduced through parameters allows universals to be all but undetectable in particular languages. It does not, however, allow them to be broken.

This can be contrasted with a longstanding approach to universals in which the linguist attempts to discover a typology of the languages of the world by seeing what they have in common; this leads to what are variously called 'implicational', 'statistical', or 'Greenbergian' universals. An example is the **Accessibility Hierarchy** (Keenan and Comrie, 1977). All languages have relative clauses in which the subject of the relative clause is related to the Noun as in the English:

72. Alexander Fleming was the man who discovered penicillin.

A few languages do not permit relative clauses in which the object in the relative clause relates to the Noun. For example the English:

73. This is the house that Jack built.

would not be permitted in Malagasy. Still more languages do not allow the indirect object from the relative clause to relate to the Noun. The English sentence:

74. John was the man they gave the prize to.

would be impossible in Welsh, for instance. Further languages cannot have relative clauses that relate to the Noun via a preposition, as in:

75. They stopped the car from which the number plate was missing.

or via a possessive; the English sentence:

76. He's the man whose picture was in the papers.

would not be possible in Basque. Unlike many languages, English even permits, though with some reluctance, the relative clause to relate via the object of comparison as in:

77. The building that Canary Wharf is taller than is St Paul's.

Or, to take an example from a novel:

78. To Harold's annoyance, the other thing that he was not more of than Sneezy was strong.

The Accessibility Hierarchy is represented in terms of a series of positions for relativization:

Subject > Object > Indirect Object > Object of Preposition > Genitive > Object of Comparison.

All languages start at the left of the hierarchy and have subject relative clauses; some go one step along and have object clauses as well; others go further along and have indirect objects; some go all the way and have every type, including objects of comparison. It is claimed that no language can avoid this sequence; a language may not have, say, subject relative clauses and object of Preposition relative clauses but miss out the intervening object and indirect object clauses. The Accessibility Hierarchy was established by observations based on many languages; it is an implicational universal. There is as yet no compelling reason within UG theory why this should be the case, no particular principle or parameter involved; it is simply the way languages turn out to be. Implicational universals such as the Accessibility Hierarchy are data-driven; they arise out of observations; a single language that was an exception could be their downfall, say one that had object of Preposition relative clauses but no object relative clauses. Universals within UG are theory-driven; they may not be breached but they need not be present. There may indeed be a UG explanation for a particular data-driven universal such as the Accessibility Hierarchy; this would still not vitiate the distinction between the theory-driven UG type of universal and the data-driven implicational universal.

So it is not necessary to show that a universal occurs in dozens of languages. UG research often starts from a property of a single language, such as structure-dependency in English. If the principle can be ascribed to the language faculty itself rather than to experience of learning a particular language, it can be claimed to be universal on evidence from one language alone; 'I have not hesitated to propose a general principle of linguistic structure on the basis of observations of a single language' (Chomsky, 1980b, p. 48). Newton's theory of gravity may have been triggered by an apple but it did not require examination of all the other apples in the world to prove it. Aspects of the theory of UG are disprovable; a principle may be attributed to UG that further research will show is peculiar to Chinese or to English; tomorrow someone may discover a language that breaches structure-dependency. The purpose of any scientific theory it that it can be shown to be wrong; 'in science you can accumulate evidence that makes certain hypotheses seem reasonable, and that is all you can do – otherwise you are doing mathematics' (Chomsky, 1980b, p. 80). Structure-dependency is a current hypothesis, like gravity or quarks; any piece of relevant evidence from one language or many languages may disconfirm it. But of course, the evidence does have to be relevant: not just the odd sentence that seems to contradict the theory but a coherent alternative analysis.

The Language Faculty

Already lurking in the argument has been the assumption that language knowledge is independent of other aspects of the mind. Chomsky has often debated the necessity for this separation, which he regards as 'an empirical question, though one of a rather vague and unclear sort' (Chomsky, 1981b, p. 33). Support for the independence of language from the rest of the mind comes from the unique nature of language knowledge. The principle of structure-dependency does not necessarily apply to all aspects of human thinking; it is not at all clear that such UG principles could operate in areas of the mind other than language. Speakers can entertain mathematical or logical possibilities that are not structure-dependent; they can even imagine rules that are not structure-dependent by means of their logical faculties, as the asterisked sentences of linguists bear witness. Nor do the principles of UG seem to be a prerequisite for using language as communication; it might be as easy to communicate by means of questions that reverse the linear order of items as by questions that are based on structure-dependent movement; a language without restrictions on the types and positions of heads in phrases might be easier to use. Structure-dependency and the head parameter are facts unique to language; the language faculty has particular properties that do not belong to other faculties; 'syntax seems to observe a property of "structure-dependency", unable to make use of linear and arithmetical properties that are much easier to implement outside the language faculty' (Chomsky, 1995a, p. 16). Further arguments for independence come from language acquisition; principles such as structure-dependency do not appear to be learnable by the same means that, say, children learn to roller-skate or to do arithmetic; language acquisition uses special forms of learning rather than those common to other areas.

   Chomsky does not, however, claim that the proposal to integrate language with other faculties is inconceivable, simply that the proposals to date have been inadequate; 'since only the vaguest of suggestions have been offered, it is impossible, at present, to evaluate these proposals' (Chomsky, 1971, p. 26). In the absence of more definite evidence, the uniqueness of language principles such as structure-dependency points to an autonomous area of the mind devoted to language knowledge, a 'language faculty', separate from other mental faculties such as mathematics, vision, logic, and so on. Language knowledge is separate from other forms of representation in the mind; it is not the same as knowing mathematical concepts, for example.

Thus the theory divides the mind into separate compartments, separate modules, each responsible for some aspect of mental life; UG is a theory only of the language module, which has its own set of principles distinct from other modules and does not inter-relate with them. This contrasts with cognitive theories that assume the mind is a single unitary system, for example connectionism (McLelland et al., 1986) or John Anderson's ACT* model which sees the mind as a single elaborate network (Anderson, 1983), and which therefore traces structure-dependency back to a general cognitive property. The separation from other faculties is also reflected in its attitude to language acquisition; it does not see language acquisition as dependent on either 'general' learning or specific conceptual development but *sui generis*. Thus it conflicts with those theories that see language development as dependent upon general cognitive growth; Piaget for instance argues for a continuity in which advances in language development arise from earlier acquired cognitive processes (Piaget, 1980).

In some ways its insistence on modularity resembles a nineteenth-century tradition of 'faculty' psychology, which also divided the mind into autonomous areas (Fodor, 1983). The resemblance is increased by a further step in the argument. We speak of the body in terms of organs – the heart, the lungs, the liver, etc. Why not talk about the mind in terms of mental organs – the logic organ, the mathematics organ, the common sense organ, the language organ? 'We may usefully think of the language faculty, the number faculty, and others as "mental organs", analogous to the heart or the visual system or the system of motor coordination and planning' (Chomsky, 1980a, p. 39). The mistake that faculty psychology made may have been its premature location of these organs in definite physical sites, or 'bumps', rather than its postulation of their existence. On the one hand 'The theory of language is simply that part of human psychology that is concerned with one particular "mental organ", human language' (Chomsky, 1976, p. 36); on the other 'The study of language falls naturally within human biology' (Chomsky, 1976, p. 123). For this reason the theory is sometimes known as the biological theory of language

(Lightfoot, 1982); the language organ is physically present among other mental organs and should be described in biological, as well as psychological terms, even if its precise physical location and form are as yet unknown. 'The statements of a grammar are statements of the theory of mind about the I-language, hence statements about the structures of the brain formulated at a certain level of abstraction from mechanisms' (Chomsky, 1986a, p. 23). The principles of UG should be relatable to physical aspects of the brain; the brain sciences need to search for physical counterparts for the mental abstractions of UG – 'the abstract study of states of the language faculty should formulate properties to be explained by the theory of the brain' (Chomsky, 1986a, p. 39); if there are competing accounts of the nature of UG, a decision between them may be made on the basis of which fits best with the structure of brain mechanisms.

The language faculty is concerned with an attribute that all people possess. All human beings have hearts, all human beings have noses; the heart may be damaged in an accident, the nose may be affected by disease; similarly a brain injury may prevent someone from speaking, or a psychological condition may cause someone to lose some aspect of language knowledge. But in all these cases a normal human being has these properties by definition. Ultimately the linguist is not interested in a knowledge of French or of Arabic or of English but in the language faculty of the human species. It is irrelevant that some noses are big, some small, some Roman, some hooked, some freckled, some pink, some spotty; the essential fact is that normal human beings have noses. All the minds of human beings include the principles that movement is structure-dependent and that heads are on a certain side of phrases; they are part of the common UG. It is not relevant to UG theory that English has a particular set of properties, French another, German another; what matters is what they have in common.

The words 'human' or 'human being' have frequently been used in the discussion so far. The language faculty is indeed held to be specific to the human species; no creature apart from human beings possesses a language organ. The evidence for this consists partly of the obvious truth that no species of animal has spontaneously come to use anything like human language; whatever apes do in captivity, they appear not to use anything like language in the wild (Wallman, 1992). Some controversial studies in recent years have claimed that apes in particular are capable of being taught languages. Without anticipating later chapters, it might be questioned whether the languages used in these experiments are fully human-like in utilizing principles such as structure-dependency; they may be communication systems that use none of the distinctive features of human language. It may on the other hand be possible that they are learnt via other faculties than language at the animal's disposal; in a human being some aspects of language may be learnable by some other means than the language faculty; a linguist may know that Japanese has Verbs on the right as academic knowledge without having any knowledge of Japanese in the language faculty; similarly patterns of learning used by the animal for other purposes may be adapted to learning certain aspects of language. The danger in this argument is that it could evade the issue; how is it possible to tell 'proper' language knowledge gained via the language faculty from 'improper' language knowledge gained in some other way? Presumably only by returning to the first argument: if it embodies principles of UG and has been acquired from 'natural' evidence, then it is proper; none of the systems learnt by animals seem proper in this sense either because they fail to reflect abstract features of language or because they are artificially 'taught'.

The species-specificness of UG nevertheless raises difficult questions about how it could have arisen during evolution; Piaget, for instance, claims 'this mutation particular to the human species would be biologically inexplicable' (Piaget, 1980, p. 31). While the possession of language itself clearly confers an immense advantage on its users over other species, why should structure-dependency or the head parameter confer any biological advantage on their possessor? Indeed one puzzle is why human languages are actually different: it would seem advantageous if the whole species spoke the same language. Presumably our lack of distance from human languages makes them seem so different; the differences between Japanese and English might seem trivial to a native speaker of Martian.

Principles and Rules

So far it has been suggested that the theory relies heavily on the notion of the individual's knowledge of principles as they apply to the language, partly through variable parameters, interconnected with a knowledge of how the lexical items of the language are used in the syntax. Knowledge of language does not consist of rules as such but of underlying principles from which individual rules are derived; the concept of the rule, once the dominant way of thinking about linguistic knowledge, has now been minimized. 'What we know is not a rule system in the conventional sense. In fact, it might be that the notion of rule in this sense . . . has no status in linguistic theory' (Chomsky, 1986a, p. 151).

Let us apply this reasoning to the Verb Phrase rule that has already been introduced, namely:

VP ⟶ V (NP)

This states that a Verb Phrase always contains a Verb and optionally contains a Noun Phrase. That is to say, English has both transitive sentences with objects (V + NP) such as:

79.   He breeds fox-terriers.

and intransitive sentences without objects such as:

80.   The ship sank.

Firstly, the part of the rule is redundant that reflects how the head parameter is set in English. The speaker knows the general fact about English, that the head is on a particular side of the phrase; thus there is no need for the rule to specify that V is on the left of (NP) because this follows from the general principle. Secondly, the lexical items of the language are specified in terms of their possibilities of syntactic occurrence, according to the Projection Principle. So the optional element NP need not be mentioned in the rule as the lexical entry for each verb shows whether it can be followed by an NP – the entry for *sleep* specifies that it cannot be followed by NP, and so on; this aspect of the rule is also redundant. Finally, as suggested earlier, all phrases of a particular type always have a head of that type; it is not necessary to state that VPs have head Verbs, NPs have head Nouns, and so on, because this is a general fact about language. The information in the VP rule is reduced either to general principles or to the properties of lexical entries; the rule itself is no longer needed. Rules are idiosyncratic phenomena that account for specific aspects of one language, such as the Verb Phrase in English. Principles account for properties of all rules and all languages; UG is concerned with establishing a single principle that applies to all rules in English, such as the head parameter, rather than with devising large numbers of rules repeating the same piece of information. This is the major conceptual shift of the theory: rules are to be explained as the interaction of principles and lexical properties rather than existing in their own right. 'One can formulate algorithms that project rule systems from a choice of values for the parameters of UG, but it is not obvious that this is a significant move or that it matters how it is done' (Chomsky, 1986a, p. 151). Rules can still be used as labels for the combination of principles involved in a particular point; the VP rule is a convenient summary of a complex interaction between the head parameter, the principle of head type, and the Projection Principle; but it is nothing more. This change from rules to principles is then a major development in Chomskyan thinking, the repercussions of which have often not been appreciated by those in psychology and other areas, who still assume Chomskyan theory relies heavily on 'rules'. To reiterate, 'a language is not, then, a system of rules, but a set of specifications for parameters in an invariant system of principles of Universal Grammar (UG)' (Chomsky, 1995b, p. 388).

So rules are artifacts of the interaction between the principles and the lexicon. The information stated in rules should be reinterpreted as general principles that affect all rules rather than as a property of individual rules. 'There has been a gradual shift of focus from the study of rule systems, which have increasingly been regarded as impoverished, . . . to the study of systems of principles, which appear to occupy a much more central position in determining the character and variety of possible human languages' (Chomsky, 1982a, pp. 7–8). The theory is not concerned with specific syntactic points such as 'passive', or 'relative clause', or 'question', which are simply shorthand labels for particular interactions of principles and parameters. The passive is not looked at as an independent construction but as a complex of many principles, each of which will also have effects elsewhere in the syntax. 'The basic assumption of the P&P model is that languages have no rules at all in anything like the traditional sense, and no grammatical constructions (relative clauses, passives, etc.) except as taxonomic artifacts' (Chomsky, 1995b, p. 388).

The reliance on principles rather than rules has consequences also for the interpretation of the term **generative grammar** that has been associated with the Chomskyan approach since it first appeared. 'Generative' means that the description is rigorous and explicit; 'when we speak of the linguist's grammar as a "generative grammar" we mean only that it is sufficiently explicit to determine how sentences of the language are in fact characterized by the grammar' (Chomsky, 1980a, p. 220). The chief contrast between traditional grammar statements and the rules of generative grammar lay not in their content so much as their expression; generative rules were precise and testable without making implicit demands on the reader's knowledge of the language.

The justification for rewrite rule systems was that they formalized grammar into a rigorous enclosed set of definitions; a rule such as:

S $\longrightarrow$ NP VP

essentially defined a sentence (S) as consisting of an NP and a VP. The reader then hunted for the definition of NP:

NP $\longrightarrow$ (Det) N

namely that a Noun Phrase (NP) consists of a determiner (Det) and a Noun (N). And so on, until this process of hunting for definitions concluded in the dictionary where the meanings of the eventual lexical items themselves were defined. One of the famous traps people fall into when talking about Chomskyan theory, called the Generative Gaffe by Botha (1989), is to use the term 'generative' as a synonym for 'productive' rather than for 'explicit and formal'.

Principles do not lend themselves, however, to the same formal treatment as rules. The rival theory of Head-driven Phrase Structure Grammar (HPSG) (Pollard and Sag, 1994) claims firmly to be part of generative grammar on the grounds that it uses formal explicit forms of statement, but challenges the right of the current Chomskyan theory to be called 'generative'; generative grammar 'includes little of the research done under the rubric of the "Government Binding" framework, since there are few signs of any commitment to the explicit specification of grammars or theoretical principles in this genre of linguistics' (Gazdar et al., 1985, p. 6); it is noteworthy for instance that one introduction to 'generative grammar' (Horrocks, 1987) devotes about half its pages to Chomskyan theories, including GB, while a survey chapter on 'generative grammar' (Gazdar, 1987) dismisses Chomsky in the first two pages. Thus, though the theory still insists that grammar has to be stated explicitly, this is no longer embodied in the formulation of actual rules; the rigour comes in the principles and in the links to evidence.

Although Chomsky later claimed 'true formalization is rarely a useful device in linguistics' (Chomsky, 1987), the theory nevertheless insists on its scientific status as a generative theory to be tested by concrete evidence about language. It sees the weakness of much linguistic research as its dependence on a single source of data – observations of actual speech – when many other sources can be found. A scientific theory cannot exclude certain things in advance; the case should not be prejudged by admitting only certain kinds of evidence. 'In principle, evidence . . . could come from many different sources apart from judgments concerning the form and meaning of expression: perceptual experiments, the study of acquisition and deficit or of partially invented languages such as Creoles, or of literary usage or language change, neurology, biochemistry, and so on' (Chomsky, 1986a, pp. 36–7). Some of these disciplines may not as yet be in a position to give hard evidence; neurology may not be able to show how language is stored physically in the brain: in principle it has relevant evidence to contribute and may indeed do so one day. Fodor (1981) contrasts what he calls the 'Wrong View' that linguistics should confine itself to a certain set of facts with the 'Right View' that 'any facts about the use of language, and about how it is learnt . . . could in principle be relevant to the choice between competing theories'. When UG theory is attacked for relying on intuitions and isolated sentences rather than concrete examples of language use or psycholinguistic experiments, its answer is to go on the offensive by saying that in principle a scientific theory should not predetermine what facts it deals with; E-language approaches are deficient in the range of evidence they account for compared to I-language theories.

The question of evidence is sometimes expressed in terms of 'psychological reality'. Language knowledge is part of the speaker's mind; hence the discipline that studies it is part of psychology. Chomsky has indeed referred to 'that branch of human psychology known as linguistics' (Chomsky, 1972a, p. 88). Again it is necessary to forestall too literal interpretations of such remarks. A rewrite rule such as:

$$S \longrightarrow NP\ VP$$

did not have any necessary relationship to the performance processes by which people produce and comprehend sentences since it is solely a description of language knowledge. To borrow a distinction from computing, the description of knowledge is 'declarative' in that it consists of static relationships, not 'procedural' in that it does not consist of procedures for actually producing or comprehending speech. The description of language in rules such as these may at best bear some superficial resemblance to speech processes. With knowledge expressed as principles and parameters, the resemblance seems even more far-fetched; it is doubtful whether every time speakers want to produce a VP they consider in some way the interaction of the head parameter, the head requirement, and the lexical entries of verbs. Conventional psychological experiments with syntax tell us about how people perform language tasks but nothing directly about knowledge.

They can provide useful indirect confirmation of something the linguist already suspects and so give extra plausibility perhaps. But they have no priority of status; the theory will not be accepted or rejected as a model of knowledge because of such evidence alone. Chomsky insists that the relevant question is not 'Is this psychologically real?' but 'Is this true?' He sees no point in dividing evidence up into arbitrary categories; 'some is labelled "evidence for psychological reality", and some merely counts as evidence for a good theory. Surely this position makes absolutely no sense . . . ?' (Chomsky, 1980a, p. 108). The linguist searches for evidence of structure-dependency and finds that questions such as:

81.   Is John the man who is tall?

are possible and questions such as:

82.   *Is John is the man who tall?

are impossible. The linguist may then look for other types of evidence – how speakers form questions in an experiment, the sequence in which children acquire types of question, the kinds of mistake people make in forming questions. All such evidence is grist to the mill in establishing whether the theory is correct; 'it is always necessary to evaluate the import of experimental data on theoretical constructions, and in particular, to determine how such data bear on hypotheses that in nontrivial cases involve various idealizations and abstractions' (Chomsky, 1980b, p. 51). Psychological experiments provide one kind of data, which is no more important than any other. A speaker's claim that:

83.   Is John the man who is tall?

is a sentence of English and:

84.   *Is John is the man who tall?

is not provides a concrete piece of evidence about language knowledge. What matters is not whether the sentence has ever been said but whether a sentence of that form could be said and how it would be treated if it were. It may well be that such evidence is incomplete and biased; in due course it will have to be supplemented with other evidence. But we have to start somewhere. The analysis of this easily available evidence is rich enough to occupy generations of linguists. It is simplest to start from the bird in the hand, our own introspections into the knowledge of language we possess; when that has been dealt with, other sources can be tapped.

To sum up, the distinctive feature of Chomsky's I-language approach is that its claims are not unverifiable assertions but are checkable statements. The theory can easily be misconceived as making abstract statements unconnected to evidence, which can be countered by sheer assertion and argument. Much criticism of Chomskyan concepts attempts to refute them by logic and argument rather than by attacking their basis in precise data and evidence. A case in point is Chomsky's well-known argument that children are born equipped with certain aspects of language. This is based on the fact that children know things about language that they could not have learnt from the language they have heard, as we see in chapter 3; it can be refuted by showing that the alleged fact is incorrect: either children could learn everything about language from what they hear or adults do not have the knowledge ascribed to them. 'An innatist hypothesis is a refutable hypothesis' (Chomsky, 1980a, p. 80). It cannot be dismissed by pure counter-argument. The discussion in this book interweaves general aspects of the theory with specific examples of its actual content because Chomsky's general ideas are based on specific claims about language and cannot be adequately understood without looking at these claims. A principle of language is not a proposal for a vague abstraction but a specific hypothesis about the facts of human language, eventually coming down to precise claims about the grammaticality or ungrammaticality of specific sentences, as with structure-dependency. UG is a scientific theory based on specific evidence about language. As such, it is always progressing towards better explanations for language knowledge. Indeed the principles sketched here are now seen as superficial, as the explanations in later chapters will cumulatively demonstrate.

2

Concepts of Principles and Parameters Theory

This chapter will discuss the following topics:

— The framework of principles and parameters theory
— Relating sound and meaning
— Movement
— Modules of the theory
— Government
— The pro-drop (null subject) parameter
— Binding Theory
— Core and periphery.

The Framework of Principles and Parameters Theory

The general approach adopted in this book is to treat the Chomskyan theory of Universal Grammar as a single contemporary whole without reference to its historical origins. Nevertheless some allusions have to be made to the different versions that have been employed over the years and the history of the theory needs to be briefly sketched, partly so that the reader is not confused by picking up a book with other terminology.

Development has taken place at two levels. On the one level there are the general concepts about language and language acquisition on which the theory is based. The origins of such ideas as competence and performance, or the innateness of language, and the rejection of behaviourist views of language described in the last chapter, can be traced back to the late fifties or mid-sixties. They have grown from these original seeds continuously rather than being superseded or abandoned. On this level then the UG theory is recognizable in any of its incarnations.

On the other level there are ideas about the description of syntax that fall into definite phases. The different periods in Chomskyan thinking about syntax became known by the names of particular books or concepts. Each of them was characterized by certain concepts, which were often rejected by the next period; hence it is often difficult to translate the statements of one generation into those of the next. Unlike the general ideas, there are shifts in the syntax which lead to a series of apparent discontinuities and changes of direction.

The original model, **Syntactic Structures**, took its name from the title of Chomsky's 1957 book, which established the notion of generative grammar itself and the concept of rewrite rules; it argued for a separation between phrase structure rules that generated the basic structure and transformations which altered these in various ways; hence a popular name for it was 'transformational generative grammar'. This theory was superseded by the model first known as **Aspects** after Chomsky's 1965 book *Aspects of the Theory of Syntax*, later called the **Standard Theory**; this was distinctive for its recognition of deep and surface structure in the sentence, related by transformations, and for the introduction of the competence/performance distinction. During the 1970s this led into the **Extended Standard Theory (EST)**, which refined the types of rules that were employed. This in turn developed into the **Government/Binding (GB) Model** (Chomsky, 1981a), which introduced the concepts of principles and parameters; it was presented most readably in *Knowledge of Language* (Chomsky, 1986a). Some aspects of this model have since been modified, primarily in *Barriers* (Chomsky, 1986b).

Though 'Government/Binding theory' is a common label for this model of syntax, Chomsky himself finds it misleading because it gives undue prominence to the two elements of Government and Binding, whose status 'was not fundamentally different from others that entered into the discussion or others that did not' (Chomsky, 1987). Hence the label of 'principles and parameters theory' has come to be seen as closer to its essence. Development has not stopped; Chomsky's writings, such as Chomsky (1993) and Chomsky (1995b), are starting to put together another major revision of the theory, known as the **Minimalist Programme**, an outline of which is presented in chapter 9 below.

This chapter gives an overview of principles and parameters theory and an informal presentation of some key areas; chapter 3 looks at general ideas of language acquisition within the framework suggested in this chapter. Chapters 4–8 give a fuller, more technical account of the extended GB/Barriers framework. Non-technical readers can then get some concept of what the theory is about by reading chapters 1–3; specialists can persevere through to chapter 8; the more dedicated can attempt the latest theory, Minimalism, in chapter 9. While the content is mostly seen through Chomsky's own writings, it should not be forgotten that these build on and incorporate the work of many other linguists.

Relating Sound and Meaning

One of Chomsky's insights is that 'each language can be regarded as a particular relationship between sounds and meaning' (Chomsky, 1972a, p. 17). The sentence:

1.   The moon shone through the trees.

consists on the one hand of a sequence of sounds, on the other of a set of meanings about an entity called 'the moon' and the past relationship of its light to some entities called 'trees'. Similarly the Japanese sentence:

2.   Ohayoh gozaimasu.

is related to its Japanese pronunciation on the one side and to its meaning 'Good morning' on the other.

The sounds are the external face of language, its contact with the world through the physical forms of speech; they have no meaning in themselves. *Moon* means nothing to a speaker of Japanese, *gozaimasu* nothing to an English speaker. The meanings are the internal face of language, its contact with the mind; they are abstract mental representations, independent of physical forms. The overall issue in linguistics is always finding the relationship between the external sounds and the internal meanings, as shown in figure 2.1.

'sounds' ⟷ 'meanings'

Figure 2.1   The sound–meaning link

If language could be dealt with as pure sounds or as pure meanings, its description would be comparatively simple. The difficulty of the task is due to the complex and often baffling links between them: how *do* you match sounds with meanings? The answer is the 'computational system' (Chomsky, 1993) present in the human mind that relates meanings to sequences of sounds in one direction and sequences of sounds to meanings in the other. To describe a sentence such as:

3. Gill teaches physics.

the grammar must show how the sentence is pronounced – the sequence of sounds, the stress patterns, the intonation, and so on; what the sentence actually means – the individual words, the syntactic structures, and so on; and how these are related to one another via syntactic devices. It needs a way of describing actual sounds – a phonetic representation; it needs a way of representing meaning – a semantic representation; and it needs a way of describing the syntactic structure that connects them – a syntactic level of representation. Syntactic structure plays a central mediating role between physical form and abstract meaning. Figure 2.2 depicts the bridge from sounds to meanings via the intervening computational system of syntax.

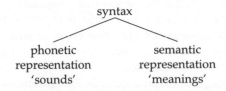

Figure 2.2   The sound–meaning bridge

Principles and parameters theory captures this bridge between sound and meaning through the technical constructs **Phonetic Form** (PF), realized as sound sequences, and **Logical Form** (LF), representations of certain aspects of meaning, which are connected via syntax, as shown in figure 2.3.

Phonetic Form and Logical Form have their own natures, for which distinct PF and LF components are needed within the model. They

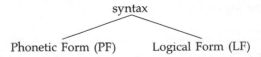

Figure 2.3   The bridge between Phonetic Form and Logical Form

form the contact between the grammar and other areas, at the one end physical realizations of sound, at the other further mental systems: 'PF and LF constitute the "interface" between language and other cognitive systems, yielding direct representation of sound on the one hand and meanings on the other as language and other systems interact . . .' (Chomsky, 1986a, p. 68). Hence PF and LF are known as the interface levels. Most research in principles and parameters theory has concentrated on the central syntactic component rather than on PF or LF. If syntax is a bridge, independent theories of PF or LF are beside the point: however elegant the theories of PF or LF in themselves, they must be capable of taking their place in the bridge between sounds and meanings. The same is true of language acquisition: the central linguistic problem is how the child acquires the syntactic interface rather than sounds or meanings. Phonetic Form and Logical Form are treated in this book as incidentals to the main theme of syntax. Nevertheless this does not mean that considerable work on theories of LF and PF has not been carried out over the years. The PF component, for example, grew from *The Sound Pattern of English* (Chomsky and Halle, 1968) into a whole movement of generative phonology, as described in Roca (1994) and Kenstowicz (1994).

The bridge between sounds and meanings represented in figure 2.3 is still not complete in that LF represents essentially 'syntactic' meaning. 'By the phrase "logical form" I mean that partial representation of meaning that is determined by grammatical structure' (Chomsky, 1979, p. 165). LF is not in itself a full semantic representation but represents the structurally determined aspects of meaning that form one input to a semantic representation, for example the difference in interpreting the direction:

4.   It's right opposite the church.

as:

5.   It's [right opposite the church].

meaning 'exactly opposite the church', or as:

6.   It's right [opposite the church].

meaning 'turn right opposite the church'.

The simplest version of linguistic theory needs two levels to connect the computational system with the physical articulation and

perception of language on the one hand and with the cognitive semantic system on the other. The recent minimalist approach indeed
claims that 'a particularly simple design for language would take the
(conceptually necessary) interface levels to be the only levels' (Chomsky, 1993, p. 3), as we see in chapter 9.

Movement

However, earlier principles and parameters theory still found it necessary to make use of more than these two interface levels. The last chapter contrasted the underlying form of passives and questions before
movement takes place with the derived form after it takes place:

7.   The hospital is where?

compared with:

8.   Where is the hospital?

These are examples of the two levels of syntactic representation required by the GB version of principles and parameters theory: the
underlying D-structure at which all the elements in the sentence are
in their original location and the S-structure at which they have been
moved. Thus the D-structure:

9.   You are seeing what at the cinema?

is connected to the S-structure:

10.   What are you seeing at the cinema?

by movement of *what* and *are* to the beginning of the sentence, shown
by the arrows:

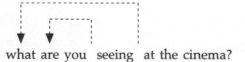

what are you seeing at the cinema?

While the terms D-structure and S-structure originated historically
in 'deep' and 'surface' structure respectively, they were specialized in
their scope within GB theory. The bridging level between sounds and

meanings is S-structure, leading on the one hand to Phonetic Form, on the other to Logical Form. S-structure is related by movement to the D-structure that expresses the key structural relationships in the sentence. S-structure 'is the sole point of interaction among the three fundamental levels' (Chomsky, 1991c, p. 45). However, S-structure still needs to indicate the original locations of the elements that are moved; otherwise the semantic and phonological interpretation would go awry. This is achieved by **traces**, symbolized as t, which mark the original places in the sentence from which elements have moved. The fuller S-structure of the English question is:

11.   What$_1$ are$_2$ you t_2 seeing t_1 at the cinema?

including t_1 to mark the original position from which *what* has moved and t_2 to mark that of *are*. The items to which the traces are linked are shown by having the same number as a subscript. S-structure is not just the 'surface' structure of the sentence but is enriched by traces of movement marking the original locations of elements that have moved. In the GB version of principles and parameters theory, the S-structure level of syntactic representation is where the effects of movement can still be seen, as these are necessary for determining both the phonetic form of the sentence in the PF component and its logical form in the LF component.

Syntactic Movement

the relationship between the two levels of syntax:
— D-structure where the underlying form of the sentence is given before movement
— S-structure where the related form of the sentence after movement is described, including traces (t) of the original positions of the moved items

e.g. D-structure   John will see who
     S-structure   Who$_2$ will$_1$ John t_1 see t_2
     surface structure Who will John see?

Extension: Chapter 6

Movement can now be integrated with the bridge between PF and LF into the so-called **T-model**, labelled for its upside-down T shape,

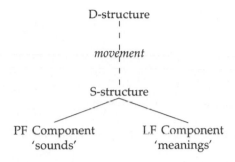

Figure 2.4   The T-Model

as in figure 2.4. The bridge between sounds and meanings is maintained in the link between PF and LF; the intervening computational system is now more complex, having two distinct levels. D-structure is related to S-structure by movement: S-structure is interpreted by the PF and LF components in their respective ways to yield the phonetic and semantic representations.

Clearly this division into D-structure and S-structure only applies to languages such as English where movement distorts an underlying D-structure into an S-structure. Japanese does not have syntactic movement (as always with one or two problematic exceptions, for example one analysis of movement (Kubo, 1989)); it does not then require these two levels. Nevertheless Japanese does require movement in the LF component in order to get what is usually assumed to be the correct LF representation of questions, namely one in which the questioned element has to be at the beginning of the sentence. In a Japanese question such as:

12.   Restoran wa doko   desu ka?
      (Restaurant   where is)
      Where is the restaurant?

the question-word *doko* does not move; so there is no difference in this respect between S-structure and D-structure and the distinction between the two levels is superfluous. One parameter of UG is then whether movement takes place in syntax or in LF in a particular language – whether in fact a language needs the two levels of D-structure and S-structure. It should also not be forgotten that in a sense the notions of S-structure and D-structure are optional extras which minimalism is trying to eliminate, as we see in chapter 9.

Modules of the Theory

At this point we need to introduce something which is both a strength
of the theory and a major difficulty in understanding it, namely its
modularity. In the last chapter one sense of modularity was already
introduced in the theory's insistence that the language faculty is separate from all the other faculties of the mind. The actual grammar is
also, however, modular in a slightly different sense in that it consists
of a number of separate parts, often themselves called theories; the
last chapter showed how the description of a single sentence in terms
of principles and parameters means simultaneously invoking several
different aspects of the grammar; the VP *likes books* is the product of
an interaction between the principle that the head of a VP must be
a V, the Projection Principle that the V *like* must have an object NP,
and the head parameter setting that the head *likes* must come before
the complement *books*. The description of a single sentence or a single
phrase involves the simultaneous application of all relevant principles
and parameter settings. So, in the theory as a whole, each module
affects any aspect of the sentence that comes within its brief. The
presentation of the theory to the reader is difficult since each part
joins together in a complex web that will not support itself till all
the links are made. The reader might adopt Coleridge's principle of
'willing suspension of disbelief': do not worry if some module does
not seem completely coherent at first sight; it will make better sense
when all the interlinking modules are in place.

D-structure requires an account of the phrase structure, achieved
by the theory of **X-bar syntax**, named after its claim that the heads of
phrases have different numbers of 'bars', to be explained in chapter 4.
This is in essence a way of capturing the familiar phrase structure
insights depicted in trees in terms of principles and parameters. One
of the principles of X-bar syntax has already been introduced, namely
that the location of all heads within phrases can be specified once
in the grammar of each language by setting the value of the head
parameter. X-bar syntax integrates the lexicon with the syntax via the
Projection Principle: 'An X-bar structure is composed of projections
of heads selected from the lexicon' (Chomsky, 1993, p. 6). On the one
hand it is concerned with the characteristics of the lexical categories,
Nouns, Verbs, Prepositions, and Adjectives. On the other the syntactic
structure of the sentence reflects the properties of the lexical items
of which it is composed; the Verb *like* must be followed by an NP
complement, for instance. The Projection Principle that projects the

characteristics of lexical entries onto the syntax links D-structure to S-structure and LF to the lexicon by specifying the possible contexts in which a particular lexical item can occur.

X-bar syntax
—describes the structure of phrases

The head parameter
—specifies whether a language has heads that come first or last in the phrase

The Projection Principle
—requires the syntax to take into account the specifications for each lexical item given in its entry in the lexicon

Extensions: Chapter 4

Syntax is also concerned with the semantic relationships between the parts of the sentence – who is doing what to whom – called in principles and parameters theory θ-**roles** (theta roles or thematic roles). These form a crucial part of the syntactic meaning of the sentence relevant to LF. A sentence such as:

13.   Sally gave Jim a record.

has three θ-roles: *Sally* refers to the person who is carrying out the action (the **Agent** role), *the record* to the object affected by it (the **Patient**), *Jim* to the person who receives it (the **Goal**). Principles and parameters theory handles θ-roles in θ-**theory** (**theta theory**). Again θ-theory takes into account how lexical items behave; for example the Verb *give* always has a Goal θ-role:

14.   She gave the money to charity.

but *drink* does not:

15.   *He is drinking it to somebody.

Interacting with X-bar syntax and the Projection Principle, θ-theory concerns the assignment of θ-roles to elements of the structure of the sentence. A Verb such as *give* assigns three θ-roles to NPs:

16.   He gave the suspect a bad time.

That is to say *he, the suspect* and *a bad time* are all NPs bearing θ-roles projected from the Verb *give*. θ-roles express certain meaning relationships between elements, a type of meaning directly relevant to the LF component and indirectly relevant to the semantic component. It is also important that each Noun Phrase has such a relationship, a θ-role, guaranteed by a requirement of θ-theory known as the **θ-criterion**.

θ-Theory (Theta theory)
— deals with the assignment of semantic roles (θ-roles), such as Agent, Patient and Goal, to elements in the sentence

θ-Criterion
— constrains θ-assignment by making certain all elements get a θ-role and every θ-role is assigned

Extensions: Chapter 5

Overall, principles and parameters theory consists of an interlocking network of sub-theories in which each interacts with all the others; these will be detailed in the following chapters. The analysis of any sentence or 'rule' inherently involves the whole theory rather than a single sub-theory. A sentence cannot be simply described as 'passive' or seen as the product of a passive rule but is always treated as a combination of multiple factors. The over-riding goal of principles and parameters theory is never to deal with isolated phenomena but always with a continuous interaction of principles and sub-theories. 'The task is to show that the apparent richness and diversity of linguistic phenomena is illusory and epiphenomenal, the result of interaction of fixed principles under slightly varying conditions' (Chomsky, 1995b, p. 389).

Government

Some principles of language have effects that are confined to a particular sub-theory. Others, however, affect every part. For example, while structure-dependency is particularly relevant to movement, it enters into virtually all aspects of language. Even more widespread is the concept of government. This refers to a syntactic relationship of high abstraction between a 'governor' and an element that it governs. A Verb governs its object NP as in:

17.   Kate likes me.

where the Verb *likes* governs the NP *me*. A Preposition also governs its NP. In:

18.   The traffic warden spoke to her.

the Preposition *to* governs the NP *her*. The possible governors are the categories Noun, Verb, Adjective, and Preposition – in fact all lexical heads of phrases. This chapter illustrates the idea of government and some of its uses; a technical definition will come in chapter 7. The term 'government' is derived from the familiar usage of traditional grammar, for example 'Nouns are governed, as it is called, by verbs and prepositions' (Cobbett, 1819, p. 67).

If the relationship of government obtains between two elements in the sentence, there is a one-way flow of influence from the governor to the governed. So the fact that the Preposition *to* governs the NP means that the pronoun has the form *her* rather than *she*:

19.   to her

not:

20.   *to she

In more technical terms, the object of the Preposition appears in the Accusative Case (*her*) rather than in the Nominative Case (*she*) and it is the fact that the NP is governed by the Preposition which determines this. Similarly the objects of Verbs also appear in the Accusative rather than the Nominative Case:

21.   Kate likes me.

versus:

22.   *Kate likes I.

The verb *like* governs the NP object and thus determines that it appears as the Accusative form *me* rather than the Nominative form *I*.

This is the domain of the sub-theory known as **Case Theory**, to be developed in chapter 6.

The question of what, if anything, governs the subject and therefore determines its Case is one which has interested Chomsky. To discuss this requires introducing an element in the sentence called **Inflection**. This is abbreviated to INFL or to I; while, as we shall see in chapter 4, the letter I stands for the head of the phrase IP, we shall use INFL here for ease of reading. The element INFL represents *inter alia* the grammatical elements tense and agreement. **Tense** is associated with time reference, such as past or present, and mostly concerns the Verb, as in the following pair of sentences:

23.   You play the piano very well.
24.   You played the piano very well.

The first sentence (23) is present tense (which has no inflection in the 2nd person in English), the second sentence (24) past tense (which requires an *-ed* inflection).

Agreement has to do, among other things, with whether the subject is singular or plural in number:

25.   He plays the piano very well.
26.   They play the piano very well.

In the first example (25), where the subject is singular, the Verb has the agreement inflection *-s* attached; in the second example (26), where the subject is plural, there is no visible agreement morpheme. Technically, the Verb agrees with the subject by taking the agreement inflection *-s* if the subject is both singular and third person. The usual abbreviation for the Agreement feature of INFL is **AGR**. INFL is therefore an abstract element that brings together information from other constituents in the sentence about agreement and tense.

Sentences with tense and AGR are called **finite clauses**. Thus:

27.   Mervyn plays the piano very well.

is a finite clause because it contains the ending *-s* to show both present tense and singular AGR. Sentences which do not have tense and agreement are called **non-finite clauses**, for example the infinitival clause:

28.   (He considers) Mervyn to play the piano very well.

Non-finite clauses such as *Mervyn to play the piano very well* only appear inside other clauses, such as *he considers*. Nevertheless they still have an INFL constituent. Though the Verb *play* lacks any inflection, it is preceded by the 'infinitival marker' *to*. The INFL element is here an independent element *to* which precedes the Verb, not a morpheme attached to the verb. INFL can thus be either finite or non-finite. When INFL is finite, it may contain the features of tense and agreement (AGR), which are realized as an inflection attached to the Verb such as *-ed*. When INFL is non-finite, it may contain the infinitival marker *to*.

As far back as *Syntactic Structures* (Chomsky, 1957), Chomsky assumed that the inflectional element forms an independent constituent of the sentence. One reason is that the infinitival marker *to* is clearly separate and independent. Also, even though tense and agreement are realized as inflections, they may sometimes be attached to a preceding auxiliary rather than to the main verb. In:

29. Mervyn is/was playing the piano very well.

and:

30. Mervyn has/had played the piano very well.

whether the sentence is singular or plural, or past or present, is shown by the form of the auxiliaries *be* and *have*, not by that of the Verb *play*. So INFL is an independent element that can end up in different places in the sentence. Assuming that the underlying position of INFL is between the subject and the VP, the underlying structure of the sentence is:

31. Mervyn INFL play the piano very well

If INFL is finite and contains *past*, it will be realized as:

32. Mervyn played the piano very well.

But if INFL is non-finite and contains the infinitival marker *to*, it will be realized as:

33. Mervyn to play the piano very well

which of course needs to be put within another structure (*He considers . . .*) to be grammatical.

Let us return to the issue of what governs the subject. Normally in finite clauses the subject appears in Nominative rather than Accusative Case:

34. He plays the piano.

not:

35. *Him plays the piano.

However, in the special case of non-finite clauses, the subject *him* can appear in the Accusative:

36. Susan wants [him to play the piano].

The subject only appears in Nominative Case when there is a finite INFL. Therefore we can surmise that a finite INFL (i.e. one with tense and agreement) governs and determines the Case of the subject; a non-finite INFL does not.

To sum up, INFL is a separate and independent element in the sentence which comes between the subject and the VP. It can be either finite or non-finite; when it is finite, it can contain tense and agreement, and when it is non-finite, it can contain the infinitival marker *to*. Only finite INFL governs the subject and determines its Case as Nominative; hence finite INFL can be added to the list of governors along with Noun, Verb, Adjective, and Preposition, the difference being that it is not a lexical item in itself. This relationship between government and case assignment plays an important part in many other aspects of the grammar to be discussed in later chapters.

Government

A syntactic relationship between a governor and an element that is governed.

Governors: Noun, Verb, Adjective, Preposition, finite INFL

Affects: Case – *him* vs *he*, etc.
Agreement – *he likes/they like*

Extensions: Chapters 6 and 7

The Pro-drop (Null Subject) Parameter

While the principles of UG lay down absolute requirements that a human language has to meet, the parameters of UG account for the syntactic variation between languages. English does not just instantiate UG principles; it also has particular settings for all the UG parameters; it selects a particular type of movement and sets the head parameter one way. 'The grammar of a language can be regarded as a particular set of values for the parameters, while the overall system of rules, principles, and parameters, is UG which we may take to be one element of human biological endowment, namely the "language faculty"' (Chomsky, 1982a, p. 7).

Let us illustrate how parametric variation works through the **pro-drop parameter**, called after *pro*, the phonologically empty subject which is present in these sentences. This concerns whether a language has declarative finite sentences without apparent subjects, known as null-subject or subjectless sentences, hence it is also often known as the 'null subject parameter'. A starting point can be the Beatles' line:

37. I am the walrus.

In Italian this could be translated as a null-subject sentence:

38. Sono il tricheco. (am the walrus)

But in English the null-subject counterpart is ungrammatical:

39. *Am the walrus.

A pro-drop language such as Italian can have finite null-subject declarative sentences; a non-pro-drop language such as English cannot (putting aside the entirely different imperative construction which can also be subjectless). This difference applies to a range of sentences, e.g. Italian:

40. Parla. (speaks)

or the once familiar notice on trains:

41. E pericoloso sporgersi. (is dangerous to lean out)

both of which permit subjectless sentences.

Needless to say, exceptions can be found in English. Some regional varieties may permit subjectless sentences. The first page of the Trinidadian novel *The Dragon Can't Dance* (Lovelace, 1985) includes the sentence:

42.   Is noise whole day.

Some writing styles may also allow subjects to be omitted, for example diaries (Cook, 1990a; Haegeman, 1990). Dulcie Domum, the pseudonymous writer of a weekly diary *Bad Housekeeping* in the *Guardian* newspaper, used a large range of null-subject sentences each week, for example:

43.   'Recoil, apologising foolishly . . . Then bit lip . . . so tip-toe to study . . . Inform her that . . . Then divine from her saucy expression that . . . but am rather perplexed . . .'

The performance tendency to omit initial words from sentences in casual speech may also clip a first person pronoun from the beginning of an utterance as in:

44.   Flew in from Miami Beach.

It is important to theories of language acquisition whether children learning English produce null-subject sentences and whether native speakers of Italian use them in English, as we shall see in subsequent chapters.

In Italian it is also possible to say:

45.   Cade la notte. (falls the night)

But English speakers cannot say:

46.   *Falls the night.

with the meaning 'Night falls'. English declarative sentences have the order subject–Verb; inversion is usually kept for questions. Italian can have the order Verb–subject even in declaratives. Some languages with null-subject sentences, such as Italian and Spanish, also permit Verb–subject order; the languages that behave like English do not.

However interesting these differences between English and Italian may be, they would not be important if they could not be generalized to Universal Grammar. The group of pro-drop or 'null-subject' languages, to which Italian and Spanish belong, permits both subjectless sentences and inverted declaratives. The other group of non-pro-drop languages, such as English and French, does not allow finite declarative sentences without subjects or with Verb–subject order. Other languages can be assigned to these two groups; Chinese, for example, appears to be a pro-drop language; if asked:

47. Shi shen mo?
     (what are you?)

it is possible to answer:

48. Shi ge haixiang.
     (am the walrus)

without an initial *wo* (I) as subject. Pro-drop is therefore a generalization about human languages, a parameter of UG on which they vary. The main aspects of language affected by the pro-drop parameter are the two features mentioned, although other features have also been claimed to belong to the same phenomenon, such as the possibility in Italian, but not in English, of saying:

49. Che credi che verrà?
     *Who do you believe that will come?

The same information about pro-drop is summarized in the following chart for some sample languages, using the equivalent Verbs to English *speak*.

Differences between pro-drop and non-pro-drop languages				
		Subject–Verb	*Null subject*	*Verb–subject inversion*
Italian	pro-drop	lui parla	parla	parla lui
Arabic	pro-drop	huwa yatakallamu	yatakallamu	yatakallamu huwa
Chinese	pro-drop	ta shuo	shuo	*shuo ta
German	non-pro-drop	er spricht	*spricht	*spricht er
French	non-pro-drop	il parle	*parle	*parle il
English	non-pro-drop	he speaks	*speaks	*speaks he

However, discussing the pro-drop parameter through specimen sentences from different languages exemplifies it rather than explains it. Several different explanations have been put forward in principles and parameters theory; the one used in this chapter is chosen because it illustrates the importance of government; it is based on van Riemsdijk and Williams (1986). Chapter 8 looks at more recent versions.

A division was made earlier between lexical categories such as Noun and Verb and non-lexical categories such as INFL. A further type of category needs to be introduced, the **empty category**. The symbol *e* is used to represent an empty category in general; we have already encountered one specific type of empty category, namely *t*, the trace of movement. Pro-drop languages have declarative sentences without apparent subjects, as in the Italian:

50. Sono di   Torino.
     (am   from Turin)
     I am from Turin.

Principles and parameters theory treats such sentences as having an empty category in subject position, rather than having no subject at all; the basic assumption is that all sentences have subjects. This follows from a principle called the **Extended Projection Principle**, to be encountered later. These subjects may not be visible in pro-drop languages; while the structure of the sentence requires a subject position, in pro-drop languages this may be filled by an empty category. This empty category is clearly different from the empty category *t* introduced by movement and is known as *pro*. The D-structure of the Italian sentence is then:

51. *pro* sono di Torino

pro is an empty category that does not appear in the surface of the sentence:

52. Sono di Torino

According to the same view, Verb–subject inversion sentences such as the Italian:

53. Cade la   notte.
     (falls the night)
     Night falls.

also have an initial subject position occupied by an invisible *pro*. So the D-structure of the inversion sentence is similarly:

54. *pro* cade la notte

with the surface form:

55. Cade la notte.

In both types of construction the empty subject position is filled at D-structure by the empty category *pro*.

The inflectional element INFL stood out earlier from the other governors N, V, A and P in not necessarily being a lexical category, i.e. an actual word. This affects its power to govern. Government theory is extended through the **Principle of Proper Government** which holds that lexical categories govern properly, non-lexical categories do not. So N, V, A, P are automatically proper governors; INFL is not. This leads to a crucial principle that will recur in various forms in this book, namely the **Empty Category Principle**:

An empty category must be properly governed.

Any empty category, whether *t* or *pro* or any of the others coming later, must be in the structural relationship of government to a proper governor.

In pro-drop languages a sentence may have a null subject; it follows that in these languages the empty category *pro* is properly governed. As we have seen, finite INFL governs the subject and therefore in pro-drop languages finite INFL must be a proper governor; it has the same properties as the lexical categories. The empty category of *pro* is 'licensed' by the AGR feature of INFL. Let us for the moment refer simply to AGR rather than INFL. In the D-structure:

56. *pro* AGR sono di Torino

the AGR category must be a proper governor for the empty category *pro*. In non-pro-drop languages, a sentence may not have a null subject; the empty category *pro* is not properly governed, and so AGR is not a proper governor. The English D-structure:

57. *pro AGR speak

is ungrammatical because the AGR constituent cannot properly govern *pro*: it does not have lexical properties. The values for the pro-drop parameter amount to a choice of whether AGR is a proper governor or not – whether it acts like a lexical category. Put another way, in pro-drop languages AGR can behave like a lexical category such as N; in non-pro-drop languages, it cannot; 'the pro-drop parameter amounts to the choice at the level of the grammar between having AGR with and without nominal features' (van Riemsdijk and Williams, 1986, p. 303). The choice whether the AGR part of INFL has lexical properties accounts for many phenomena associated with pro-drop in human languages.

Many pro-drop languages have a rich system of inflectional elements not found in many non-pro-drop languages; in the Latin sentence:

58.   Amata est.
      (loved was)
      She was loved.

the form of the participle *amata* (loved) indicates that the subject is singular and feminine, although no subject is actually present in the sentence. An English sentence minus its subject does not provide any of this information. Intuitively it seems that languages compensate for the lack of information consequent on having null subjects by having richer information elsewhere in the sentence. Unfortunately for this hunch the null-subject language Chinese has no inflections; so this intuition is not entirely correct; Chinese also only has Verb–subject order with certain verbs such as *lai* (come):

59.   Lai   le   ren
      (come aspect-particle person)
      someone came

but not with *shuo* (speak), as we saw on the earlier chart:

60.   *Shuo   ta
      (speaks he)

Whether there is a null subject depends partly on discourse processes (Huang, 1984). Hence Chinese may not be fully a pro-drop language. Nor is the reverse prediction correct; as Bouchard (1984) points out, languages with 'rich' morphology, such as French, are not necessarily pro-drop. It remains, however, a fact that there is a close connection between pro-drop and presence of inflections, which will be dealt with further in chapter 8.

The pro-drop parameter

The pro-drop parameter, sometimes called 'the null subject parameter', 'determines whether the subject of a clause can be suppressed' (Chomsky, 1988, p. 64).

Definition: a parameter with two settings
either INFL is a proper governor
or   INFL is not a proper governor

The Empty Category Principle: an empty category must be properly governed.

Examples:

English *he speaks*   **speaks*   **speaks he*
Italian   *lui parla*   *parla*   *parla lui*

Gloss: a language that has INFL as a proper governor will permit null subjects (since the empty category *pro* is properly governed); a language that does not have INFL as a proper governor will not (as *pro* will not be properly governed).

Extensions: Chapter 8

Binding Theory

Let us turn to Binding Theory, which deals with whether expressions in the sentence may refer to the same entities as other expressions. As with pro-drop the following introductory discussion necessarily distorts the picture by isolating Binding from the other principles of UG; it is put in a wider context in chapter 7.

One of the topics in traditional grammar was how pronouns related to their antecedents. As Cobbett puts it, 'Never write a personal pronoun without duly considering *what noun* it will, upon a reading of the sentence, be *found to relate to*' (Cobbett, 1819, p. 73). Binding Theory is basically concerned with the same issue of how pronouns and other types of noun relate to each other but it extends the antecedent/ pronoun relationship to other categories in a rigorous fashion; Binding Theory 'is concerned with connections among noun phrases that have to do with such semantic properties as dependence of reference, including the connection between a pronoun and its antecedent' (Chomsky, 1988, p. 52). Take a sample sentence:

61.   McCabe shot him.

This implies that there is some entity to which *McCabe* may be used to refer; the noun *McCabe* relates a piece of language to a postulated piece of the world, hence it may be called a **referring expression**. This person is not otherwise mentioned overtly. To know who is being talked about means knowing which person called McCabe is referred to from other information than that contained in the sentence. The same applies to *him*, known as a **pronominal**; another person is being talked about who is not mentioned; we have to deduce for ourselves who was shot. But we are clear that *McCabe* and *him* do not refer to the same person. Some structural relationship, or lack of relationship, between *McCabe* and *him* prevents them referring to the same entity.

Let us extend the discussion to *himself*, known as an **anaphor**. In the sentence:

62.   McCabe shot himself.

while *McCabe*, as before, refers to someone outside the sentence, *himself* refers to the same person as *McCabe*. This information depends not on knowing who McCabe is but on knowing the syntactic relationship between *McCabe* and *himself*, that is, on the internal structure of the sentence. Binding Theory accounts for the differences in the interpretations of *McCabe, him,* and *himself* – how the speaker knows when two such expressions may refer to the same person and when they may not. The convention to show that two expressions co-refer is to assign them the same 'index' in a subscript, as was done earlier with traces. The fact that *McCabe* and *himself* may refer to the same person is shown by giving them both the index i:

63.   McCabe$_i$ shot himself$_i$.

Binding Theory describes when different expressions may be co-indexed – when *him* or *himself* may refer to the same person as *McCabe*. If an expression is in a certain structural relationship to another and is co-indexed with it, it is 'bound' to it. In the examples *himself* is bound to *McCabe* and has the same index; *him* is not bound to *McCabe* and has a different index. All syntactic theories will therefore need to account for the types of relationship seen here – to have a Binding Theory – although the terminology and framework may differ.

One possible way of explaining Binding is to consider the class of word involved. Three word-classes are relevant: **referring expressions, anaphors** and **pronominals**. Nouns such as *McCabe* are classed as referring expressions (r-expressions) in that their reference is necessarily to something in the discourse outside the sentence rather than to some other element in the sentence. The word *himself* belongs to the class of anaphors, made up of subgroups such as reflexives – *herself, themselves,* and so on – and reciprocals such as *each other.* The word *him* belongs to the class of pronominals among which are also numbered *she, him, them,* and so on.

The reference possibilities for r-expressions are straightforward since they always refer out of the sentence (with one or two exceptions); *McCabe* indicates there is supposed to be someone called McCabe existing outside the sentence. Anaphors, however, always have antecedents in the sentence rather than outside it; the anaphor *himself* must be bound to the noun *McCabe,* yielding the possible sentence:

64.   McCabe$_i$ shot himself$_i$.

Pronominals do not have antecedents that are nouns within the same clause; the pronominal *him* cannot refer to the same person as *McCabe.* The difference between:

65.   McCabe shot him.

and:

66.   McCabe shot himself.

is that the former contains a pronominal *him* with no antecedent in the sentence, the latter an anaphor *himself* that has an antecedent. This explains, for example, why *Jane* and *her* do not refer to the same person in:

67.   Jane sponsored her.

but Jane refers to the same person as *herself* in:

68.   Jane$_i$ sponsored herself$_i$.

This analysis falls down when confronted with more complex data, such as:

69.   McCabe said that Jensen shot himself.

Here *himself* does not refer to the same person as *McCabe* despite being in the same sentence. The important category seems to be the clause rather than the sentence; *himself* is bound to an NP within the same clause, as can be seen if square brackets are introduced to distinguish the embedded clause from the main clause:

70.   McCabe said [that Jensen$_i$ shot himself$_i$]

Anaphors such as *himself* must have antecedents within their own clause; they are 'bound' inside it.

The pronominal *him* is the opposite in that it must not have an antecedent within the same clause. Hence:

71.   McCabe said that Smith shot him.

can have two possible interpretations. In one *him* is bound to *McCabe* in the main clause, i.e.:

72.   McCabe$_i$ said [that Smith shot him$_i$]

In the other some third party altogether is involved, say *Jensen*.

73.   McCabe$_j$ said [that Smith shot him$_i$]

But *him* cannot have *Smith*, the subject of its own clause, as an antecedent. Pronominals such as *him* are ambiguous since they either have an antecedent within another clause or refer outside the sentence altogether. They are said to be 'free' within their own clause since their reference must always go outside it.

So the crucial difference between anaphors, pronominals and referring expressions is the area of the sentence within which they can be bound; anaphors are 'bound' within the clause, pronominals may be bound by NPs in other clauses or be free to take their reference outside the sentence; referring expressions are always free. Binding Theory is then chiefly concerned with giving more precision to the area within which binding may or may not take place. The discussion so far has used the concept of clause; Binding Theory in fact uses a slightly different concept called the **local domain**, of which the clause is one example. Using this term, we can now sum up in terms of the actual Binding principles.

A. **An anaphor is bound in a local domain**
B. **A pronominal is free in a local domain**
C. **A referring expression is free.**

This is one form of the Binding principles used in *Knowledge of Language* (Chomsky, 1986a, p. 166), with the omission of a qualification in Principle C; more informal versions of A and B are given in Chomsky (1988, pp. 52, 76).

Let us work through some example sentences to see how these principles operate. In:

74. Jane wanted [the girl to help herself]

Principle A applies because *herself* is an anaphor and is therefore bound to *the girl* within the local domain of the embedded clause, not to *Jane* in the main clause. Principle C also requires the referring expression *Jane* to refer to someone outside the sentence. So the sentence can be shown as:

75. Jane$_j$ wanted [the girl$_i$ to help herself$_i$]

To take a second sentence, in:

76. Kate asked the woman to see her.

Principle C again requires the referring expression *Kate* to be free and hence to refer outside the sentence. Principle B requires the pronominal *her* to be free in its local domain (the embedded clause); it may either take *Kate* in the main clause as its antecedent, as in:

77. Kate$_i$ asked [the woman to see her$_i$]

or refer to someone not otherwise mentioned. A third example sentence is:

78. McCabe said he shot himself.

By Principle A the anaphor *himself* is bound to *he* within the embedded clause:

79.   McCabe said [he$_i$ shot himself$_i$]

By Principle B the pronominal *he* is free within its local domain (the embedded clause) and so may co-refer with *McCabe* outside the embedded clause or may refer to someone else not mentioned.

80.   McCabe$_j$ said [he$_j$ shot himself]

That is to say, the full binding relationship can be seen as:

81.   McCabe$_i$/$_j$ said [he$_i$ shot himself$_i$]

To find which expression binds another in a sentence, the speaker must know not only the syntactic category (anaphor or pronominal) to which the words *her* or *herself* belong but also the relevant local domain. Though the concepts required are abstract, they are necessitated by the data; they are hypotheses that may be refuted or refined by better data.

The reason why 'local domain' is used in the definition of the Binding Principles rather than 'clause' can be seen in sentences such as:

82.   Henry believes [himself to be innocent].

On the analysis given so far, the main clause is *Henry believes* ... and the embedded clause is ... *himself to be innocent; himself* is an anaphor and so by Principle A it should be bound within the local domain of the embedded clause. Yet this is clearly not the case, as the co-indexing shows:

83.   Henry$_i$ believes [himself$_i$ to be innocent].

himself is in fact bound to *Henry* which is outside the embedded clause. Principle A clearly needs a specification of local domain that excludes such clauses. The main feature of this embedded clause is that it is infinitival and has an anaphor as its subject. We have already seen that there is no government relationship between the subject and a non-finite I and this indicates that government has yet another role to play, this time in defining the local domain for binding. These observations will be sharpened in later chapters.

As always, principles and parameters theory integrates the principle with the lexical specification. The principles depend upon a knowledge of which words are anaphors and which are pronominals. The lexical entries in the speaker's lexicon must indicate which category each item belongs to, effectively yielding a list such as:

he	[+pronominal]	[−anaphoric]
himself	[−pronominal]	[+anaphoric]
each other	[−pronominal]	[+anaphoric]

And so on. Additionally the lexical entries for certain verbs such as *believe* need to specify the type of sentence that may follow them, in ways to be developed later.

Binding Theory is typical of the approach in several ways. Firstly, it exemplifies the close relationship between syntax and lexical items already seen in the Projection Principle; a full knowledge of Binding Theory in the speaker's mind involves the interaction of syntactic and lexical knowledge. Syntax is not a separate area from vocabulary but is interwoven with it; abstract principles relate to actual lexical items. Secondly, it drives home that the theory is not about rules – the properties of isolated syntactic constructions – but about principles that apply to many constructions. Binding Theory is not concerned just with *himself*, or with reflexives; it applies to many areas, among which are reflexives, pronominals, nouns, and so on. Thirdly, Binding demonstrates the interconnectedness of the theory. Structure-dependency comes into play, for example, as the speaker needs to relate structural constituents in the sentence. In particular the Binding Principles cannot be stated in isolation from the notion of subject and from Government, as we shall see in chapter 7. The modules of the theory interact to yield the description of any sentence. Hence every minor modification to a single aspect of the theory has repercussions everywhere: 'small changes in the characterisation of the principles and concepts have wide-ranging and complex consequences for some particular language under discussion and for others as well' (Chomsky, 1986a, p. 128).

Finally Binding Theory demonstrates that UG is not concerned with information specific to one language, say English; the Binding Principles are couched at a level of abstraction that may be used for any human language. Though the actual sentences of Chinese, Arabic or Russian may be very different, they are all covered by the same Binding Principles. Binding is a property, not of English alone, but of all languages. So in the Arabic sentence:

84.   qa:lat Fatima inna Huda: qatalat nafsaha:.
      (said Fatima that Huda killed herself)
      Fatima said that Huda killed herself.

the anaphor *nafsaha* (herself) may be bound to *Huda* within the local domain, but not to *Fatima*, i.e.:

85.   qa:lat Fatima inna Huda:$_i$ qatalat nafsaha:$_i$.

In Chinese, too, in the sentence:

86.   Hailun renwei   Mali hui gei taziji chuan yifu.
      (Helen consider Mary for herself   put on clothes)
      Helen thinks that Mary dresses herself.

the anaphor *taziji* (herself) is bound to *Mali* in the same domain, by Principle A, i.e.:

87.   Hailun renwei Mali$_i$ hui gei taziji$_i$ chuan yifu.

Languages differ over the lexical items that may be used as anaphors or pronominals, and in the details of the syntax, but each of them nevertheless observes Binding. Rather than a statement about a single construction in a single language, we have arrived at some principles of language. Of course these principles may be wrong; some other more inclusive explanation may subsume Binding; the aim is to make statements about language that are precise enough to be tested. Indeed we shall see in chapter 8 how the Binding Principles need to be parameterized in order to include a wider range of languages. But the purpose is always to see any construction in any language as a variation on a theme set by UG. The relationship between UG and the grammar of a particular language is that between an abstract set of principles that can be realized in different ways and a particular example of their realization. The waltz rhythm, for example, is realized differently in Strauss's *The Blue Danube*, the Beatles' *She's Leaving Home*, and Max Roach's *The Drum Also Waltzes*; despite their superficial differences, they have an underlying similarity. English grammar incorporates structure-dependency in one way, Italian in another, Chinese in another, but all of them are alternative versions of the same principle. The realization of Binding Theory in English defines it in terms of English sentence structure; it includes unique lists of English words that are anaphors and pronominals. Italian may have a slightly different version defined in terms of Italian sentence structure; it has totally different lists of anaphors and pronominals. Binding Theory nevertheless forms part of both languages. The speaker's knowledge of English or Italian is a knowledge of how they fit UG. A grammar is a realization of the resources of UG – structure-dependency, the head parameter, and so forth; it is one of the possible permutations of UG; languages vary in the ways they use the principles but not in the principles themselves. Part of the human language faculty consists of knowledge about how a language uses the Binding Principles.

Binding Theory

'The theory of *binding* is concerned with the relations, if any, of anaphors and pronominals to their antecedents' (Chomsky, 1982a, p. 6).

Binding Principles (Chomsky, 1986a, p. 166 adapted):

A: An anaphor is bound in a local domain
B: A pronominal is free in a local domain
C: A referring expression is free

Examples:

(1) *McCabe said that Jensen₁ shot himself₁.*
(2) *McCabe₁ said that Smith shot him₁.*

Gloss: in (1) the anaphor *himself* must refer to the same person as *Jensen* because it is within the same local domain (Principle A); in (2) the pronominal *him* may refer to the same person as *McCabe* because it is in a different local domain (Principle B).

Extension: Chapter 8; for further information on whether McCabe shot Jensen or vice versa see C. McCabe, *The Face on the Cutting Room Floor*, reprinted Penguin (1986)

Binding Theory therefore has close links to the behaviour of certain lexical items; to be able to make the Binding Principles work for English you need to know that *himself, herself, each other, one another*, etc. are anaphors, and that *him, her, they*, etc. are pronominals. So Binding Theory led to a proposal by Wexler and Manzini (1987, p. 47) that 'parameterisation is essentially lexical'; parameters are not properties of principles but of individual lexical items in the lexicon. Learning Binding means learning that *him* is a pronominal subject to Principle

B, *herself* is an anaphor subject to Principle A, and so on for all the other relevant words in the language. This is called the **lexical parameterization hypothesis**; out of it has emerged a whole approach to syntax and to acquisition, as we see in chapters 3 and 8.

Core and Periphery

UG asserts that at some fundamental level all human languages conform to a particular pattern: even the variations in the pattern are systematic. Their conformity is not due to common historical origins, nor to the communicative needs of the user, but to the properties of the language faculty, the UG at the heart of grammatical competence. Knowledge of a language means knowing how it fits the general properties of UG with which the mind is equipped. We don't know English as such or Arabic as such: we know the English version of UG or the Arabic version of UG. UG is 'a system of sub-theories, each with certain parameters of variation. A particular (core) language is determined by fixing parameters in these sub-theories' (Chomsky, 1982a, p. 2).

Logically, the potential number of human languages is infinite; the permutations and combinations could vary without rhyme or reason. This was indeed taken as axiomatic by some earlier linguists; 'language is a human activity that varies without assignable limit' (Sapir, quoted in Chomsky, 1986a, p. 21). In terms of UG theory such apparent diversity conceals an underlying identity; all languages are similar at the abstract level of principles such as Binding or vary within tight limits, as with the head and pro-drop parameters. These common characteristics might be coincidence, no more than statistical accidents. Or they might reflect the nature of the mind that knows them. UG theory specifies not so much what a human language may be like as what it may *not* be like. One way of viewing UG is, in a way, not as permitting various types of language but as preventing various types of language. The principle of structure-dependency excludes from the class of human languages those rules that are structure-independent. The examples in this chapter suggest that if a language breached the Binding Principles it would not be a human language at all. Each of the principles and parameters of UG constrains the possibilities of human language. UG 'permits only a finite number of core languages (apart from the lexicon): there are finitely many parameters and each has a finite number of values' (Chomsky, 1986a, p. 149). One of the powerful consequences of the framework is that the number of possible human languages could now in principle be counted. UG puts severe limitations on what a human language may be; there are only a certain small number of languages possible because the combinations of the different values for the various parameters are limited; each possible human language must have one of these combinations. Human languages are limited to the 'finitely many (in fact relatively few) possible core grammars' (Chomsky, 1982b, p. 17).

So the language faculty itself only accepts languages that conform to the requirements of UG. In particular this limits the scope of language acquisition; learners do not need to investigate a vast number of possible grammars for the language they are learning because they can safely assume that it will have the characteristics of UG. The principles and the range of values for each parameter effectively rule out many of the possibilities in advance. Again the presence of UG in the mind does not so much facilitate learning as limit the learner's choice to a small subset of possibilities out of the vast number that are logically possible; languages that contravene UG principles cannot literally be conceived by the human language faculty. To sum up, 'UG now is construed as the theory of human I-languages, a system of conditions deriving from the human biological endowment that identifies the I-languages that are humanly accessible under normal circumstances' (Chomsky, 1986a, p. 23).

UG theory also recognizes that various aspects of a language may be unconnected to UG. For example, in English the usual form of the past tense morpheme is *-ed*, pronounced in three ways according to the phonetic environment: /d/ *planned*, /t/ *watched*, and /id/ *waited*. But English also has a range of irregular past forms, some that form definite groups such as vowel change (*bite/bit, ring/rang*), or lack of change (*hit/hit*), others that have no general pattern (*go/went, am/was*). These irregular forms are learnt late by native children, give problems to L2 learners, and vary from one region to another – UK *dived* versus US *dove*. There is no reason why UG should have to explain this range of forms; they are simply odd facts of English that any English speaker has to learn, unconnected to UG. Interestingly, the fact that such forms may be learnt by associationist networks has often been used as a test case by advocates of connectionism to show the lack of need for 'rules' (Rumelhart and McLelland, 1986). As these forms are peripheral to UG, whether they are learnable or not by such means has no relevance to the claims of the UG model.

The knowledge of any speaker contains masses of similar oddities that do not fit in with the overall pattern of the language. 'What a particular person has in the mind/brain is a kind of artifact resulting from the interplay of accidental factors . . .' (Chomsky, 1986a, p. 147). UG theory avoids taking them all on board by raising a distinction between **core** and **periphery**. The **core** is the part of grammatical competence covered by UG; all the principles are kept, all the parameters set within the right bounds. The **periphery** includes aspects that are not predictable from UG. It is unrealistic to expect UG theory to account for myriads of unconnected features of language knowledge. It deals instead with a core of central language information and a periphery of less essential information; 'a core language is a system determined by fixing values for the parameters of UG, and the periphery is whatever is added on in the system actually represented in the mind/brain of a speaker-hearer' (Chomsky, 1986a, p. 147). The theory of UG is far from a complete account of the speaker's entire knowledge of language; it deals with the core aspects that are related to UG, not with the periphery that is unrelated to UG.

As structure-dependency, for instance, is an aspect of core grammar, all languages must observe it. But this does not imply that no peripheral aspects of the language breach it, hard as they may be to imagine. Similarly a non-pro-drop language does not necessarily have a subject in every sentence. A further glance at Beatles' songs quickly produces:

88.   Can't buy me love.

with no apparent subject, and

89.   In the town where I was born lived a man who sailed to sea.

which seems to have Verb–subject order. It may be that the explanation for these is the processes of performance. But in principle core grammar would not have to be reformulated to accommodate these even if they were true exceptions; they can be left on the periphery. UG does not pretend to account for the whole of knowledge, only the core; it idealizes away from the totality of language knowledge to those parts that humans share.

Such idealization involves the methodological danger of providing an easy way to dispose of inconvenient counter-examples: if some feature of a language seems to contravene our concept of UG, it can be put down to peripheral rather than core grammar, and the UG proposal maintained despite exceptions. Earlier, for example, this escape hatch was used when arguing that, despite the existence of some subjectless sentences, English is a non-pro-drop language. This increases the problem of finding appropriate evidence; actually occurring sentences can be dismissed not just because they are performance but also because they are peripheral. The laudable aim is to concentrate on the key points that languages have in common, on the central features of the language faculty. But such abstraction brings the danger of insulating the theory from relevant as well as irrelevant evidence.

The distinction between periphery and core is not absolute but a continuum of '**markedness**'. Some aspects of grammar are totally derived from UG, some less derived, some quite unrelated. '**Markedness**' means departure from the usual 'neutral' form in one way or another; the black sheep is marked, the white sheep unmarked because sheep are expected to be white; the albino crow is marked because crows are expected to be black. The more something departs from UG the more it is marked; the central core is unmarked – the neutral, expected form of human language. The unmarked version of the head parameter is that all phrases consistently have their heads on the same side; a completely marked language would vary head position inconsistently. A language may have an unmarked core where the head position is consistent but more peripheral elements where it varies, English being a case in point. For example, a current British fad is to reverse the normal Adjective–Noun order in commercial names, as in *Network SouthEast* for part of the railway network. So one form of markedness is simply whether the parameter applies in the way laid down by UG. It might be that a language does not completely fit, at a cost to be seen later.

But another sense of markedness refers to the choice between settings for a parameter. One interpretation of the pro-drop parameter is whether INFL is a proper governor; it is a switch with two settings, each of which might be equally part of UG. Or one setting might be closer to the core, one more peripheral. How could a choice be made between these two possibilities? Once again we come back to language acquisition. Language learners have the pro-drop switch ready in their minds. The switch might be initially neutral, in which case neither setting is more marked than the other; it makes no difference which language they are learning as it is equally easy to switch in either direction. Or they might start with the switch set one way; depending on the language they encounter, they have either to keep it the same way or turn it the other way. If the switch is initially set to pro-drop, learners acquiring Spanish have nothing to acquire since Spanish is a pro-drop language; those learning English have to acquire something extra and vice versa if the switch is initially set the other way. How can we tell which is the case? One way is to see whether the child learning English ever uses null-subject sentences, as is indeed true. This suggests that the initial setting is pro-drop. A complementary approach is to consider the types of evidence that the child requires in order to set the switch; the less evidence that is required the easier the parameter is to set and the least marked the setting. Thus markedness is linked to learnability.

Finally it will have become apparent that much of the discussion is not about language as such but about grammar. The speaker knows a core grammar that incorporates the principles of UG and has particular values for the parameters, conforming to English or French, or whatever language it may be. The speaker's language knowledge extends far outside these limits, and includes marked peripheral information. While 'grammar' is a precise definite term, 'language' is a looser, weaker concept that relates to it in some way. Chomsky calls language an epiphenomenon; 'the notion "language" itself is derivative and relatively unimportant. We might even dispense with it with little loss ... the fundamental concepts are *grammar* and *knowing a grammar* ...' (Chomsky, 1980a, p. 126). What the speaker knows is a grammar, not a language; the term 'language' is an artefact derived from more basic issues; 'The grammar in a person's mind/brain is real; it is one of the real things in the world. The language (whatever that may be) is not' (Chomsky, 1982b, p. 5). Hence UG theory tends to use the term 'grammatical' competence rather than 'linguistic' competence.

3

General Concepts of
Language Acquisition

This chapter will discuss the following topics:

— General ideas of language acquisition
— First language acquisition
— Second language acquisition and Universal Grammar.

Since chapter 1 we have been essentially answering the first of Chomsky's questions for linguistics: what constitutes knowledge of language? Chapter 2 described the overall structure of the knowledge of language represented in the human mind and some of its detail in terms of principles and parameters. This inevitably leads on to the second question for linguistics: how is knowledge of language acquired? For what is learnt is governed by the properties of the mind that is acquiring it; knowledge of language cannot be divorced from language acquisition. The principles and parameters that constitute knowledge of language must therefore relate to acquisition. If they are the final form of language knowledge, there is no point in elaborating a theory of acquisition in which they play no part; similarly there is no point in making an elegant description of language that could not be acquired by a human being. Hence all the aspects of the theory raised in the last chapter inevitably also form part of acquisition. We are not concerned with language knowledge in a vacuum but with knowledge acquired by an ordinary human mind with all its strengths and weaknesses. And furthermore acquired by virtually *every* human mind regardless of intelligence, size, race, sex, class, or other variables.

This chapter provides an introduction to the general ideas of the Universal Grammar theory of language acquisition. The advantage of the principles and parameters model over earlier models is that it can draw an explicit link between competence and acquisition; the form of the grammar can now mirror the needs of acquisition; this connection forms an intrinsic design feature of principles and parameters theory. The two questions of knowledge and acquisition have merged to some extent; an answer to the one cannot be separated from an answer to the other. This chapter introduces the broad sweep of Chomskyan ideas on language acquisition primarily through the concepts already familiar from the previous two chapters; chapter 8 takes the discussion to a more technical level when the details of the syntactic model have been elaborated, and considers some current topics of research. The present chapter starts with general ideas about acquisition, goes on to illustrate them from first language acquisition, and then looks at their relevance for second language acquisition.

General Ideas of Language Acquisition

To some extent, Chomsky's ideas are now so taken for granted that their originality has been obscured. For, prior to Chomsky's work of the late fifties, language was considered to be not knowledge but behaviour, as incorporated in the structuralist linguistics tradition best known from Bloomfield's book *Language* (Bloomfield, 1933). Bloomfield had seen language acquisition as initiated by the child more or less accidentally producing sounds such as *da*; these sounds become associated with a particular object such as a doll because of the parents' reactions, so that the child says *da* whenever a doll appears; then the child learns to talk about *doll* even when one is not present – 'displaced speech'. The adult is a crucial part of the process; the child would never learn to use *da* for 'doll' without the adult's reaction and reinforcement. This Bloomfieldian version of language acquisition was the commonplace of linguistics before Chomsky.

What Chomsky specifically repudiated, however, was the more sophisticated behaviourist theory of B. F. Skinner, put forward in *Verbal Behavior* (Skinner, 1957). A sympathetic account of Skinner's approach can be found in Paivio and Begg (1981). Skinner rejected explanations for language that were inside the organism in favour of explanations in terms of outside conditions. Language is determined by *stimuli* consisting of specific attributes of the situation, by *responses* the stimuli call up in the organism, and by *reinforcing stimuli* that are their consequences. Thus the object 'doll' acts as a stimulus for the child to respond *Doll*, which is reinforced by the parents saying *Clever girl!*

or by their handing the child the doll. Or the child feels thirsty – the stimulus of 'milk-deprivation', responds by saying *Milk*, and is reinforced with a bottle of milk. As with Bloomfield, language originates from a physical need and is a means to a physical end. The parents' provision of reinforcement is a vital part of the process.

Chomsky's classic critique of Skinner in his review of *Verbal Behavior* (Chomsky, 1959) presaged many of his later ideas. Chapter 1 introduced the key Chomskyan notion of **creativity**; people regularly understand and produce sentences that they have never heard before. How could they be acting under the control of stimuli? To take Chomsky's examples, you do not need to have experienced the situation before to take appropriate action if someone says *The volcano is erupting* or *There's a maniac in the next room*.

Nor is a stimulus usually as simple and unambiguous as milk-deprivation or a volcano erupting. Chomsky imagines the response of a person looking at a painting. They might say *Dutch* or *Clashes with the wallpaper, I thought you liked abstract art, Never saw it before, Tilted, Hanging too low, Beautiful, Hideous, Remember our camping trip last summer?*, or anything else that comes to mind. One stimulus apparently has many responses. There can be no certain prediction from stimulus to response. One of the authors went to a supermarket in Kassel, prepared with language teaching clichés about buying and selling; the only German that was addressed to him was:

1. Könnten Sie mir bitte den Zettel vorlesen, weil ich meine Brille zu Hause vergessen habe?
    Could you please read the label to me because I've left my glasses at home?

In other words, human language is basically unpredictable from the stimulus. The important thing about language is that it is stimulus-*free* not stimulus-*bound* – we can say anything anywhere without being controlled by precise stimuli.

It is also hard to see what reinforcement means in the circumstances of children's actual lives, rather than in a laboratory. The child rarely encounters appropriate external rewards or punishment; 'it is simply not true that children can learn language only through "meticulous care" on the part of adults who shape their verbal repertoire through careful differential reinforcement' (Chomsky, 1959, p. 42). The burden of Chomsky's argument is, on the one hand, that Skinnerian theory cannot account for straightforward facts about language, on the other that the apparent scientific nature of terms such as 'stimulus' and 'response' disguises their vagueness and circularity – how do we know the speaker was impressed by the 'Dutchness' of the painting rather than by some other quality? Only because they said *Dutch*: we are discovering the existence of a stimulus from the response rather than predicting a response from a stimulus.

This early demolition of Skinner has remained Chomsky's main influence on psychology, rather than his later work; introductions to psychology seldom mention post-1965 writing.

States of the language faculty

From these early days on, Chomsky started developing an alternative 'nativist' approach to language acquisition that would emphasize language as knowledge and that would cover its unique aspects. One way in which Chomsky has conceptualized language acquisition is in terms of initial and final 'states' of the mind. In the beginning is the mind of the new-born baby who knows no language, termed the **initial zero state** or S_0. At the end is the adult native speaker with full knowledge of the language. This final state is, to all intents and purposes, static; the speaker may become more or less efficient at using language, or may add or lose a few vocabulary items, but competence is essentially complete and unchanging once it has been attained. The adult native speaker's knowledge is therefore termed the **steady state** or S_s – fully developed static competence: 'we take an I-language to be an instantiation of the initial state' (Chomsky, 1995a, p. 18). Acquiring language means progressing from not having any language, S_0, to having full competence, S_s:

$$S_0 \longrightarrow S_s$$

'a person proceeds from a genetically determined initial state S_0 through a sequence of stages S_1, $S_2 \ldots$, finally arriving at a "steady state" S_s which then seems to change only marginally' (Chomsky, 1980b, p. 37).

An E-language approach would interpret this as an invitation to follow large numbers of children from S_0 to S_s, say the 128 children involved in the Bristol study (Wells, 1985). An I-language approach, however, sees language acquisition as a logical problem that can be solved in principle without looking at the development of actual children in detail. The final stage S_s consists of a core grammar instantiating the principles and parameters of UG, which is the common possession of all human beings, and of peripheral grammar and a mental lexicon of idiosyncratic items, which are more variable.

The Language Acquisition Device

The UG model is thus concerned with language acquisition in a logical sense. Chomsky (1959, p. 58) provided a germ out of which the theory grew; 'in principle it may be possible to study the problem of determining what the built-in structure of an information-processing (hypothesis-forming) system must be to enable it to arrive at the grammar of a language from the available data in the available time'. Chomsky (1964) put this metaphorically as a black box problem – something goes into a black box, something comes out of it; by looking at what goes in and what comes out, it is possible to arrive at some understanding of the process concealed inside the black box itself. Suppose we see barley and empty bottles going in one door of a distillery, bottles of Scotch whisky coming out the other; we can deduce what is going on inside by working out what must be done to the barley to get whisky. Given a detailed analysis of the whisky and of the barley we could deduce the process through which one is transformed into the other. Children hear a number of sentences said by their parents and other caretakers – the **'primary linguistic data'**; they process these in some fashion within their black box, called the **Language Acquisition Device** (LAD), and they acquire linguistic competence in the language, i.e. a 'generative grammar'. We can deduce what is going on inside the child's LAD by careful examination and comparison of the language input that goes in – the material out of which language is constructed – and the knowledge of language that comes out – the grammar. 'Having some knowledge of the characteristics of the acquired grammars and the limitations on the available data, we can formulate quite reasonable and fairly strong empirical hypotheses regarding the internal structure of the language acquisition device that constructs the postulated grammars from the given data' (Chomsky, 1972a, p. 113). In the case of the whisky we could go into the distillery to check on our reasoning; it is not of course possible to open the child's mind to confirm our deductions in the same fashion.

The diagram of this process proposed by Chomsky (1964) was as shown in figure 3.1, here adapted slightly.

The LAD is 'a procedure that operates on experience acquired in an ideal community and constructs from it, in a determinate way, a state of the language faculty' (Chomsky, 1990, p. 69). It has to operate for any child anywhere; it must tackle the acquisition of Chinese as readily as the acquisition of English, the acquisition of Russian as readily as that of Sesotho.

Figure 3.1 The LAD model of L1 acquisition

The LAD conceptualization was a powerful metaphor for language acquisition; McCawley (1992) indeed insists that it is true of *any* theory of language acquisition, not just of Universal Grammar. It embodied the central tenet of the theory by treating language acquisition as the acquisition of knowledge. While this may now seem obvious, it was nevertheless totally at odds with the accounts of language acquisition that had been provided before the 1960s, which talked in terms of behaviour. The LAD metaphor said that it was not how children behaved that mattered; it was not even what they actually said: it was what they *knew*.

In the early days the LAD led to a neat way of putting the goals of linguistics in terms of three 'levels of adequacy' (Chomsky, 1964) that foreshadowed the goals of linguistics described in chapter 1. The first level that a linguistic theory has to meet is **observational adequacy**: a theory is observationally adequate if it can deal with the basic facts observed in samples of language, that is to say with the primary linguistic data of adult speech as heard by the child, alias the input to the LAD. The second level is **descriptive adequacy**: a theory achieves descriptive adequacy if it deals properly with the linguistic competence of the native speaker, i.e. the generative grammar that comes out of LAD. The third level is **explanatory adequacy**: a theory is explanatorily adequate if the linguistics theory can provide a principled reason why linguistic competence takes the form that it does, i.e. if it can explain the links between linguistic competence and primary linguistic data that are concealed within the LAD. Explanatory adequacy was presented as a method of deciding between two descriptions of linguistic competence that both seem descriptively and observationally adequate. The preferred description of the output, whenever there is a choice, is that which children can learn most easily from the language data available to them: 'a linguistic theory that aims for explanatory adequacy is concerned with the internal structure of the device . . . ; that is, it aims to provide a principled basis, independent of any particular language, for the selection of the descriptively adequate grammar of each language' (Chomsky, 1964, p. 29).

This 1964 LAD model can be rephrased within principles and parameters theory. The LAD itself can be seen as synonymous with the language faculty, i.e. Universal Grammar. The knowledge that emerges from LAD consists of a grammar couched in principles and parameters form; the knowledge that the child needs consists of structure-dependency, the Projection Principle, etc. The grammar contains the appropriate settings for the parameters of pro-drop, and so on; and it has thousands of lexical entries specifying how each word can behave in the sentence. The adaptation into UG terms can be expressed as in figure 3.2, now conventional in slight variations in the literature, for example Haegeman (1994, p. 15) and Atkinson (1992, p. 43).

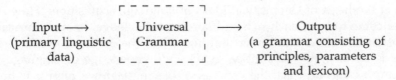

Input ⟶   Universal   ⟶   Output
(primary linguistic   Grammar   (a grammar consisting of
data)   principles, parameters
                                     and lexicon)

Figure 3.2 The Universal Grammar model of L1 acquisition

The UG revision alters the relative importance of the levels of adequacy. Explanatory adequacy had seemed an optional extra only to be employed in the unlikely event that there were two competing grammars that were descriptively adequate. As most energy went into the descriptions themselves, there was seldom a straightforward choice between competing grammars that needed to be resolved by this means; acquisition never had a real role in deciding on the right linguistic theory. The current UG theory, however, integrates acquisition with the description of grammar by making explanatory adequacy central; the description of the grammar goes hand in hand with the explanation of how it is learnt. In principle any element in the grammar has to be justified in terms of acquisition; any principle or parameter that is proposed for the speaker's knowledge of syntax has to fit into an account of acquisition. So all the technical apparatus of principles and parameters theory dealt with in the last chapter from pro-drop to binding must be integrated with the theory of language acquisition.

The poverty-of-the-stimulus argument

The black box LAD model leads to further interesting ideas about acquisition. To return to the distillery, barley is going in and whisky is coming out, but where does the water come from that makes up

43 per cent of distillery strength whisky? The only thing that could come out of the distillery that had not visibly gone in must have originated within the distillery itself. So there is presumably a spring or a water supply inside the distillery that the observer cannot see from the outside.

Suppose something comes out of the LAD that didn't go in: where could it come from? Only from the structure of the mind itself. If the adult's grammar S_s has principles that could not be constructed from the primary linguistic data then they must have been added by the UG itself. The things that are missing from the input are added by UG; the black box is not just processing the input; it is contributing things of its own. This is the conundrum called 'Plato's problem' which is at the heart of Chomskyan ideas of language acquisition: 'How do we come to have such rich and specific knowledge, or such intricate systems of belief and understanding, when the evidence available to us is so meagre?' (Chomsky, 1987). Our knowledge of language is complex and abstract; the experience of language we receive is limited. Human minds could not create such complex knowledge on the basis of such sparse information. It must therefore come from somewhere other than the evidence they encounter. Plato's own solution was to say it originated from memories of prior existence; Chomsky's is to invoke innate properties of the mind. This argument has a clear and simple form: on the one hand there is the complexity of language knowledge, on the other there are the impoverished data available to the learner; if the child's mind could not create language knowledge from the data in the surrounding environment, given plausible conditions on the type of language evidence available, the source must be within the mind itself. This is therefore known as the '**poverty-of-the-stimulus**' argument, meaning that the data in the stimulus are too thin to justify the knowledge that is built out of them.

Let us go over the poverty-of-the-stimulus argument informally before putting it in more precise terms. Part of the linguistic competence of a native speaker is demonstrably the principle of structure-dependency. Some recent research, for example Cook (1994), has used an instrument called the MUGtest (Multi-parameter Universal Grammar test); this asks for grammaticality judgements on a range of sentences involving different parameters and has been used with speakers of English from several backgrounds, both as L1 and L2. Native speakers of English indeed rejected sentences involving rules that violated structure-dependency in questions, such as:

2.   *Is Sam is the cat that brown?

99.6 per cent of the time. How could they have learnt this from their parents? What clues might children hear that would tell them that English is a structure-dependent language? Children never hear examples of English sentences based on rules that break structure-dependency since these do not exist outside the pages of linguistics books. Nor is it likely that parents correct them when they get structure-dependency wrong, partly because children do not produce such errors, partly because parents would probably not know what they were if they did. Perhaps it is just the sheer unfamiliarity of the sentence that offends them. Yet native speakers encounter new and strange sentences all the time, which they immediately accept as English, even if they do not fully understand them, say:

3. On later engines, fully floating gudgeon pins are fitted, and these are retained in the pistons by circlips at each end of the pin. (Haynes, 1971, p. 29)

It is not that a sentence involving a rule that breaches structure-dependency is novel or necessarily incomprehensible: we know it is *wrong*. The child has been provided with no clues that structure-dependency exists – but has nevertheless learnt it. The source of structure-dependency is not outside the child's mind. The environment does not show that structure-dependency exists. As structure-dependency came out of the black box but did not go in as part of the input, it must be part of the black box itself: structure-dependency must already have been present in the child's mind. Thus structure-dependency is an innate aspect of the human language faculty.

There are four stages to the poverty-of-the-stimulus argument (Cook, 1991):

Step A. *a native speaker of a particular language knows a particular aspect of syntax.*

The starting point is the knowledge of the native speaker. The researcher has to select a particular aspect of language knowledge that the native speaker knows. Instead of structure-dependency, one might take the Binding Principles or any of the aspects of language knowledge presented in the last two chapters.

Step B. *this aspect of syntax could not have been acquired from the language input typically available to children.*

The next step is to show that this aspect of syntax could not have been acquired from the primary linguistic data, the speech that the child hears. This involves considering possible sources of evidence in the language the child hears and in the processes of interaction with parents. These will be itemized in greater detail below.

Step C. *this aspect of syntax is not learnt from outside.*

If all the types of evidence considered in Step B can be eliminated, the logical inference is that the source of this knowledge is not outside the child's mind.

Step D. *this aspect of syntax is built-in to the mind.*

Hence the conclusion is that the aspect of syntax must originate within the child's mind. Logically, as the aspect did not come from without, it must come from within, i.e. be a built-in part of the human language faculty.

Steps C and D are kept distinct here because there could be explanations for things which are known but not learnt other than the innate structure of the mind. Plato's memories of previous existence are one candidate, telepathy another. We will assume, however, that the proper explanation for linguists to explore is innateness.

The steps of this argument could be repeated over and over for other areas of syntax. Take the example of Binding Principle A, which concerns the binding of anaphors such as *herself* within a local domain. Step A is to claim that the native speaker knows that in:

4. Helen said that Jane voted for herself.

Jane binds *herself* so that *herself* refers to the same person as *Jane*, i.e.:

5. Helen said that Jane$_i$ voted for herself$_i$.

Cook (1990b) indeed found that 91.1 per cent of native speaker answers interpreted these sentences in this way.

Step B is to see whether children could have worked this out from the speech they are likely to have encountered. Suppose children wrongly understand that *herself* is bound by *Helen*, i.e.:

6. *Helen$_i$ said that Jane voted for herself$_i$.

Nothing would tell the children that they are wrong; no context could let them unerringly distinguish the binding of anaphors and of pronominals. They would happily go on making the mistake for ever more. Steps C and D therefore follow on, to say that, as Binding Principle A is not derived from the environment, it must be an innate part of the child's mind.

Nor does the argument depend upon the technical details of the syntax. It may be, as Culicover (1991) and Freidin (1991) have argued, that structure-dependency derives from other general principles; it may be that the analysis of Binding given in the last chapter needs substantial revision. But the point is still true; if no means can be found through which the child can acquire these from the usual evidence he or she may receive then they must be built in to the mind, however controversial the linguist's analysis itself may be. The poverty-of-the-stimulus argument is fundamentally simple; whenever you find something that the adult knows which the child cannot acquire, it must be already within the child. The form of the argument has in fact been used in other areas; the field of molecular phylogeny, for example, reconstructs early species by working backwards from the protein structure of present-day creatures. Indeed arguments within several religions claim that the world is so beautiful or so complex that it could not have come into existence spontaneously and must therefore be due to a creator; the 'argument by design' was used by Paley (1802, quoted in Gould, 1993) as a stick with which to beat evolutionary theories: 'The marks of design are too strong to be got over. Design must have had a designer. That designer must have been a person. That person is GOD.'

The crucial steps in the argument are: first, that some aspect of language is indeed part of the native speaker's linguistic competence; second, that the child does not get appropriate evidence. A later part of this chapter elaborates on the evidence problem; the last chapter has already presented a reasonable range of the phenomena that form part of linguistic competence and on which the argument can draw.

The principles and parameters theory and language acquisition

The overall model of language acquisition proposed by Chomsky can be put quite simply. Universal Grammar is present in the child's mind as a system of principles and parameters. In response to evidence from the environment the child creates a core grammar S_s that assigns

The poverty-of-the-stimulus argument

The poverty-of-the-stimulus argument, otherwise known as Plato's Problem, claims that the nature of language knowledge is such that it could not have been acquired from the actual samples of language available to the human child

Step A. a native speaker of a particular language knows a particular aspect of syntax
Examples: structure-dependency (chapter 1), Binding Principles (chapter 2), etc.

Step B. this aspect of syntax could not have been acquired from the language input typically available to children

Step C. this aspect of syntax is not learnt from outside

Step D. this aspect of syntax is built-in to the mind

values to all the parameters, yielding one of the allowable human languages – French, Arabic, or whatever. To start with, the child's mind is open to any human language; it ends by acquiring a particular language. The principles of UG are principles of the initial state, S_0. The Projection Principle, Binding, Government, and the others, are the built-in structure of the language faculty in the human mind. No language breaches them; since they are underdetermined by what the child hears, they must be present from the beginning. They are not learnt so much as 'applied'; the child's grammatical competence automatically incorporates them. The resemblances between human languages reflect their common basis in principles of the mind; Japanese incorporates the Binding Principles, as do English or Arabic, because no other option is open to the child. While we are concentrating here on acquisition of syntax, Chomsky extends the argument to include 'fixed principles governing possible sound systems' (Chomsky, 1988, p. 26) and 'a rich and invariant conceptual system, which is prior to any experience' (Chomsky, 1988, p. 32); these guide the child's acquisition of phonology and vocabulary respectively.

Parameter-setting allows the child to acquire the circumscribed variation between languages. A speaker of English has set the head parameter to head-first, a speaker of Japanese to head-last. Acquiring a language means setting all the parameters of UG appropriately. As we have seen, they are limited in number but powerful in their effects. To acquire English rather than Japanese the child must set the values for pro-drop, the head parameter, and a handful of others. The child does not acquire rules but settings for parameters, which, interacting with the network of principles, create a core grammar. 'The internalised I-language is simply a set of parameter settings; in effect, answers to questions on a finite questionnaire' (Chomsky, 1991b, p. 41). Rather than a black box with mysterious contents, Chomsky is now proposing a carefully specified system of properties, each open to challenge.

In addition to the core grammar, the child acquires a massive set of vocabulary items, each with its own pronunciation, meaning and syntactic restrictions. While the acquisition of core grammar is a matter of setting a handful of switches, the child has the considerable burden of discovering the characteristics of thousands of words. 'A large part of "language learning" is a matter of determining from presented data the elements of the lexicon and their properties' (Chomsky, 1982a, p. 8). So the child needs to learn entries that specify that *sleep* is a Verb which requires a subject; that *give* is a Verb that requires a subject, an object and an indirect object; that *himself* is an anaphor: and so on for all the items that make up the mental lexicon of a speaker of English. This **lexical learning hypothesis** (Wexler and Manzini, 1987) claims that parameters belong to lexical entries rather than to principles. It reduces all language acquisition to the learning of lexical properties. This is the logic behind such remarks as 'there is only one human language apart from the lexicon, and language acquisition is in essence a matter of determining lexical idiosyncrasies' (Chomsky, 1991c, p. 419); this will be discussed in terms of acquisition in chapter 8.

As well as the aspects derived from UG principles, the child acquires parts of the language that depart from the core in one way or another, for example the irregular past tense forms in English. Grammatical competence is a mixture of universal principles, values for parameters, and lexical information, with an additional component of peripheral knowledge. Some of it has been present in the speaker's mind from the beginning; some of it comes from experiences that have set values for parameters and led to the acquisition of lexical knowledge. To sum up in Chomsky's words, 'what we "know innately" are the principles of the various subsystems of S_0 and the manner of their interaction, and the parameters associated with these principles. What we learn are the values of the parameters and the elements of the periphery (along with the lexicon to which similar considerations apply)' (Chomsky, 1986a, p. 150).

Let us see what this entails through two examples. Native speakers of English know that

7.   His father plays tennis with him in the summer.

is a possible sentence. What have they acquired? First they have set the head parameter to head-first, so that *play* appears to the left of *tennis, in* to the left of *the summer*. This setting was presumably acquired by noticing that English phrases have a head-first tendency. They also know that the Verb *play* can be followed by an object NP. This comes from the built-in Projection Principle and from the lexical entry for *play*, which is derived from observations of sentences. They also know that an actual lexical subject – *his father* – must be included; they have set the value of the pro-drop parameter to non-pro-drop. The fact that *him* must refer to someone other than *his father* derives from their built-in knowledge of Binding Principles, together with the specific lexical knowledge that *him* is a pronominal, acquired from experience.

Now take the Japanese sentence:

8.   Kare wa tegami o eki   de yomimasu.
     (he   letter   station on read)
     He read the letter on the station.

Japanese speakers have set the value for the head parameter to head-last, as seen in the Verb *yomimasu* (read) occurring to the right of *tegami o eki de* and in the Postposition *de* (on) occurring to the right of *eki* (station). They have learnt that the Verb *yomimasu* requires a subject and an object. Government and Case Theory have been learnt in relationship to the case particles *wa* (subject) and *o* (object) which are assigned to the appropriate constituents. Japanese learners have followed the same route as English learners but with a different result.

First Language Acquisition

Let us now see how this applies to first language acquisition in more detail.

The evidence available to the L1 learner

A constant theme in Chomsky's writings is the nature of the evidence available to the child, taking up arguments suggested by Gold (1967), Baker (1979), and others. Children have to acquire a language from the evidence they encounter. Without any evidence at all, they will acquire nothing; with evidence, they will acquire Chinese or Arabic or any human language they encounter. The 'logical problem of language acquisition' hinges upon the types of evidence they meet and the uses they put it to. This can be illustrated by looking at how one might learn to play games such as chess or snooker. Let us take snooker as an example – the reader who does not know the game will find the example even more convincing! After years of watching snooker on television, Joe Smith knows from observation some of the sequences of colours in which balls are hit by the players: for example every other ball has to be red and the last ball of all has to be black. If he started to play snooker tomorrow, he could copy the sequences he has already observed, but he would not be able to tell if a new sequence, say two red balls in succession, was illegal, or simply one he had by chance not encountered before. He would have no idea what sequences are actually impossible because, given the standard of competition play, he has only seen sequences in which the rules are obeyed rather than those in which they are broken. While he might pass as a snooker player for a few minutes, an adequate knowledge of snooker involves knowing what *not* to do as well as what to do. To learn snooker properly, he would need to get some other type of evidence. One possibility is to see players breaking the rules, unlikely in television snooker. Furthermore, to recognize a sequence as a mistake, something must indicate that it is wrong, such as a penalty from the referee or the hissing of the crowd or a remark from the commentator; otherwise it would simply be another permissible sequence to add to his stock. A further possibility is to learn from the mistakes he makes while actually playing; he hits a black ball followed by a blue and sees if his opponent tells him it is wrong. Or he might deduce from the fact that he has never seen a particular colour sequence, say blue followed by black, that it is illegal; this would not help him to distinguish sequences that are impossible from those that are rare or unlikely. Finally he might buy a guide to snooker and read up the actual rules given there; this solution, however, is no use if he were unable to read or could not grasp the type of information given in the rule, as would be the case for the child acquiring the first language. Overall it would be impossible for him to learn the rule of colour sequences from just watching games in progress.

This analogy illustrates the general properties of the evidence that are necessary for acquisition. On the one hand there is **positive evidence** of actually occurring sequences, i.e. sentences of the language. On the other is **negative evidence** such as explanations, corrections of wrong sequences, or ungrammatical sentences, that shows what may *not* be done. A knowledge of correct snooker sequences appears to be unlearnable from positive evidence alone but needs additional evidence from impossible sequences, correction, ability to read the rulebook, ability to comprehend abstract explanation, and so on. But these possibilities are not available in first language acquisition; except for positive evidence, the other forms detailed above are seldom encountered by the child. The foundation of UG accounts of language acquisition is that evidence other than positive evidence by and large cannot play a critical role; the child must learn chiefly from positive examples of what people actually say rather than examples of what they *don't* say. Again, this comes back to the poverty-of-the-stimulus argument; to acquire language knowledge from experience, the mind needs access to evidence other than actual sentences; as this is not available, the knowledge cannot be acquired but must already be there.

Chomsky (1981a, pp. 8–9) recognizes three logically possible types of evidence for acquisition. First comes 'positive evidence (SVO order, fixing a parameter of core grammar; irregular verbs, adding a marked periphery)'. The occurrence of particular sentences in the speech children hear tells them which sort of language they are encountering and so how to set the parameters; hearing sentences such as:

9.   The hunter chopped off the wolf's head.

they discover that English is head-first; hearing sentences such as:

10.   Mukashi   ojihisan to   obaasan ga koya ni sunde
      mukashi   imashita.
      (once upon old   and old   cottage in were
      a time   man   woman   living)
      Once upon a time an old man and an old woman were living
      in a cottage.

they discover Japanese is head-last. Positive evidence can set a parameter to a particular value.

Chomsky's second type of evidence is 'direct negative evidence (corrections by the speech community)'. The child might conceivably say:

11. Man the old.

and a parent correct:

12. No dear, in English we say 'The old man'.

The third of Chomsky's types is 'indirect negative evidence'; the fact that certain forms do *not* occur in the sentences the children hear may suffice to set a parameter. An English child is unlikely to hear many subjectless declarative sentences:

13. *Speaks.

or subject–Verb inversion:

14. *Speaks he.

save for performance mistakes. At some point the cumulative effect of this lack might make English children decide that English is a non-pro-drop language. Chomsky claims that 'There is good reason to believe that direct negative evidence is not necessary for language acquisition, but indirect negative evidence may be relevant' (Chomsky, 1981a, p. 9). This division into three types of evidence will be used in later discussion with some qualifications.

The argument partly depends on two requirements which, though Chomsky does not name them explicitly himself, can be called **occurrence** and **uniformity**. It is not enough to show that some aspects of the environment logically could help the child; we must show that it *does* occur. While it is at least conceivable that parental explanation of the Binding Principles might be highly useful to the child, it is inconceivable that it actually occurs. If a model of acquisition depends crucially on children hearing a particular structure or on their being corrected by their parents, it is necessary to show that this actually happens; to meet the **occurrence** requirement, speculations about the evidence that children might encounter need support from observations of what they *do* encounter.

All children with very few exceptions learn language. Suppose a learning theory suggests that acquisition depends upon the provision of particular types of evidence and that observations of children confirm these do occur. This explanation would still be inadequate if a single child is found who acquires language without this type of evidence. Some children are corrected by their parents, some are not, yet all acquire language, so acquisition cannot crucially depend upon correction. Since language knowledge is common to all, the **uniformity** requirement stipulates that a model of acquisition must only involve properties of the situation known to affect all children. Uniformity is a stronger form of occurrence; it is not enough to show that a certain type of evidence is available to one child; it must be available to *all* children. A model of language acquisition cannot rely on a particular feature of the environment unless it is available to all children. Children are capable of acquiring their first language despite wide differences in their situations within a single culture and across different cultures. Baby-talk words such as *puff-puff* or *bow-wow* are used by some parents in Britain and shunned by others; some children are told *Open the window*, some asked *Could you open the window?*; yet, although children differ in the extent to which they are able to use language, they nevertheless appear to attain the same grammatical competence. So long as the environment contains a certain amount of language, it appears not to be crucial to the acquisition of grammatical competence what this sample consists of; any human child learns any human language, whatever the situation. As Gleitman (1984, p. 556) succinctly puts it, 'Under widely varying environmental circumstances, learning different languages, under different conditions of culture and child rearing, and with different motivations and talents, all non-pathological children acquire their native tongue at a high level of proficiency within a narrow developmental frame'.

Finally there is a third, weaker, requirement. Given that children have a particular type of evidence available to them, we must still demonstrate that they take advantage of the opportunity afforded to them; this can be called the **take-up requirement**.

Requirements on the language evidence for the child

— **positive evidence requirement**: in principle children must be able to learn language simply from examples of language spoken by others (positive evidence), without correction, explanation etc. (negative evidence)

— **occurrence requirement**: any type of evidence needed by the child must be shown to occur in normal language situations; for example correction does not normally occur

— **uniformity requirement**: the type of evidence must be available uniformly to *all* children regardless of variations in culture, class, etc. (since all children acquire their L1)

— **take-up requirement**: children must be shown actually to make use of this type of evidence

Some insufficient ways of acquiring a first language

Let us go through some alternatives to the innate UG position. This section brings together various points against non-UG positions, derived from Chomskyan thinking in general rather than a specific source. To give concreteness, wherever possible the discussion uses examples of the language of young children and their parents taken from the Bristol transcripts, made available as part of the project described in Wells (1985).

Imitation   Children might learn by imitating the behaviour of those around them. Children brought up among Italian-speaking people speak Italian not English; their knowledge of language reflects their experience. If this counts as imitation, the child learns by imitating. However, often the term 'imitation' has been applied more specifically to speech exchanges in which children repeat the speech of adults (e.g. Clark and Clark, 1977, p. 334), as in:

15.   TV: It's Tuesday.
       Child: It's Tuesday.

The basis of this acquisition model is that children parrot what is said to them.

   In terms of the present discussion children can only imitate what they actually hear. Imitation provides positive evidence, with all its deficiencies; principles such as Binding could not be learnt by imitation because children would never discover what *not* to say. Furthermore speakers can produce new sentences that have never been produced before or understand sentences that they have never met before: language knowledge is creative. However often children imitated the speech of others, they would be unable to produce new things they had never heard before. Imitation in this sense cannot account for the vital creative aspect of language use. The defence to this charge is that children in some way generalize to new circumstances they have not met before; Chomsky insists that generalization is not an adequate explanation because it conceals 'a vast and unacknowledged contribution ... which in fact includes just about everything of interest in this process' (Chomsky, 1959, p. 58). In addition this book has maintained throughout that what native speakers know and what children learn is an I-language. What children hear, however, is E-language sentences, not I-languages. They couldn't acquire competence from such evidence, as I-language cannot be acquired from examples of E-language alone.

Imitation is rare in transcripts of English-speaking children but is common for example among the Kahuli of Papua New Guinea (Ochs and Schieffelin, 1984). The occurrence requirement therefore seems culturally determined; that is to say, imitation does not occur in all the situations children are raised in, and so the uniformity requirement that all children must encounter it is not met. Direct imitation in the form of repetition of adult sentences is unlikely to lead to acquisition. However, to some extent this may be a straw man argument; staunch supporters of direct imitation are thin on the ground. Deferred imitation in which the child repeats an adult remark some time later may have a greater frequency in the child's speech than direct imitation and hence meet the occurrence requirement, though it may be hard to detect in the child's speech. Nor is frequency in itself necessarily important; even if the child only imitated once a day, it might still be the key to acquisition. Nevertheless it is still true that children cannot imitate what they do not hear; if they never hear relevant sentences, they will never be able to imitate them.

Explanation   Hypothetically, the Binding Principles, for example, could be taught to the child through parents explaining that there are two classes of words, anaphors and pronominals, which behave in different ways. Explanatory evidence in principle could compensate for the inadequacy of positive evidence. The minds of students learning foreign languages or computing languages are often presumed to work in this way by their teachers. But it is totally implausible for first language acquisition. Firstly, such conscious knowledge of language, essentially similar to the linguist's knowledge, is different from unconscious competence and must be the property of some faculty of the mind other than language. It is also doubtful whether young children could acquire such abstract and complex conscious knowledge: a child that is old enough to understand the explanation is hardly in need of it. Secondly, the occurrence requirement requires a search for such explanations in the speech of parents to children. Not only have few instances of syntactic explanation by parents been found in transcripts, but also most parents do not possess sufficient conscious knowledge of abstract UG principles to be able to give explanations of them. Chomsky's point about second language learning is equally applicable to first language acquisition: 'one does not learn the grammatical structure of a second language through "explanation and instruction" beyond the most elementary rudiments, for the simple reason that no one has enough explicit knowledge about this structure to provide explanation and instruction' (Chomsky, 1972a, pp. 174–5). Finally, the uniformity requirement requires all children to encounter syntactic explanation, which seems unlikely. So, while some aspects of language might well be learnt through explanation, for example, polite forms of address for different relatives, its difficulty and its rarity suggest it is hardly the prime means of learning principles of syntax.

Correction and Expansion Adults might, however, provide negative evidence by explicitly correcting the child's malformed sentences, i.e. by reinforcement. A child might say:

   16. Book the blue.

and the parent might dutifully correct:

   17. No we don't say that. We say 'the blue book'.

Like explanation, correction could in principle compensate for deficiencies in the positive evidence; even if parents themselves don't supply negative evidence, they might react to the child's own mistakes. This view of language acquisition as a process of teaching by adult correction is one that seems to be commonly held by parents.

For correction to be feasible, the occurrence requirement has to be met by evidence that children produce ungrammatical sentences, and that adults correct them. Starting with the children's speech, examples can be found such as:

   18. I broked it in half.
   19. She be crying because her fur will get wet, wouldn't she?
   20. What did my mummy do at you?

Since these are ungrammatical in terms of adult competence, the sheer occurrence of ungrammatical sentences is demonstrated. If children learn the head parameter for the order of elements in phrases by correction, however, they must produce sentences that specifically violate the appropriate setting. The child would have to make mistakes such as the concocted example:

   21. Man old the go will.

so that the adult can point out:

22.   No. You should say 'The old man will go'.

While the real children's sentences above are typical and familiar to every parent, sentences that go against the typical order within the phrase are hard to find; Roger Brown (1973, p. 77) for example comments that 'the child's first sentences preserve normal word order'. Put conservatively, children do not seem to make many mistakes with UG word order principles; from the first time they use a principle, they get it right. While the occurrence requirement is met in that children do produce ungrammatical sentences, they have not been shown to produce sentences that actually violate UG – which explains why sentence 21 was concocted, not real. The closest perhaps is a student who reported observing a child saying:

23.   What does sheep make a noise?

which seems to violate structure-dependency because part of the constituent *what* seems to have moved, rather than the whole constituent *what noise*. Chomsky asserts: 'Though children make certain kinds of errors in the course of language learning, I am sure that none make the error of forming the question "Is the dog that in the corner is hungry?" despite the slim evidence of experience and the simplicity of the structure independent rule' (Chomsky, 1971, p. 30). Though it is impossible to prove the negative point that relevant mistakes never occur, they are, to say the least, extremely hard to find. This conclusion may be overturned by new evidence; Platt and MacWhinney (1983) for example demonstrate that 4-year-old children are more tolerant of their own mistakes than those of others or of babies, though again the mistakes studied do not appear typical of UG principles.

Even if the occurrence requirement were met in the child's speech, the occurrence of correction in the parents' speech still has to be shown. A preliminary point is that, if parents are to correct the mistake, they have to be able to detect it. But some mistakes are not apparent to the listener. If the child said:

24.   Peggy hurt her.

with the meaning:

25.   *Peggy$_i$ hurt her$_i$.

the fact that *her* was incorrectly being used as an anaphor could not be detected if the listener finds an alternative plausible interpretation which happens not to be the one intended. Berwick and Weinberg (1984, p. 170) make the same point in terms of parsing: 'If an antecedent can be found, the sentence will be grammatical, otherwise not: in both cases the sentence will be parsable.'

Let us start by using correction to refer to explicit comments by the adult on the form of the child's speech. Take the following exchange between a Bristol mother and child:

26. Child: I yeard her.
    Mother: You *heard* her.
    Child: Yeard her.
    Mother: Not yeard. Heard.

Such examples bear witness that correction does indeed occur; the problems are how often it occurs and what is corrected. The above example was one of only five in six transcripts amounting to some three hours of recording of diverse activities. A second example was:

27. Child: I'm calling it a flutterby.
    Mother: That's wrong, isn't it?

The remaining three concerned *please* and *thank you* as in:

28. Child: Find some more.
    Mother: Please. Ask him properly and he might.

In only one of these five does an adult directly point out what is wrong with the child's speech and even this example may be simply correction of pronunciation: if this is typical, explicit correction of syntax is a rare phenomenon. Howe (1981) found only one occurrence of correction of well-formedness in 1,711 mothers' replies to children. Brown (1973, p. 412) comments: 'in general the parents seemed to pay no attention to bad syntax, nor did they even seem to be aware of it.' When Brown and Hanlon (1970) correlated the grammaticality of the children's speech with approval or disapproval by the mother, they found that some sentences were frowned on:

29. Child: And Walt Disney comes on Tuesday.
    Mother: No he does not.

simply because they were factually untrue, while other sentences were praised:

30.   Child: Draw a boot paper.
      Mother: That's right. Draw a boot on paper.

where the meaning was obvious even if the grammar was wrong. Often then grammatical sentences are corrected and ungrammatical sentences are approved, as the examples above show – only one correction out of five applied to an ungrammatical sentence. Hirsh-Pasek, Treiman and Schneiderman (1984) found a ratio of 3 to 1 for approval of well-formed versus ill-formed sentences and 5 to 1 for disapproval of well-formed versus ill-formed, suggesting that something other than grammaticality is involved.

Even if children get appropriate correction, the take-up requirement still needs to be met: do children actually pay any attention to correction? A famous exchange reported in McNeill (1966) is:

31.   Child: Nobody don't like me.
      Mother: No, say 'nobody likes me'.
      Child: Nobody don't like me.
      [eight repetitions of this dialogue]
      Mother: No, now listen carefully; say 'nobody likes me'.
      Child: Oh! Nobody don't likes me.

Firstly one is struck by the sheer ineffectiveness of the mother's repetition; the take-up requirement is not met. Secondly one feels slightly uncomfortable with the dialogue: why is the mother not reassuring the child that someone *does* like them? For the usual adult response to children's speech is to comment not on its grammaticality, but on what it means (Brown and Hanlon, 1970).

However, there may again be an element of tilting at windmills in the argument: even if parents seldom correct the syntactic structure of their children's sentences overtly, correction could take more subtle forms. For instance the child's sentence given above:

32.   Draw a boot paper.

was not corrected directly by the mother but it *was* expanded:

33.   That's right. Draw a boot on paper.

Hirsh-Pasek et al. (1984) found that children's ill-formed sentences were about twice as likely to be repeated by parents as well-formed ones. A person who denies the value of direct correction will point to the apparent approval conferred on the sentence by the adult. But the very fact that a sentence is repeated singles it out to the child as needing attention, let alone the intonation pattern used by the mother. Nor should the apparent infrequency of correction itself be a reason for dismissing it, a confusion of quantity with quality. The real argument once again is whether the type of knowledge postulated in UG is learnable through correction; in principle, this still seems as remote as ever. Chomsky originally stated that 'It is simply not true that children can learn language only through "meticulous care" on the part of adults who shape their verbal repertoire through careful differential reinforcement . . .' (Chomsky, 1959, p. 42). Provided that the word 'language' is restricted within the UG scope, this seems still tenable. As a postscript it should be noted that the results from a questionnaire given to parents in the Bristol project showed that, the more they believed they corrected, the slower the language development of their children (Wells, 1985, p. 351).

Turning to expansion, there has indeed been a widespread feeling that children benefit when adults expand their sentences. Bellugi and Brown (1964) described exchanges such as:

34. Child: Baby highchair.
     Mother: Baby is in the highchair.

as showing a process of 'imitation with expansion'; the mother expands the child's sentence and supplies anything missing while preserving the content words in their original order. However, Cazden (1972) reported a controlled experiment in which children whose sentences were expanded did *not* gain grammatically from the experience. Furthermore, in a large-scale experiment Nelson, Carskadden and Bonvillain (1973) found that children who received expanded sentences progressed less well than those who received straightforward replies.

There are two main arguments why expansion is insufficient to acquire the aspects of grammar covered by the principles and parameters theory. One is the availability of expansions. Hirsh-Pasek et al.'s results are age-specific in that adults expanded the 2-year-olds' sentences but not those of 3- to 5-year-olds; at best only the early aspects of syntax could be acquired in this way. Wells (1985) found that parents expanded more when they knew the microphone was switched on: it may have been something they felt they ought to do rather than something they actually did.

The second argument against expansion would be the child's sheer difficulty in using expansions for acquisition. To appreciate that the adult is correcting a piece of syntax, the child has to disentangle the specific point from everything else included in the adult's expansion and to decide whether the adult is expanding a correct or an incorrect sentence. If expansion provides a type of negative evidence, it is not very efficient – a further example of I-language not being deducible from E-language without extra information.

Social interaction   The interaction between the child and the parents has often been seen in recent years as the mainspring of language acquisition. Correction, approval or imitation are different types of social exchange between the child and the parent; even if these do not carry sufficient weight separately, perhaps the child learns through a number of such routines. Jerome Bruner for instance attaches particular importance to 'formats'; a format is 'a standardized initially microcosmic interaction pattern between an adult and an infant that contains demarcated roles that eventually become reversible' (Bruner, 1983, pp. 120–1), an example being the complex evolution of peekaboo games. Or take the following Bristol exchange:

35.   Father: Are you a mucky pup?
      Child: No.
      Father: Yes you are.
      Child: No.
      Father: Yes you are.

This seems a well-practised routine; the child may learn question formation in English by seeing how the question:

36.   Are you a mucky pup?

relates to the declarative sentence:

37.   Yes you are.

Many, if not most, researchers into child language since the late 1970s have connected the child's linguistic development on the one hand to the development of semantic meanings, on the other to social interaction. Bruner (1983, p. 34) talks of 'two theories of language acquisition;

one of them, empiricist associationism, was impossible; the other, nativism, was miraculous. But the void between the impossible and the miraculous was soon to be filled in', in his view by showing how the child mastered 'the social world as well as the physical' (p. 39).

The arguments against social routines providing adequate evidence will be familiar by now; they provide positive evidence rather than negative evidence; there is a leap from familiar routines to the creative use of language. This is not to deny that such exchanges are vital for building up the use of language, pragmatic competence; 'it would not be at all surprising to find that normal language learning requires use of language in real-life situations, in some way' (Chomsky, 1965, p. 33). But UG theory aims to explain grammatical rather than pragmatic competence; principles of UG are incapable of being learnt by social interaction. Whatever degree of importance one assigns to principles such as structure-dependency or Binding, it is clear they are not learnable through routines, however elaborate.

Dependence on other faculties The other major alternative is that language acquisition depends upon general cognitive development. The basic issue is the autonomy of the language faculty. It is not denied that in actual use the production and comprehension of language depends upon other mental faculties and physical systems, although it is tricky to disentangle them. What *is* denied is that language acquisition depends upon other faculties. Piaget typically claims that the symbolic function of language depends upon the general semiotic function that develops out of the sensorimotor stage of cognitive development. The book *Language and Learning* (Piattelli-Palmarini, 1980) provides a useful debate between Chomsky and Piaget on the issue of autonomy. Chomsky points to the complexity of the knowledge that is learnt – structure-dependency and the binding of *each other* – and denies that this could be the product of sensorimotor intelligence or of general learning theories. 'The common assumption to the contrary, that is that a general learning theory does exist, seems to me dubious, unargued, and without any empirical support or plausibility at the moment' (Chomsky, 1980b, p. 110). His usual argument is that, whatever else cognitive development can account for, it cannot explain the acquisition of language knowledge; as no one has proposed a precise way in which principles such as structure-dependency are acquired, they must be learnt in a manner specific to language. If one accepts Chomsky's premise that language consists of abstract principles such as structure-dependency and Binding, an attempt to show they are derived from other faculties must show their existence elsewhere and show how they are acquired, which he claims has not been done. The insufficiency of general cognitive development as a basis for language acquisition is demonstrated not so much by providing direct evidence as by challenging its advocates to show how language knowledge is learnable by such means.

The discussion has sketched standard arguments against five alternatives to the UG position. The positions outlined are of course considerably more sophisticated than the brief versions given here. But overall the discussion has found no way in which principles of UG are learnable from the environment. The chart below summarizes the argument. Positive evidence alone is insufficient to acquire the principles of UG. The alternatives to innateness are insufficient because they rely on positive evidence, or they occur too rarely or too inconsistently, or they cannot explain creativity, or they cannot handle the type of knowledge that is acquired. UG theory, however, is only concerned with core grammar, not with the many other aspects of language the child has to acquire. The arguments apply to the acquisition of the syntactic core: peripheral grammar, pragmatic competence, social competence, communication skills, and so on, may well be acquired by means such as the formats of Bruner. Indeed in some way these complement Chomsky's approach by showing how the ability to use language may be acquired: 'The study of grammar will ultimately find its place in a richer investigation of how knowledge of language is acquired' (Chomsky, 1972b, p. 119).

Some insufficient ways of acquiring UG from the environment in the L1

	positive evidence	other evidence	occurrence requirement	uniformity requirement
imitation	+		−	−
explanation		+	−	−
correction		+	−	−
social interaction	+		+	−

So where does UG come from? The remaining possibility is that UG does not come from *anywhere*; it is already there. Important aspects of language are not acquired from experience; they are already present in the mind. 'The solution to Plato's problem must be based on ascribing the fixed principles of the language faculty to the human organism as part of its biological endowment' (Chomsky, 1988, p. 27).

The distinctive quality of Chomsky's theory compared with other models is not innateness as such. Even a theory that children learn by associating pairs of words and objects attributes to them the innate ability to form such associations. 'Every "theory of learning" that is even worth considering incorporates an innateness hypothesis' (Chomsky, 1976, p. 13). The differences between language learning models lie in the nature and extent of the properties they attribute to the initial state. Chomskyan theory asserts that UG is innate; rather than a black box with mysterious contents, the mind contains UG principles and parameters.

The claim for innateness could be refuted in several ways. One is to deny the poverty-of-the-stimulus argument itself. But, so long as some aspect of language is known but not acquired from the world, the argument holds. A weaker attack is to deny that particular aspects of language are present in S_s, to reject, say, structure-dependency or Binding as part of the speaker's competence. However, structure-dependency is simply an explanation why:

38.   *Is the teacher who here is good?

is wrong; the only valid way of rejecting it would be to propose an alternative explanation; until that happens it is the best explanation that is available. If a better proposal is made, then it will be superseded. It seems doubtful whether any alternative principles that could account for this knowledge could be learnt either from positive evidence or from the likely negative evidence the child meets. The same is true of other principles. No one claims that the present principles represent the last word. But, to avoid the poverty-of-the-stimulus argument, the alternative principles would have to be learnable in one of the ways outlined above, which seems unlikely.

A further form of refutation would be to accept that a given aspect of language is present in S_s but to demonstrate that it could have been acquired from experience or from some other faculty in the mind. Structure-dependency might be shown to arise naturally from some environmental factors, unlikely as this may seem. Or indeed it might come from other faculties of the mind, as Anderson (1983) suggests. But dismissing a particular grammatical point from S_s does not defeat the argument itself, which could only be gainsaid by showing it applied to *no* aspect of language. Claims about innate ideas in UG theory can always be found to be wrong; contrary evidence may show up and cause specific claims to be abandoned or modified. 'An innatist hypothesis is a refutable hypothesis' (Chomsky, 1980b, p. 80). A theory based on evidence changes as more evidence comes to light, as do theories in other disciplines; UG theory is not an unsubstantiable conjecture about the mind, but a hypothesis that is open to refutation and modification. Chomsky's argument that children are born equipped with certain aspects of language is justified by precise claims based on evidence about language knowledge; each piece of final knowledge that is not derived from experience is innate – structure-dependency, Binding, or whatever. To defeat the argument involves explaining how each and all of these principles could have been acquired from experience or from other faculties.

Grammatical competence was presented as knowledge of how the principles and parameters of UG are reflected in a particular language; knowledge of English is knowledge of how English utilizes UG. This chapter has taken UG as the initial state of the language faculty, S_0; it comes from within not from without. Acquiring English means discovering how it fleshes out the properties of UG which are already present. 'A study of English is a study of the realization of the initial state S_0 under particular conditions' (Chomsky, 1986a, p. 37). The steady state is reached by the mind using evidence to discover how UG is reflected in a particular language. When installing a new video recorder, though the clock and tuner are built-in to the machine, they still need setting to local circumstances – the time of day and the appropriate wavelengths. The final state S_s is one of the possibilities inherent in S_0, as are all the possible human languages; the contribution of experience is to decide which of these possibilities is actually realized, which wavelength is tuned to. S_0 'projects' onto the final state S_s, as a frame in a film projects onto the screen. 'We can think then of the initial state as being in effect *a function that maps experience onto the steady state*' (Chomsky, 1980b, p. 109).

Children acquire movement in English by fitting what they hear to the pre-existing principle of structure-dependency in their minds. They acquire Binding by using the principles they know and learning which words are anaphors and which are pronominals. 'Language learning, then, is the process of determining the values of the parameters left unspecified by universal grammar' (Chomsky, 1988, p. 134). They need to hear some examples of English sentences; otherwise they have no reason for learning English rather than Japanese. The evidence encountered by the child need not be very extensive; a handful of English sentences could show how the head parameter applies, which words are anaphors, and that a language is pro-drop. Positive evidence 'triggers' acquisition rather than being needed in large quantities; some language is necessary to set the process off, to show how the principle applies or the parameter should be set. Chomsky (1988) pointed out that the single sentence 'John ate an apple' is enough to set the main word order parameters for English. But, unlike an E-language model, this experience does not form the primary source of information about language; a loud noise may trigger an avalanche but the noise is distinct from the falling snow. Experience sets off a complex reaction in the organism; 'a central part of what we call "learning" is actually better understood as the growth of cognitive structures along an internally directed course under the triggering and partially shaping effect of the environment' (Chomsky, 1980a, p. 33). Thus, although an I-language theory, UG has a place for experience in language learning – otherwise all children would end up speaking the same language. 'The environment determines the way the parameters of universal grammar are set, yielding different languages' (Chomsky, 1988, p. 134), or, as it is sometimes summed up informally, *linguistic competence = Universal Grammar + primary linguistic data*. Provision of appropriate input is completely necessary; indeed with certain rare constructions accelerated learning may take place if suitable triggering is provided; Cromer (1987) shows that children given ten examples of the construction seen in *The wolf is easy to bite* every three months were, at the end of the year, on average way ahead of those not given this exposure.

The last chapter stressed the view of UG as limitations on language; UG cuts down the potentially infinite number of languages to the smaller number of possible human languages by imposing strong restrictions on their syntactic form. UG is a collection of restrictions on core grammar; the grammar of English consists of one combination of these restrictions, the grammar of Chinese of another. Children narrow down the infinite possibilities of human language to the one that they actually learn via UG. Given that a language could be anything at all, untold millions of children each year choose English, or French, or whatever language they are learning, out of the diverse possibilities; 'the system of UG is so designed that given appropriate evidence, only a single candidate language is made available . . .' (Chomsky, 1986a, p. 83). Hence the reason why children learn language speedily, easily, and uniformly, and apes and computers do not, is that UG narrows down the choices open to them.

The physical basis for Universal Grammar

Acquisition of language is, to Chomsky, learning in a peculiar sense: it is not acquisition of information from outside the organism, as we acquire, say, facts about geography; it is not like learning to ride a bicycle where practice develops and adapts existing skills. Instead it is internal development in response to vital, but comparatively trivial, experience from outside. To make an analogy, a seed is planted in the ground, which grows and eventually flowers; the growth would not take place without the environment; it needs water, minerals and sunshine; but the entire possibility of the plant is inherent in the seed; the environment only dictates the extent to which its inherited potentialities are realized. Knowledge of language needs experience to mature; without it nothing would happen; but the entire potential is there from the start. Chomsky argues that language acquisition is more akin to growing than to learning; it is the maturing of the mind according to a preset biological clock. 'In certain fundamental respects we do not really learn language; rather grammar grows in the mind' (Chomsky, 1980a, p. 134). Language is part of the human inheritance; it is in our genes. As Lenneberg (1967) pointed out, to become a speaker of a human language does not require a particular size of brain; it does not require a particular type of interaction with adults. The requirements for learning a human language are to be a human being and to have the minimal exposure to language evidence necessary to trigger the various parameters of UG.

The physical basis of UG means that it is part of the human genetic inheritance, a part of biology rather than psychology; 'universal grammar is part of the genotype specifying one aspect of the initial state of the human mind and brain . . .' (Chomsky, 1980a, p. 82). Like other inherited attributes this does not rule out variation between individuals. Most introductory linguistics books assert that all human children can learn all human languages. An 'English' child transported to Japan, a 'Japanese' child transported to England, grow up with competences identical to those of children born of Japanese or English parents. If this is due to common genetic inheritance, some individual variation might be expected; all human beings have eyes but some are brown, some blue, some green. At the moment the common features of UG in all human minds need to be established before variations that show up between individuals can be investigated. Controversial work by Gopnik and Crago (1991) has, however, claimed to find a particular language deficiency widely spread among the members of one family, suggesting a common genetic origin. For the moment it is how the human eye works that is of basic importance, not variations of colour in the iris. 'The main topic is the uniformity of development . . . it could ultimately be an interesting question whether there is genetic variation that shows up in language somewhere'

(Chomsky, 1982c, p. 25). While the bulk of Universal Grammar seems common to all human beings, this assumption is not at present based on proof that, say, 'English' native speakers of Japanese have identical competences to 'Japanese' speakers of Japanese.

The language organ is also held to be the property only of human brains: people speak; dogs do not. Various attempts have been made to refute Chomsky's claim that the language faculty is species-specific. The usual approach is to teach another species a simplified form of English, using some other means of expression than the vocal apparatus, such as gestures, or visual signs. This approach was adopted in a series of experiments with apes in the 1970s and 1980s. The general assumption was that the reason why apes could not talk was not so much their lack of mental capacity as their physical difficulties in producing the sounds of human speech, in particular the different structure of their larynx. Several projects substituted another form for spoken language, assuming that this would open the door for the apes to acquire language. Gardner and Gardner (1971) brought up a chimpanzee called Washoe in ways similar to a human child except that the language was American Sign Language, the gesture language used by the deaf; this was taught primarily by 'modelling', that is to say the human guided the chimp's hands to make the appropriate sign. Considerable success appeared to be achieved by this means. Washoe for instance produced the subject *you* sign before the object *me* sign 90 per cent of the time these were combined, i.e. she seemed to know the correct subject–object order. Washoe would also react differently to the orders in *baby mine* and *mine baby*. Rumbaugh (1977) taught an invented language to a 2-year-old chimp called Lana; this 'Yerkish' language consisted of abstract symbols on the keyboard of a computer and was displayed on a computer terminal, which was her only means of communication. She was guided through a careful sequence of increasingly complex 'sentences' by reinforcement with sweets. She too appeared very successful; the first time she was shown an orange, she produced the novel sequence *Tim give apple which-is orange*. Patterson (1981) taught a one-year-old gorilla called Koko a version of American Sign Language. Again several combinations were produced by Koko that she could not have encountered, for example *white tiger* for a toy zebra, *bottle match* for a cigarette lighter, and *cookie rock* for a stale bun. Superficially these studies seem to show that the apes are using language to communicate, that they can make use of order to signal meaning, and that they are capable of creating new utterances when the situation demands it.

But there are many reasons why this evidence cannot be held to prove the acquisition of language by apes, clearly presented in Wallman (1992). Much of the research has problems of methodology and interpretation; it is all very well to report that Koko produced *cookie rock*; what she actually did was produce two gestures interpreted by the human observers as *cookie* and *rock*; what they meant to her we do not know. It seems at best language-like behaviour that, even compared with a human child, does not begin to tap the complexity of human language. Chomsky's ironic comment compares how well human beings fly with how well apes speak; perhaps 'the distinction between jumping and flying is arbitrary, a matter of degree; people can really fly, just like birds, only not so well' (Chomsky, 1976, p. 41).

One objection is that the languages involved do not contain anything resembling the principles of UG: whatever the ape has acquired, it is not core grammar. The ape's knowledge might be peripheral or it might be functional knowledge of how to achieve things through gestures or signs but it is not language knowledge as a UG system. Chomsky's main objection is that the learning described does not resemble language acquisition in children because it is taught rather than 'picked up'. Children learn language from positive evidence rather than reinforcement by their parents. The apes, however, are all *taught* language; in the wild, apes do not develop language for themselves. The child 'does not choose to learn, and cannot fail to learn under normal conditions' (Chomsky, 1976, p. 71). The role of the environment to the child is triggering; it sets things off rather than provides precise controlled instruction. Even if the attempt to *teach* language to apes were successful, it would not prove how animals could *acquire* language. To sum up, 'the interesting investigations of the capacity of the higher apes to acquire symbolic systems seem to me to support the traditional belief that even the most rudimentary properties of language lie well beyond the capacities of an otherwise intelligent ape' (Chomsky, 1980a, p. 239).

Acquisition of principles and parameter setting in first language acquisition

This section takes some examples of how parameter setting works in first language acquisition, using the areas of syntax already introduced in chapters 1 and 2. This allows the reader to see the theory in operation. Although some of the analyses will not fully represent current theory, this will be remedied in chapter 8 after a fuller foundation has been laid.

Acquisition of Binding One area that has been studied is the Binding Theory. Since principles are innate, children should know the Binding Principles without acquiring them; what the child acquires should only be the knowledge of which words are anaphors, which pronominals, and which referring expressions, rather than the principles themselves. Comparatively few mistakes might be expected to occur with the principles and no difference in acquisition between pronominals and anaphors would be anticipated. But, oddly enough, anaphors seem to be easier for children than pronominals. Deutsch, Koster and Koster (1986) found that Dutch children aged 6 to 10 were better at reflexive anaphors (Principle A: anaphors are bound in a local domain) such as:

39. De broer van Piet wast   zich.
     The brother of   Piet washes himself.

than at pronominals (Principle B: pronominals are free in a local domain):

40. De broer van Piet wast   hem.
     The brother of   Piet washes him.

Solan (1987) had a similar result when testing English children aged 4 and 7 on sentences such as:

41. The dog said that the horse hit him/himself.

So there seems to be a discrepancy between children's knowledge of Principle A and of Principle B; they can cope with the sentences involving anaphors such as *himself* but not with those with pronominals such as *him*. Solan explained the comparative difficulty of pronominals by suggesting that children initially have access only to Binding Principle A, which covers anaphors, but not to Principle B which applies to pronominals; Finer (1987) argues that it is not so much that Principle B is missing but that children do not know it applies to particular pronominals – it is their lexical knowledge that is deficient, not their syntax. This discussion will be developed in chapter 8.

Principle C claims that referring expressions are free. This rules out sentences such as:

42. *He$_i$ complained after John$_i$ had the accident.

where the referring N *John* is bound to the pronominal *he* in the preceding higher clause. Lust, Loveland and Kornet (1980) showed that young children more often chose a referent for the pronominal *he* inside the sentence in sentences such as:

43.   When he closed the box, Cookie Monster lay down.

where Principle C permits such binding, than in sentences such as:

44.   He turned round when Snuffles found the penny.

where Principle C forbids such co-reference. Children show signs of knowing Principle C at a very young age. Further discussion can be found in Goodluck (1991, pp. 82–8).

Binding Theory has then led to interesting research into whether principles are built-in. What has been described here is not of course the full picture. Later research has led to parameterized binding which varies the concept of domain and has linked it to the notion of lexical parameterization, described in chapter 2 – perhaps children are learning how lexical items like *her* and *herself* behave in sentences rather than the principles themselves. The area shows some of the ways that UG can now be interpreted in practical terms of actual research with children. It will be updated in chapter 8.

The Pro-drop Parameter   Let us look more closely at how children acquire settings for parameters, so that they learn that Spanish is a pro-drop language, French is non-pro-drop; English is head-first, Japanese is head-last, and so on. The parameters in the child's mind can be thought of as built-in switches, each to be turned to suit the language that is heard. 'The transition from the initial state, S_0, to the steady state S_s, is a matter of setting the switches' (Chomsky, 1986a, p. 146). Acquiring the grammar of English means setting all UG parameters the English way; the setting of each switch is triggered by evidence. Continuing to use pro-drop as an example, the evidence that English children hear enables them to discover that English is a non-pro-drop language; the evidence that Spanish children hear enables them to discover that Spanish is a pro-drop language. Somewhere in the sentences children hear is the trigger that sets the value for the parameter in their minds. Children must be learning either from positive evidence alone or from indirect negative evidence, such as the lack of null-subject sentences in English. This is possible only if their choice is circumscribed; if they know there are a few possibilities, say pro-drop or non-pro-drop, they only require evidence to tell them which one they have encountered. Hearing a few sentences is sufficient to set the parameter one way or the other. The logic of indirect negative evidence, as Chomsky sees it, is 'if certain structures or rules fail to be exemplified in relatively simple expressions, where they would be expected to be found, then a (possibly marked) option is selected excluding them in the grammar, so that a kind of "negative evidence" can be available even without correction, adverse reactions, etc.' (Chomsky, 1981a, p. 9). Indirect negative evidence does not circumvent the poverty-of-the-stimulus argument because it relies on the child's expectation of certain principles; in other words it presupposes innateness.

Three logical possibilities for parameters in the initial state S_0 can be distinguished:

1 The switch is in a neutral position. The child is equally prepared for pro-drop or non-pro-drop settings. In this case the interim stages in the child's development of grammar might have either setting for pro-drop; children learning Spanish and English would have no common sequence of acquisition but would set the parameter appropriately from the moment that they first use it:

neutral initial setting ⟶ ⌐⟶ pro-drop setting (PD)
                          └⟶ non-pro-drop setting (NPD)

Figure 3.3 Neutral initial setting for pro-drop parameter

2 The switch is set to non-pro-drop. The child initially assumes that INFL does not properly govern the subject in all languages and so needs evidence to set it differently in pro-drop languages; children learning English would use one setting from the beginning and would have no need to change it; children learning Spanish would start with a non-pro-drop setting and would change with time, triggered by evidence.

non-pro-drop setting (NPD) ⟶ pro-drop setting (PD) (if necessary)

Figure 3.4 Non-pro-drop initial setting for pro-drop parameter

3 The switch is set to pro-drop, the reverse position. Those learning non-pro-drop languages are now the ones who require evidence; those learning Spanish need no extra evidence, those learning English do.

pro-drop setting (PD) ──→ non-pro-drop setting (NPD) (if necessary)

Figure 3.5   Pro-drop initial setting for pro-drop parameter

The most celebrated 1980s attempt to settle the choice between these three possibilities for the pro-drop parameter in first language acquisition was carried out by Nina Hyams (1986). By analysing published examples of children's language, she found that English children at the earlier stages indeed produced null-subject sentences such as:

45.   Read bear book.

and:

46.   Want look a man.

These were not due to the children's limited capacity to handle information since at the same time they could produce equivalent sentences with subjects such as:

47.   Gia ride bike.

and:

48.   I want kiss it.

Nor was it a performance clipping of the initial *I* since the children also had null subjects which were not at the beginning of the sentence. Hyams concluded that the third of the above alternatives is correct for pro-drop: children start from the setting for the parameter that allows null-subject sentences whether they are learning English, German or Spanish. English and German children go on to learn that their languages are non-pro-drop, setting the switch away from its initial value.

There is still no explanation for how the child does this. Let us look at the evidence available to the child. It might seem that indirect negative evidence suffices to acquire non-pro-drop; noticing a lack of null-subject sentences, the child switches to non-pro-drop. However, this involves the child keeping track not just of those sentences that occur but also of those that do not; when, say, 500 sentences have been heard and not one null-subject sentence is among them, the switch reverses. Apart from the difficulties with the occasional subjectless sentence the child will hear for accidental or dialectal reasons, this involves a striking feat of memory.

Hyams (1986) presents a solution in which the child learns from positive evidence, using a slightly different syntactic analysis from that given here. This rests primarily on a further property of non-pro-drop languages, namely the presence of 'expletives' such as *there* and *it* as subjects. A non-pro-drop language such as English uses an impersonal indefinite *it* in constructions such as 'weather' sentences:

49. It's raining.

Italian cannot use *it* in this way but must have a null-subject sentence:

50. Piove. (rains)

Similarly English has 'existential' sentences with *there* such as:

51. There's a tide in the affairs of men which taken at the flood leads on to fortune.

which also has a meaningless 'dummy' *there* in subject position. In other words it is a sign of a non-pro-drop language to have lexical expletives like *there* and *it* acting as subject; Hyams (1986) suggests that one trigger to tell the child to set the parameter away from the initial pro-drop value is the presence of such expletive subjects. When English children hear:

52. Once upon a time there were three bears.

or:

53. It's time for bed.

they realize that English is non-pro-drop and this affects the whole complex of syntactic phenomena covered by the parameter. Hyams supports this by showing that English children acquire expletive subjects at about the same time that they acquire full lexical subjects. Thus the child is setting the switch from positive evidence alone, namely the use of *there* and *it* as subjects, rather than from the indirect negative evidence of the lack of null-subject sentences.

Since 1986 Hyams has extended the analysis to other languages and substantially modified her position. Her work provides an interesting insight into how principles and parameters theory can be applied to actual data of children's language acquisition. The pro-drop parameter not only had theoretical linguistic consequences but it motivated a clear analysis of one of the most well-known aspects of children's early language, namely null-subject sentences. Chapter 8 will show that this was far from the final word; the pro-drop analysis itself has changed radically and alternative explanations are put forward for children's null-subject sentences, some of which do not involve pro-drop. Nevertheless, after Hyams' initial work, people could no longer say that principles and parameters theory was divorced from the study of actual children's speech, something which spurred a whole generation of researchers to look at actual children's language from the viewpoint of Universal Grammar.

Using a limited number of such parameters, UG cuts down on the possible core grammars the child can choose from. Ideally, given the evidence that the child has available, UG should narrow the possible grammars down to one, 'this language being a specific realization of the principles of the initial state S_0 with certain options settled in one way or another by the presented evidence (e.g., the value for the head parameter)' (Chomsky, 1986a, pp. 83–4). The evidence for fixing parameters need only be sufficient to trigger them and may be readily available. 'The parameters must have the property that they can be fixed by quite simple evidence, because this is what is available to the child; the value of the head parameter, for example, can be determined from such sentences as *John saw Bill* (versus *John Bill saw*)' (Chomsky, 1986a, p. 146). The effects of such parameters are sweeping; they are not confined to one rule or construction but apply anywhere in the grammar. Thus the pro-drop parameter is a choice in the theory of government, a principle that pervades the grammar, not just an explanation for the occurrence of null-subject sentences in some languages.

The discussion of acquisition is no longer concerned with what happens in a single language; the interest lies in finding how the child's UG can cope equally well with different languages. Most experimental or observational work with children has dealt with the acquisition of particular rules in a language – how the child learns question formation, or passives, or relative clauses. From a UG perspective such work is at best partial. Rules such as question formation are not 'pure' discrete phenomena that can be studied in their own right but involve many principles, each of which has some contribution to make. Research based on rules or on specific constructions is only a first approximation. Instead research within the principles and parameters theory needs to examine how a principle or a parameter is employed across the board in the child's grammar before it can make a final statement about acquisition. The examples given here have indeed run some risk of being construction-specific; for example the discussion of null-subject sentences may seem to concern a single sentence type rather than an underlying parameter that manifests in other aspects of the sentence as well as the subject position.

Chapter 8 provides further examples of current work in first language acquisition, in particular taking the work with pro-drop and Binding a stage further.

Acquisition of parameter settings

A parameter might:

— start in a neutral position in which any setting is possible

— start from a particular value (the unmarked setting) and need particular evidence to adopt the other setting (the marked setting)

Evidence for setting the parameter must be positive

The pro-drop parameter

Hyams (1986) suggests that there is an unmarked setting, namely the null-subject setting, as English children too go through a null-subject phase (*want look a man*), and that their evidence for changing to the marked non-pro-drop setting comes from the 'dummy' English subjects *it* and *there* (*It's raining outside, There's a car in our drive*), whose equivalent do not occur in pro-drop languages

---

Language input

What the child hears, the input, is nevertheless vital to the principles and parameters theory. What children need is raw linguistic data to get their teeth into. Without hearing any words of the language, they would have nothing to say; without hearing sentences, they would not be able to set the parameters appropriately for the language they are acquiring.

The poverty-of-the-stimulus argument, which maintains that the evidence is inherently too impoverished for the child to be able to acquire UG principles, must be firmly distinguished from an early claim made by Chomsky, namely the **degeneracy of the data**. Language acquisition is made more difficult by the fact that children hear performance, which may contain mistakes, slips of the tongue, English sentences with null subjects, and so on. Part of the positive evidence is therefore misleading and has to be filtered out by the learner. A model of language learning cannot be predicated on children hearing only grammatical sentences; it has to be able to tolerate a certain amount of ungrammaticality (Braine, 1971). However, the claim that the input data for the child are degenerate has had to be modified in the light of the 1970s research into speech addressed to children, which showed that, on the contrary, such input was highly regular. Newport (1976) found that only 1 out of 1,500 utterances addressed to children was ungrammatical. Such regularity, however, applies only to the language addressed directly to the child; children also hear adult performance addressed to fellow adults, with the usual quota of deviancies. The main argument concentrates on the poverty of language addressed to children, i.e. the fact that it does not contain the right kind of syntactic evidence, rather than on the degeneracy of the data, the fact that it is not always completely well-formed, since the data are arguably not as degenerate as was earlier thought.

Many claims and counterclaims about the speech addressed to children have indeed been made in the field at large in recent years. To take Bruner (1983) again as representative, he postulates a Language Acquisition Support System (LASS) in adults' minds that enables them unerringly to provide the appropriate environment for their children; 'Language is not encountered willy-nilly by the child; it is shaped to make communicative interaction effective – fine-tuned' (Bruner, 1983, p. 39). Even if such fine-tuning, or indeed any other adaptive linguistic behaviour by the parent, could teach the principles of UG, it would still have to meet the uniformity requirement that all parents use it, which seems unlikely.

However, input itself is nevertheless vital to the UG model, as we saw above. Without hearing an example of *see*, children cannot begin to record it as a Verb. Without hearing English sentences such as:

54.   John sees Mary.

they cannot build up the lexical entry for *see* with the object NP that has to follow it. Without hearing sentences such as:

55.   John sees himself.

they cannot discover that *himself* is an anaphor. Without hearing:

56.   It's raining.

they cannot begin to discover that English is a non-pro-drop language. Language evidence is crucial to the process of acquisition. For children to be able to create linguistic competence, they need to hear a range of sentences from adults. But the speech they hear does not need to be specially adapted to them in any other way.

Or does it? James Morgan (1986) has claimed that in some cases children will not be able to tell how to set a parameter from the straightforward evidence they hear. Let us take an idealized example to demonstrate this. Suppose a child hears:

57. The dog bites the cat.

How would the child know if this were a language with an SVO (subject–verb–object) order, like English, or one with an OVS (object–verb–subject) order, rare as the latter may be? Only if the input somehow showed this by 'bracketing' together the VP, i.e.:

58. The dog [bites the cat].

Morgan (1986) therefore argues for the importance of phonological clues such as pauses and intonation to indicate to the child where the syntactic boundaries come. He found in an experiment that speech addressed to children indeed has clearer marking of phrase boundaries through pauses and vowel lengthening than speech to adults. He argues that children need **'bracketed input'**, that is to say sentences with clear signs of particular phrase boundaries, and that parents indeed provide such input.

Much of Morgan's work is within the theory of learnability, a mathematical approach to language acquisition that has had a symbiotic connection to the UG theory. Formal learnability theory, starting with the work of Gold (1967), is concerned with what is logically necessary for language learning. Wexler and Culicover (1980) measured the input to the learner in 'degrees' going from degree-0 (no embedded clauses) through degree-1 (one embedded clause) upwards; their argument is that children need to encounter degree-2 sentences to acquire human language, i.e. sentences containing two embedded clauses. Morgan (1986) suggested that bracketed input reduced the degrees of embedding necessary to one, i.e. degree-1; children could learn a human language if they heard sentences with at most one embedded clause. Lightfoot (1989, 1991) attempted to reduce this still further within the principles and parameters theory. He claimed that all the information that the child needs to learn any kind of sentence is present in sentences with no embedded clauses, i.e. degree-0. This raises problems about the properties of embedded clauses that do not seem to be directly represented in the structure of the main clause of a sentence. Movement restrictions from one clause to another are one example; Lightfoot (1991) claims that these can be triggered by information as to whether movement within the simple clause is possible, such as that in the French:

59. Combien   as-tu   vu de personnes?
    (how many have you seen of people)
    How many people have you seen?

Another problem is Binding Theory, where the behaviour of anaphors and pronominals in sentences such as:

60. Helen said she met her.

seems unlearnable with only a single clause to play with; Lightfoot (1991) modifies his degree-0 claim by saying that it is not the single clause that is needed so much as the single binding domain, as described in the last chapter; 'a child with access only to material from unembedded binding Domains has access to certain well-defined elements of an embedded clause' (Lightfoot, 1991, p. 31). He claims that this degree-0 property is an ancillary to UG; it reflects learning strategies, not the language faculty itself. Many of the arguments in Lightfoot (1991), however, depend upon historical change in language, where the degree-0 argument can be applied; for example the change from Old English OV order to Modern English VO order was facilitated by the increasing possibility of allowing particles to separate from verbs. (Denison (1994), however, doubts whether there is sufficient evidence to be able to label Old English conclusively as SOV.)

Markedness and language development

UG is concerned with core grammar rather than with the periphery. The logical argument of acquisition deals primarily with the core, with the elements that are directly linked to UG. Peripheral elements can be learned in ways that are unconnected to UG. Politeness formulas such as *please* and *thank you* may well be learnt through active correction by the parents; historical accidents such as the irregular past tense in English are not necessarily learnt through UG or entirely from positive evidence. The same idealizations are involved in acquisition as in the description of competence; it is grammatical knowledge that is being discussed, not language performance or language use; within language knowledge the crucial areas are those that are universal.

Within the core, one possibility is that certain parameter settings are more marked than others; languages that have syntactic movement, for instance, may be closer to the unmarked form of UG than those that do not, making English unmarked, Japanese marked. With the opposite assumption, English is marked, and Japanese is not. Going back to pro-drop, the conclusion that all children start with a pro-drop setting means that non-pro-drop is more marked. Children start off with the unmarked setting for the parameters; they have to reset those which are more marked in the language they are learning.

Markedness also relates to the problem of evidence available to the child. One interpretation is that the unmarked settings of parameters are those that the child can learn from the least amount of positive evidence. Spanish learners need no evidence to set pro-drop; they have the right setting from the start. Children learning English need evidence to turn the switch away from its initial unmarked setting, if we accept Hyams' account. Children need evidence to move from unmarked to marked settings. Hence marked elements of UG need more evidence, or different types of evidence, than unmarked elements. Elements of peripheral grammar may need totally different types of evidence; for example the *was/were* distinction in English might need specific negative correction from parents. Perhaps it should be pointed out that the use of the term 'markedness' in UG is very different from its use in other theories.

Complementary to this approach to markedness is the Subset Principle, introduced within principles and parameters theory by Berwick (1985) and stated by Chomsky as:

> **if a parameter has two values + and –, and the value – generates a proper subset of the grammatical sentences generated with the choice of value +, then – is the 'unmarked value' selected in the absence of evidence.** (Chomsky, 1986a, p. 146)

Roughly speaking, children choose the setting for a parameter that fits the evidence with the fewest possible assumptions. The children's choice is conservative in that it stays as close as possible to the data they hear. They prefer a language that is a 'subset' of a larger language rather than leaping immediately to the 'larger' version. This is slightly difficult to accommodate within the discussion here since it concerns the 'languages' the children learn rather than 'grammars'. Wexler and Manzini (1987) show how the Subset Principle deals with the learning of the Binding Principles but argue it does not apply to the type of evidence for pro-drop presented by Hyams (1986). This is developed in chapter 8.

There are general problems in interpreting data from the actual language development of children in relation to markedness. The study of children's speech is potentially misleading for the logical problem of acquisition. As with adults, grammatical competence is imperfectly reflected in speech performance; children too can run out of breath, or make mistakes, or change their minds. The psychological processes used in speech comprehension and production are indirectly and partially linked to their grammatical competence. To study the competence of adults, an alternative source of evidence is available in the form of judgements about sentences, a device used frequently in this book. Such judgements are hardly feasible with small children. Nevertheless some researchers have argued in its favour: McDaniel and Cairns (1990) for instance suggest that judgements can be elicited from small children if the task is appropriately designed. However large the sample of children's utterances, it is still an inaccurate source of information about their competence.

In addition the processes involved in language performance are themselves developing at the same time as competence. Filtering out the effects of performance processes from actual samples of speech is doubly difficult with children since it cannot be assumed that only language develops. The child starts by saying one word at a time:

61.   Mine. Bath. Yes. Car. Carses. Hiding.

and goes on to a two-word stage:

62.   That baba. All gone. A lion. Little girl. See Mary.

Both stages may be the by-product of short-term memory restrictions that limit the number of items in the child's utterance rather than of anything directly to do with language acquisition; 'it might be that he had fully internalized the requisite mental structure, but for some reason lacked the capacity to use it' (Chomsky, 1980a, p. 53). The apparent progress from one word to two words may have little to do with language acquisition, more to do with the growth of 'channel capacity'. The expansion of children's general cognitive capacity allows them to produce longer and more complex sentences, but this is caused by relaxing constraints on performance rather than by increased competence. In Chomsky's words, 'much of the investigation of early language development is concerned with matters that may not properly belong to the language faculty ... but to other faculties of mind that interact in an intimate fashion with the language faculty in language use ...' (Chomsky, 1981b, p. 36). Acquisition considered as a logical problem is an abstraction from such features of development. The history of speech developing in the child reflects factors that are nothing to do with acquisition.

We can make a distinction between language **acquisition** – the logical problem of how the mind acquires S_s independent of intervening stages – and language **development** – the history of the intervening stages; the distinction reflects Chomsky's thinking, even if he does not make it in these terms. Acquisition is an idealized 'instantaneous' model in which time and experience play minimal roles; the crucial factor is the relationship between S_0 and S_s. Development reflects the complex interaction of language with the other faculties of mind that are maturing at the same time. Research into both acquisition and development is concerned with evidence, the former with evidence of what speakers know, the latter with evidence from what children say. Acquisition theory does not necessarily need support from actual studies of children's language; 'behavior is only one kind of evidence, sometimes not the best, and surely no criterion for knowledge' (Chomsky, 1980a, p. 54). While some studies such as Hyams' have attempted the complex task of linking development with acquisition, there is no compelling reason why the theory should accept them as more than supplementary evidence.

It is then possible to assign markedness as a *post hoc* consequence of developmental studies. If the pro-drop setting is used first, then, everything else being equal, this is a reason for preferring pro-drop as the unmarked setting. But everything else rarely *is* equal because of the complexity of actual development. 'We would expect the order of appearance of structures in language acquisition to reflect the structure of markedness in some respects, but there are many complicating factors: e.g., processes of maturation may be such as to permit certain unmarked structures to be manifested only relatively late in language acquisition, frequency effects may intervene, etc.' (Chomsky, 1981a, p. 9). Assigning markedness on the basis of developmental stages is circular if there is no other reason for a setting to be unmarked than its earlier occurrence; without a syntactic rationale, markedness amounts to saying 'whatever is learnt first is learnt first'.

It might also be that the language faculty itself matures. Babies have lungs and hearts that function from the time that they are born; however, the first teeth appear at around seven months, and are replaced by others at around six years; wisdom teeth appear much later. This does not mean that teeth are not biologically determined; they appear at particular stages of maturation even if absent at the beginning; 'genetically determined factors in development evidently are not to be identified with those operative at birth' (Chomsky, 1986a, p. 54). UG might be like the heart – complete and functional at birth – or like teeth – coming into operation bit by bit; these alternatives are called by Chomsky the 'growth' theory and the 'no growth' theory (Chomsky, 1987). So far as acquisition is concerned, UG is neutral between the two possibilities; the relationship between the two states, S_0 and S_s, is not affected by whether UG is initially present or not. It is, however, vital to the development argument. This is developed in chapter 8.

Let us borrow the term **wild grammar** from Helen Goodluck (1986) to refer to a grammar that does not conform to UG, by, say, breaking the principles or having illegal parameter settings. If UG is present and functioning from the start, children would never entertain wild grammars; children would not stray outside the bounds of UG at any stage of development; their learning would be error-free so far as UG is concerned. A UG principle such as structure-dependency will be used at all stages of development. This is not to say it initially figures prominently in their speech; it may be precluded for performance reasons of sentence length or complexity; a principle of Binding for example can hardly be used in one-word or two-word sentences. But, if there are no wild grammars, none of the children's grammars should violate structure-dependency or Binding at any stage; all of their interim grammars should be possible human languages. Research into language development to investigate this is necessarily complex and tentative. Anecdotal observations suggest that children rarely produce sentences that breach UG. But this is hardly surprising in view of the complexity of the sentences that are needed to show many UG principles combined with the constraints on the child's performance; there are no opportunities for breaking structure-dependency with one-word sentences, for example.

It is perfectly plausible that UG matures. Lila Gleitman has often argued for a biologically determined maturational transition from a semantic phase of language to a syntactic phase; at the first stage the child produces sentences to convey meaning without regard to their syntax; at the next stage the child abruptly switches to syntactic organization. Her evidence is based on a variety of forms of acquisition including acquisition by Down's syndrome children, blind children, deaf children and premature children (Gleitman, 1982). Chomsky's view that early stages of development are nothing to do with acquisition supports the possibility of a presyntactic phase; UG may simply not be available to the very young child, who gets by on semantics alone. Chomsky separates this line of thinking firmly from the logical problem of language acquisition; 'there is good reason to believe that the language faculty undergoes maturation – in fact, the order and timing of this maturation appear to be rather uniform despite considerable variation in experience and other cognitive faculties – but this does not bear on the correctness of the empirical assumption embodied in the idealization to instantaneous learning . . .' (Chomsky, 1986a, p. 54).

Let us review briefly the main argument for the innateness of UG. The first step is to recognize the complex and abstract grammatical competence possessed by the native speaker. The distinctive nature of this knowledge rules out its acquisition through imitation, correction and approval, social routines, or other mental faculties; grammatical explanation is ruled out for other reasons. Unless the principles and parameters of grammatical competence can be shown to be learnable by one or other of these means, they must be innate. This central argument is bolstered by other arguments about the common possession of language by the whole human species, the uniformity of acquisition despite the variety of situations, the lack of key mistakes in children's speech, and the inability of other species to acquire language. But the crucial step is the first one; once it is conceded that language knowledge is defined in terms of a grammatical competence of this kind, everything else follows.

How does it relate to other approaches to language acquisition? The UG position that has been presented is, broadly speaking, popular among linguists rather than those primarily interested in studying first language acquisition in children. One reason for this is that in a sense the study of children is unnecessary in UG theory since all that the linguist needs to do is to work backwards from S_s, the final state. The primary work is the linguistic description and the use of learnability arguments to motivate the description. E-language research with large numbers of children is secondary though it can provide some supporting evidence, if it is properly evaluated. I-language research deals with the individual mind, not the behaviour of groups. Secondly, experimental or observational research on UG issues is hard to carry out. The necessity of separating competence from performance and acquisition from development means on the one hand that actual observations of children are flawed, on the other that appropriate methodologies for experiments are extremely hard to devise.

The impression one is left with is that many workers in child language are not prepared to take the first step of accepting that the essential part of language is grammatical competence. They may concede that it is a quaint logical problem, but claim that what really interests them is how children form social relationships, how their thinking influences their language, how children with language problems can be helped, all side-issues to UG theory. To those with primarily sociological or educational aims, or indeed E-language aims in general, UG theory has comparatively little to offer; it is concerned with mental man rather than with social man and with what human beings have in common rather than their differences. UG indeed provides a core test case of the essential quality of human minds; the type of knowledge revealed as part of the structure of the brain is fascinating and profound. Supporting it with research into children's language is a valuable exercise. UG theory has a unique central place in first language acquisition studies. But it is only part of the broad picture. UG theory is concerned with the acorn rather than with the tree in all its complexity; vital as the acorn may be as the source of growth and development, for many purposes the leaves, the wood, or the blossom are more important. The danger is that UG may be seen as a threat to other ideas of language development, rather than as a complementary theory that accounts for a specific area of vital concern to those interested in the unique properties of the human mind.

Second Language Acquisition and Universal Grammar

Some people do not know one language; they know two or more. During the 1980s Second Language Acquisition research became increasingly interested in seeing the extent to which the principles and parameters model could deal with second language acquisition.

Let us start by adapting the Language Acquisition Device model to L2 learning. In principle the LAD diagram could simply be extended to take in other languages, as in figure 3.6. A second set of primary linguistic data go into the black box, a second grammar comes out containing a second version of the principles, a second batch of settings for the parameters, and a second lexicon.

But second language acquisition appears not to function in this way.

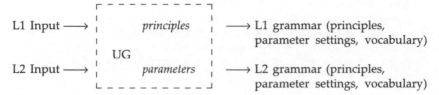

Figure 3.6 LAD extended to Second Language Acquisition

Though many people start to learn a second language, few, if any, manage to gain a knowledge of the L2 equivalent to that of the L1, unlike first language acquisition where virtually all children acquire full L1s. What is different about L2 learning? One possibility is the existence of the first language in the mind. L1 children start with the zero state S_0 and go on to the steady state S_s; they progress from an initial stage of knowing only their innate endowment to a final state of knowing everything about a particular language. L2 learners, however, already know a first language; they possess one instantiation of UG. The initial state of the child's mind, S_0, has no language-specific knowledge; the initial state of the L2 learner, which we can distinguish by calling S_i, already contains one grammar, complete with principles and actual parameter settings. Or, to make matters more complicated, the L2 may be being learnt while the learning of the L1 is still incomplete; in this case S_i contains a non-final form of the L1. With different starting points to first and second language acquisition, it is hardly surprising that the end result is different. The mind starting to learn an L2 in state S_i already contains an L1 grammar, an S_s; that is to say, $S_i = (S_0 + S_s)$; the L2 has to live alongside this other grammar. The LAD diagram misrepresents the initial state of L2 learning by treating it as the same as the initial state of L1 learning.

In L1 acquisition the final S_s is adult competence, which is by definition complete: a native speaker's competence is whatever a native speaker knows, neither more nor less. But the final state in L2 learning is hard to define. What *is* a normal L2 speaker? A person who can effortlessly pass for a native speaker in all circumstances? A person who can just about order a coffee in a restaurant? A person who can translate Shakespeare? A person who can interpret the small print in a contract? One possibility is to take the final state of L2 learners as identical to the L1 S_s: the task of L2 learners is complete when they know the L2 as well as they know the L1. Chomsky himself argues for the 'common-sense' view that only the complete knowledge of language counts, rather than intermediate states:

We do not for example say that the person has a perfect knowledge of some language L similar to English but still different from it. What we say is that the child or foreigner has a 'partial knowledge of English' or is 'on his or her way' towards acquiring knowledge of English, and if they reach this goal, they will then know English. (Chomsky, 1986a, p. 16)

But such 'ambilinguals' or 'balanced bilinguals' are rare; at best they constitute a small and untypical minority of L2 speakers. Most people are substantially less efficient in their L2 than in their L1; many learn little of the L2, sometimes despite their best efforts. It has been said that at any moment 80 per cent of the L2 learners of English in the world are beginners, implying that few go on to become intermediate or advanced speakers. If the native adult S_s is the final state of L2 learning, hardly anyone reaches it. While L1 competence is whatever it is, L2 competence is usually defined as what it is *not*, in short as if it were L1 competence. The steady state that L2 learners achieve differs from an L1 S_s and varies from one learner to another. This terminal state of L2 learning can be referred to as S_t, to distinguish it from S_s in L1 learning. So, while L1 learning can be shown as:

$$S_0 \longrightarrow S_s$$

L2 learning needs to be shown as:

$$S_i \longrightarrow S_t$$

Neither the initial nor the final states of L2 learning are the same as those of first language acquisition.

The poverty-of-the-stimulus argument and second language acquisition

Nevertheless, if L2 learners possess knowledge of language they could not have acquired from the evidence they have encountered, its source must be within their own minds. Innateness can be established in just the same way in second language learning as in first language acquisition. The poverty-of-the-stimulus argument, however, works slightly differently with second languages. Step A in first language acquisition means demonstrating the existence of a property of syntax in the mind of a native speaker, taken to be normal by definition. But L2 learners come in all varieties and levels of knowledge of the L2; some are just beginners and never likely to progress any further; others are interpreters with the future of nations hanging on their translations. There is no typical L2 learner, only diverse individuals. Is it possible to demonstrate Step A for L2 learners, say for structure-dependency? The results for the MUGtest show that advanced L2 learners of English consistently rejected sentences such as:

63. *Is Sam is the cat that brown?

Japanese teachers of English scored 97 per cent; Chinese students 86.6 per cent, and Finnish students 100 per cent. Step A is satisfied in that advanced L2 learners know structure-dependency.

Step B looks at the sources of language evidence available to the L2 learner. The occurrence and uniformity requirements function slightly differently in L2 learning theory; since S_t is itself variable, explaining how a learner acquired something means showing that the postulated situational effect actually occurs for that learner, but does not necessitate showing that it occurs for *all* learners – what is termed elsewhere the 'narrow' and 'broad' forms of the poverty-of-the-stimulus argument (Cook, 1991).

Imitation   As in L1 acquisition, sheer imitation only provides positive evidence of what is heard; repeating sentences does not in itself allow the learner to know what can*not* be said. Indeed a similar argument was responsible for the decline of language teaching methods that rely on imitation, such as audiolingualism. Repeating aloud:

64. Oscar fancies himself.

ten times does not confer knowledge of Binding Principle A.

Explanation   Grammatical explanation does not figure prominently in the experience of L1 children. L2 learning is, however, different, at least for those learners who encounter the language in the classroom. Some language teachers constantly explain rules to students; explanation forms one basis of the grammar-translation method still popular in many European settings, in particularly at university level; for example at the University of Essex all undergraduates studying a modern language have to take a descriptive course with the avowed aim of improving their practical ability as well as their academic knowledge. Carroll and Swain (1993) showed that 'metalinguistic feedback' indeed helped L2 learners to acquire the dative alternation between *Give the dog a bone* and *Give a bone to the dog*. Even if some learners never encounter grammatical explanation, undoubtedly many adult L2 learners automatically reach for a grammar book, as Burling (1981) points out.

Yet the explanations of syntax that L2 learners receive necessarily concern only those points that their teachers are aware of; structure-dependency or pro-drop are unlikely to be part of the teachers' conscious grammatical knowledge. 'It must be recognised that one does not learn the grammatical structure of a second language through "explanation and instruction" beyond the most rudimentary level for the simple reason that no one has enough explicit knowledge about this structure to provide explanation and instruction' (Chomsky, 1969). Even if grammatical explanation might work for some aspects of L2 learning, it cannot account for how people know what they are not taught, for example structure-dependency. The explanations of 'reflexives' in pedagogical grammar books for instance do not go very far towards explaining the Binding Principles the L2 learner knows. This does not exclude the possibility that L2 teaching could hypothetically be based on grammatical explanation of principles and parameters syntax, as suggested in Cook (1993) and carried out with some success in White (1992).

Correction and approval   Children rarely receive correction or approval of syntactic forms in the L1; the occurrence requirement therefore rules this out as a way of acquiring the L1. But such feedback is provided in many L2 learning situations, most conspicuously in the classroom, but also in 'natural' situations; teachers are only too aware of the insatiable demand from L2 students for correction. If correction is to be successful, the L2 learner must, furthermore, produce sentences that deviate in the appropriate way. In order to learn Binding, the learners must produce sentences such as:

65.   The Joneses asked the Smiths to help themselves.

meaning that the Joneses wanted help, i.e.:

66.   *The Joneses$_i$ asked the Smiths to help themselves$_i$.

And the correctors must point out:

67.   No, in that case you mean 'The Joneses asked the Smiths to help *them*'.

Though the language of L2 learners exhibits a variety of peculiarities, such mistakes are not numbered among them. It is not then obvious that L2 learners actually produce the necessary mistakes in terms of principles and parameters that would enable their teachers to correct them.

Turning to other areas, there are no reports that L2 learners breach principles such as structure-dependency. The corrector has to be able to identify the problem in order to correct it. Many of the possible deviations from UG are unlikely to be spotted by the ordinary native speaker. Correction cannot be ruled out as a source of evidence in the classroom; traditionally minded teachers use it frequently; conventional students often request it. But correction of the type of mistake needed to acquire UG principles seems unlikely. Correction is no more liable to lead to L2 knowledge in non-classroom settings than in L1 acquisition. As L2 learners manage to learn UG principles without such correction, it cannot be the most important element. While correction potentially meets the occurrence requirement for some areas of language for some learners, it is likely to prove an ineffective way of acquiring the central areas of UG.

Social interaction In considering social interaction it is necessary to separate those exchanges that are 'natural' from those that are 'non-natural'; though L2 learners may engage in the same routines of social interaction as L1 children, they may in addition have controlled 'artificial' exchanges, for instance those found in such teaching techniques as structure drills. Natural social exchanges seem a clear route to pragmatic competence in the L2 but they are not able to help the acquisition of UG principles in the L2 any more than they are in the L1; so, while all L1 learners encounter natural communicative interaction, some classroom L2 learners do not! Non-natural exchanges have been used by teachers in many ways ranging from grammatical correction to asking the students to talk about the differences between two pictures to the classic threefold exchange Teacher's Initiation/Pupils' Response/Teacher's Feedback. These exchanges could aim at teaching principles such as Binding, say through a carefully constructed Socratic dialogue in which the student is led to see the binding possibilities in the sentence. But this approach has not been attempted to our knowledge, and would indeed necessitate the provision of negative evidence or grammatical explanation if it were to succeed. Vital as social interaction may be to the needs of foreign language students, it is an unlikely vehicle for the acquisition of core UG grammar.

Dependence on other faculties   The use of other mental faculties was ruled out in L1 acquisition, primarily because of the uniqueness of the language principles. The same argument applies to L2 learning; there is no compelling reason why it should involve other mental faculties, certainly so far as S_ts that resemble S_ss are concerned. However, the argument is more complex in L2 learning because the learner is usually at a later stage of cognitive development and consequently the relationship between language and cognition differs from that in the native child. People such as Bley-Vroman et al. (1988) have therefore argued that the comparative inefficiency of L2 learning is because L2 learners do not have Universal Grammar available to them but acquire second languages though other mental processes. This implies that the knowledge of the L2 is very different from knowledge of the L1, and so not expressible in the principles and parameters format (since these cannot be learnt). We shall return to this debate in chapter 8.

All in all, the poverty-of-the-stimulus argument still applies to L2 acquisition, provided various provisos are borne in mind about the alternative starting and finishing points and intervening routes. If some L2 learners who have used natural means know UG principles, the source must be in their own minds. But of course this may be the knowledge they already have of a first language, S_s, rather than UG itself.

Some insufficient ways of acquiring UG from the environment in the L2

	positive evidence	other evidence	occurrence requirement	uniformity requirement
imitation	+		±	−
explanation		+	±	−
correction		+	±	−
social interaction	+		±	−

Acquisition of parameter settings in second language acquisition

Let us now parallel the discussion of first language acquisition by seeing how pro-drop is acquired in an L2. There were three possibilities for parameter setting in L1 acquisition: children might start with a neutral setting or with either of the two possible settings as a default unmarked setting. In principle the same is true for second language acquisition, with the complication that S_i already contains one setting for pro-drop, that of the L1. L2 learners might start from scratch like L1 learners or they might transfer the parameter setting from their L1, which might or might not be the same as the L2. In addition to the three diagrams seen earlier (pp. 111–12), there is also the following possibility:

L1 pro-drop setting (PD or NPD) $\longrightarrow$ L2 pro-drop setting (PD or NPD)

Figure 3.7 Additional pro-drop setting relationship in a second language

This involves four combinations;

$$
\begin{array}{ll}
\text{L1 PD} & \longrightarrow \text{L2 PD} \\
& \longrightarrow \text{L2 NPD} \\
\text{L1 NPD} & \longrightarrow \text{L2 PD} \\
& \longrightarrow \text{L2 NPD}
\end{array}
$$

Figure 3.8 Parameter setting alternatives for pro-drop in a second language

If the two languages have the same setting (PD or NPD), L2 learning would resemble L1 learning by accident and nothing could be shown by this similarity. Only if the L1 and L2 settings differ and L2 learners start off from the unmarked setting, could it be shown that L2 learning is the same as first language acquisition. Thus, if Spanish or Italian learners of English (PD → NPD) lack subjects, this could either mean that they are transferring their L1 pro-drop setting or that they are starting from the unmarked pro-drop setting established by Hyams. In reverse, if English learners of Spanish (NPD → PD) showed a lack of subjects in Spanish, this could not be transfer but might be the use of the unmarked setting.

A considerable amount of L2 research into pro-drop took place in the mid-1980s to establish the issue of whether the L1 setting influenced the L2. White (1986) compared French learners of English (NPD → NPD) with Spanish learners of English (PD → NPD). A grammaticality judgements test showed that Spanish learners of English tolerated sentences such as:

68. *In winter, snows a lot in Canada.

much more than French learners. Her conclusion was: 'L1 parameters influence the adult learner's view of the L2 data, at least for a while, leading to transfer errors' (White, 1986, p. 69). The MUGtest (Cook, 1994) shows similar results for the learning of English: Japanese teachers of English (PD → NPD) rejected:

69.   *Is French.

61 per cent, Poles (PD → NPD) 84 per cent.

In the reverse direction, however, Liceras (1989) tested French- and English-speaking learners of Spanish (NPD → PD) on sentences which exemplified the lack of expletive 'dummy' subjects in pro-drop languages. L2 learners found it quite easy to spot that the expletive subjects were not needed. Her conclusions were that 'resetting the pro-drop parameter from English and French to Spanish is not difficult with respect to null subjects' (Liceras, 1989, p. 126). So L2 learners start neither from the L1 setting nor from what Hyams for one regarded as the unmarked L1 setting.

Second language acquisition clearly provides an interesting area for principles and parameters research, which will be developed further in chapter 8. As we see from the poverty-of-the-stimulus argument, if something is known that is not learnt, it must be built into the human mind, even if it only manifests itself in the learning of a second language.

4

The X-bar Theory of Phrase Structure

This chapter will discuss the following topics:

— X-bar theory of phrase structure
— The structure of lexical phrases
— The structure of functional phrases
— Levels of structural representation and movement.

Chapters 4 to 7 present the principles and parameters theory in more detail, illustrated chiefly from English; this chapter covers the X-bar theory of constituent structure, to be expanded in chapter 5. A logical order of presentation would treat each component of the theory separately. However, since the theory is an interlocking arrangement of principles and sub-theories which interact in diverse ways, no part can be considered in isolation from the rest. Nor can the theory be tackled through particular grammatical rules such as 'passive' or 'questions', as such constructions represent the interaction of principles and particular parameter settings rather than being syntactic areas in their own right. Inevitably therefore the theory will not make complete sense to the reader until all its parts are assembled: to describe how a plane flies you need to know about the whole machine, not just about the wings or the engines on their own.

X-bar Theory of Phrase Structure

First some of the general properties of phrase structure need to be stated, which come at the heart of syntax. Phrase structure is a way of capturing the structural relationships of the sentence through the concept 'consists of'. A phrase consists of one or more constituents; a phrase A may consist of the constituents B and C, as seen in the following tree diagram:

1.

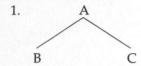

These constituents may in turn be made up of others, say B consisting of D and E, C of F:

2.

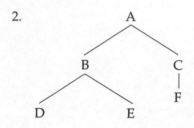

The phrase structure of the sentence is a hierarchy, with each constituent successively consisting of other constituents, until only non-expandable items are left. The 'consists of' relationship can be expressed as rewrite rules (A → B C) or as bracketting ([_A B C]), as we saw in chapter 2. An item that comes above another item in the tree (and is not on a separate branch) is said to 'dominate' it: A dominates everything in tree (2) – B, C, D, E and F; B dominates D and E but not F; C dominates F. An item that comes immediately above another item is said to 'immediately dominate' it; thus A immediately dominates B and C but A does not immediately dominate D and E. Items that are immediately dominated by the same element are known as 'sisters'; E is a sister to D, B a sister to C.

When there is no need to specify the internal structure of a phrase for the purposes of a particular discussion, that part of the tree is simplified into a triangle connecting the final elements, say *g* and *h*, viz.:

3.

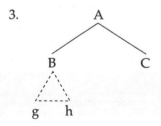

This tree might then be appropriate in a discussion of A to which the internal structure of B is irrelevant and would be distracting. Since the tree representation of principles and parameters theory gets progressively unwieldy, this short cut will be resorted to whenever possible here.

So far the discussion could apply to almost any model of phrase structure. Within principles and parameters theory, phrase structure is a comparatively simple system derived from a few principles and the setting of certain parameters. The form of phrase structure employed is **X-bar syntax**, a model of syntax not exclusive to this theory but used widely, for example within Generalized Phrase Structure Grammar (Gazdar et al., 1985). As always, the emphasis is on expressing the general principles of Universal Grammar rather than the peculiarities of a particular language or of a particular rule. X-bar syntax replaces large numbers of idiosyncratic rewrite rules with general principles; it captures properties of *all* phrases, not just those of a certain type; and it bases syntax on categories that tie in with the lexicon.

X-bar syntax is distinctive in claiming that every phrase conforms to certain requirements. In particular it insists that phrases must be 'endocentric': a phrase always contains at least a head as well as other possible constituents. Thus a Noun Phrase (NP) such as *the bird* contains a head *bird*; a Verb Phrase (VP) *sees the cat* contains a head *sees*. An essential requirement of X-bar syntax is that the head of the phrase belong to a particular category related to the type of phrase. A Noun Phrase contains a Noun head, i.e.:

$$NP \rightarrow \ldots N \ldots$$

and a Verb Phrase contains a Verb head:

$$VP \rightarrow \ldots V \ldots$$

never vice versa with a V acting as head of an NP or an N acting as head of a VP, as in the ungrammatical sentence:

4.   *The see cats the bird.

The head of a phrase is not related arbitrarily to the phrase type; it is not chance that an NP contains an N rather than a V, a VP a V rather than an N. The general principle that all phrases contain a particular type of head can be formalized as:

$$XP \rightarrow \ldots X \ldots$$

The X in both places stands for the same category; any phrase XP must have a head X of the same type – VPs contain V heads, NPs N heads, and so on for all phrases. It is a principle of X-bar theory that phrases have heads of the same category as the phrase itself.

The Structure of Lexical Phrases

The types of head in lexical phrases are related to word-classes. The four lexical phrases used in X-bar syntax are: Verb Phrase (VP), Noun Phrase (NP), Adjective Phrase (AP) and Prepositional Phrase (PP). Each of these contains the appropriate head V, N, A, P, that is to say a lexical category corresponding to one of the four major word-classes in the lexicon. Lexical phrases invariably have heads that are lexical categories linked to lexical entries.

Let us give examples of phrase structure for each type of lexical phrase. The PP (Prepositional Phrase) *from England* has a head P *from* and an NP *England* within it.

5.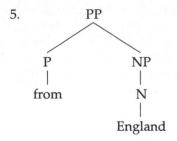

In the NP *doctors from England* the lexical category which is the head of the phrase is the N *doctors*:

6.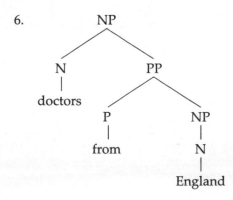

The VP (Verb Phrase) *drink milk* has as its head the V *drink* and contains within it an NP *milk*:

7.

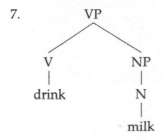

Finally the AP (Adjective Phrase) *jealous of Peter*, as in *He was jealous of Peter*, contains an Adjective (A) head *jealous* and a PP *of Peter*:

8.

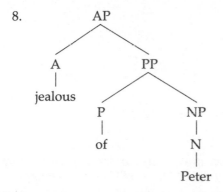

Each phrase consists of a head and other elements, which are phrases themselves; each phrase is built up around a lexical category such as N from which it takes its name and its main properties.

Looking at a whole sentence:

9.   The detective confronted Max with the evidence.

demonstrates how the structure depends on lexical heads of phrases. The first NP *the detective* contains a head N, which is the lexical item *detective*. The VP contains a head V, the lexical item *confront*. The PP contains a head P, the lexical item *with*. The phrase structure of the sentence is linked to the lexicon, not just because the sentence eventually consists of actual words, but also because the heads of the phrases within the sentence must be lexical categories and must suit the particular structure of which they form part. An NP is a phrase containing a head N; a PP is a phrase containing a head P; and so on. In some ways this resembles a traditional analysis in terms of parts of speech in that the sentence is largely made up of lexical categories. A major part of phrase structure consists of arrangements of lexical categories at different levels of abstraction; any phrase is in a sense the elaboration of the properties of its head.

X-bar theory claims that the phrase level, i.e. XP where X stands for any of the categories, and the category level, i.e. X, are insufficient to capture all the details of phrase structure; a further intermediate level is required. Take the sentence:

10.   The Education minister will resign her post on Tuesday.

Given the analysis used so far (and ignoring *will* to make life simpler), the VP would require a tree something like:

11.

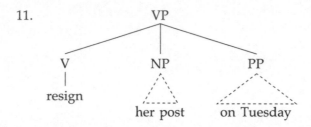

This untypically involves three branches rather than the binary branching more usual in the theory. But it also fails to distinguish the relationship between the V *resign* and the NP *her post* from the relationship between the V and the PP *on Tuesday*. The object NP *her post* relates to the lexical entry for *resign* which is a transitive Verb that requires an object. The PP *on Tuesday*, however, is not a compulsory part of the projection of *resign* but an optional extra. It would be convenient if the structure of the VP distinguished those elements that are optional from those that are a compulsory part of the phrase by including them at a separate level.

A further argument for an intermediate level is provided by the *so* test. We can amplify the sentence:

12.   The Education Minister will resign her post on Tuesday.

with a second clause:

13.   And so will the Prime Minister.

What constituent does *so* replace? It is not the Verb alone:

14.   *And so will the Prime Minister her post.

Nor is it the whole VP, for we can say:

15.   And so will the Prime Minister on Wednesday.

It seems to be a constituent somewhere between VP and V. This inter-mediate constituent is necessarily going to be a kind of V, i.e. a pro-jection of V. Let us distinguish it as V' with a bar; the VP now has levels of structure going from VP through V' to V, as in:

16.

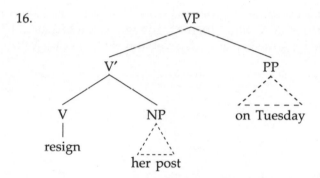

The PP can now be detached from the head V, and the close relation-ship between V and object NP can be expressed through sisterhood in the V' phrase, as well as accounting for the *so* test.

But VPs are only one type of phrase. X-bar syntax extends the same solution to all other phrases; they all have an intermediate level. This level recognizes the continuity of lexical categories within each phrase by consisting of a lexical category with a single bar. The lexical cat-egories are the basic symbols N, V, A and P; a different number of 'bars' are assigned to the lexical category at each level of the phrase above the basic lexical category. Bars are currently symbolized as ', i.e. N' and V'; a former convention depicts bars as lines above the letter, i.e. N̄, presumably abandoned because of its incompatibility with a conventional keyboard. The bar symbol then gives X-bar theory its name.

By convention the top level category has two bars (and categorial features as well); a VP is V", an NP is N", and so on. Each double-bar phrase contains a single-bar category head (and categorial features as well); a V" contains a V', an N" an N', and so on. The principle can be expressed as:

$$X'' \to \ldots X' \ldots$$

where X stands for any category that can be the head of a phrase. A double-bar phrase is a maximal phrase in that no further levels of structure are possible within the phrase itself.

Each single-bar phrase in turn contains a zero-bar lexical category head (and categorial features); thus a V' contains a V, an N' an N, and so on. Again the principle can be put as:

$$X' \to \ldots X \ldots$$

where X stands for the same category as before. A zero bar is the head itself, usually written as X rather than X^0. Leaving some blanks to be filled by elements of structure at each level, the skeleton of a VP is:

17.

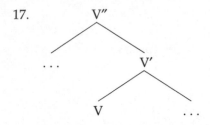

The links between syntax and the lexicon are consistently maintained through the bar notation; V builds into V' and from there into V'', N into N' and into N'', and so on. The bar system resembles army uniforms: sergeants have more stripes than privates; high-ranking US generals more stars than those below them. Conventionally the two-bar level is still normally referred to by the name of the phrase; it is less cumbersome to refer to an NP rather than to an N''; nevertheless in this system the phrase label NP, etc. is always shorthand for a double-bar category. The single-bar level will not invariably be needed to analyse a particular sentence, even if it is always potentially there. It may be left out of tree diagrams simply to make presentation easier.

The sentence:

18.   A woman played the flute.

can introduce the notion of **complements**. Some elements in the phrase are closely connected with the lexical category itself – the transitive V *play* is closely related to a following object in the VP such as *the flute* describing what is played; 'phrases typically consist of a head . . . , and an array of complements determined by the lexical properties of the head' (Chomsky, 1986a, p. 81). Complements are always complete phrases in themselves; the complete NP *the flute* is a complement in the VP *played the flute*. Several of the example phrases used earlier can be analysed as head and complements, for example *drink milk* (V head *drink* + NP complement *milk*), *from England* (P head *from* + NP complement *England*), and *jealous of Peter* (A head *jealous* + PP complement *of Peter*). The X-bar structure of the phrase needs to include the level at which the close relationship between the zero category head and its complement can be captured; complements are sisters of the lexical head and are governed by it, as we see in chapter 7. The rule for expanding X' can be expressed more completely as:

X' → X complement(s)

or as:

X' → complement(s) X

depending on the relative position of the head and complements in a language. This applies to the four lexical phrase types; the VP has a Verb head and a complement:

19. **played** [the flute]

The NP has an N head and a complement:

20. **proof** [of his guilt]

The PP likewise has a P head and a complement:

21. **with** [a stick]

Finally the AP too can have an A head and a complement:

22. **full** [of himself]

The head parameter from chapter 1 can now be set within X-bar syntax. The rule for expanding X' had to be given in two forms to show that complements could occur before or after heads. The choice between these two is that between **head-first** and **head-last** in the phrase, precisely the difference in word order captured by the head parameter. To say that English is head-first means that the verb V occurs on the left of the complement in the V':

23.   **buy** [a book]
      V   complement

It also means that the preposition P occurs on the left of the complement in the P':

24.   **on** [the boat]
      P   complement

It means that the adjective A occurs on the left in the A':

25.   **afraid** [of dogs]
      A   complement

And it also means that the noun N occurs on the left of the complement in the N', as in:

26.   **claim** [that he's right]
      N   complement

The head-last setting for the head parameter found in Japanese means that the V will be on the right of the complements within V':

27.   [Hon-o]   **katta**
      complement V
      (book   bought)
      He bought a book.

The P is on the right in the P' (hence it is known technically as a Postposition):

28.   [Fune]   **ni**
      complement P
      boat   on
      On the boat.

The A is on the right in the A':

29. [inu o]   **kowagatte**
    complement A
    dog   afraid
    (afraid of the dog)

And the N is on the right in the N':

30. [Zibun ga tadashi-to-iu] **shichoo**
    complement   N
    self   right   claim
    (the claim that he was right)

If a language is consistent, that is to say if all its phrases have the same head parameter setting, a major part of its word order phenomena can be described by stating whether its setting for the head parameter is head-first or head-last.

As well as heads and complements, phrases contain a third main element in their structure, namely a **specifier**. While complements belong alongside the X in the phrase, i.e. are sisters of X, specifiers belong alongside the X'. The Determiner *the* for example is a specifier in the NP *the book*. The structure of *the book* is therefore:

31.

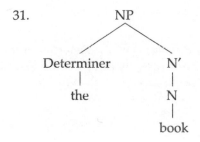

The overall principle is that a double-bar phrase may consist of a head X' and possible specifiers, whether:

X" → X' specifier

or:

X" → specifier X'

Again the principle does not spell out the order of specifier and head X'. Putting the X-bar principles together and labelling the positions gets the structure:

32.

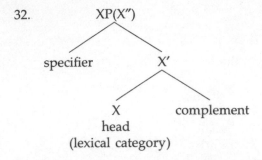

X-bar theory claims that all types of phrase need these two internal levels of structure. It proposes that all phrases in all languages share a simple cell-like structure with two levels to each phrase: one (X'') consists of the head and possible specifiers; the other (X') consists of the head (X) and possible complements. Note that specifier and complement are not themselves syntactic categories but functional labels for positions in the structure that may be filled by actual syntactic categories such as NPs and VPs.

Let us flesh this out with the English NP:

33.   his fear of the dark

This is an N'' (NP) having a specifier consisting of the Determiner *his*, and an N' *fear of the dark*; this N' in turn consists of an N, the lexical item *fear*, and a complement, the PP *of the dark*. Both the specifier and complement positions in the phrase are filled:

34.

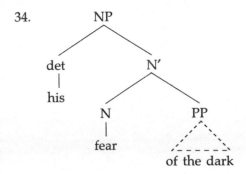

The analysis of complements and specifiers does not exhaust all the possibilities of the phrase. In addition a phrase may have adjuncts. One example has already been seen in the sentence:

35.   The Education Minister will resign her post on Tuesday.

where the PP *on Tuesday* is an adjunct. A more detailed example is given by the relative clause:

36.   The man [who paid the bill] was John.

The NP *the man who paid the bill* has a specifier *the* and a head N *man*. The relative clause *who paid the bill* cannot be a specifier as that position is filled; it cannot be a complement since the N *man* does not specify a complement. Hence it is a phrase (technically a CP as we shall see) acting as an adjunct – a part of the structure of the phrase that does not belong to the basic X-bar elements of head, specifier and complement but is 'adjoined' to the X', typical examples being adverbs and relative clauses.

So how does the adjunct fit in? An N' may be expanded in two ways; one is to expand it into another N' and an adjunct as in:

N' → N' Adjunct

The other is to expand it into an N and its complement:

N' → N Complement

The first of these options ends up with an N' so that again there are the same two possibilities for expanding N', either into N' and an adjunct, or into N and its complement; this may go on ad lib. Expanding an item into another item of the same type, i.e. an N' into an N', is an example of the general property known as **recursion** – a rule calling on itself. In principle recursion may go on indefinitely; there is no limit to the number of adjuncts in the sentence, unlike the number of complements which is laid down by the lexical entry for the head. The reason is that every N' may be expanded into another N', which itself may be expanded into an N', and so on. A sentence may be expanded in this way until the paper runs out:

37.   The man [who paid the bill] [wearing a stripy scarf] [of medium build] [with a gold tooth] . . .

Each adjunct is added to the NP by recursively expanding an N' into
another N' with the adjunct as its sister:

38.

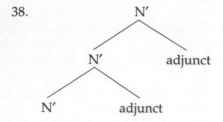

Without this recursiveness of adjuncts, the theory would be unable to
explain how sentences can expand indefinitely in part of the structure
outside the core positions of head, specifier and complement.

The subject of the sentence can now be brought into this framework.
The VP as presented so far has had a specifier position that has been
unfilled. According to current theory, this is where the subject belongs
in the D-structure of the sentence: the subject is the specifier of the VP.
This is a different location from that used in earlier versions of principles and parameters theory, or indeed in earlier Chomskyan models
of syntax, and has been introduced by, for example, Kuroda (1988),
Koopman and Sportiche (1991), and Chomsky and Lasnik (1993); the
reader is warned that older books will introduce the subject in other
places. So, setting aside the tense inflection *-ed*, the sentence:

39.   A woman played the flute.

can now be represented as:

40.

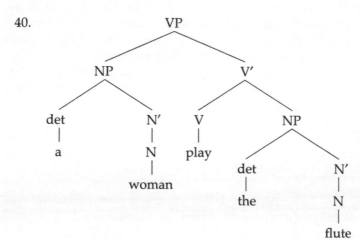

Like the rest of Chomskyan theory, X-bar syntax strives for the maximum generality. It makes statements about phrase structure that are true for all phrases rather than for one rule or one phrase type. Thus it expresses cross-category generalizations about the need for a head, for a particular type of head, and for an intermediate level within the phrase, independently of whether the phrases are NPs, VPs, or any other type of phrase. It relies on two main structural relationships within the phrase: one is the link between the head and the complements that are its sisters; the other is between the specifier and the head. The order of elements within the phrase is generalized so that a single statement specifies on which side of the head complements occur in all phrases of the language. The fact that P comes before NP in a PP *on the train*, and that V comes before NP in a VP *lost the race*, are covered by the generalization that heads come before complements in English; 'the phrase structure system for a particular language is largely restricted to specification of the parameters that determine the ordering of head–complement, head–adjunct, and SPEC–head' (Chomsky and Lasnik, 1993, p. 527). Once the parameters of X-bar theory have been set, one has captured the phrase structure of the language; rather than a list of rules, the phrase structure consists of settings for parameters and some account of 'language-specific idiosyncrasies' (Chomsky, 1982a, p. 10).

X-bar theory: lexical phrases

Definition: a theory of the phrase structure, affecting D-structure, S-structure, and LF

Principles:

— a phrase always contains a head of the same type, i.e. NPs Ns, VPs Vs, etc.

— X" $\longrightarrow$ specifier X'
a two-bar category consists of a head that is a single-bar, a specifier position, and a possible adjunct

— X' $\longrightarrow$ X complement(s)
a single-bar category contains a head with no bars and possible complements

— X' $\longrightarrow$ X' adjunct
a single-bar category can also contain a further single-bar category and an adjunct

Lexical categories: N Noun, V Verb, A Adjective, P Preposition

The Structure of Functional Phrases

Let us now start to expand this style of analysis, taking as an example
the sentence:

41.   The child finds the toy.

As presented above, the Verb Phrase (VP) *the child find the toy* consists
of an NP and V', and the V' consists of a V and an NP; the NPs *the
toy* and *the child* consist of a Determiner and an N', as follows:

42.

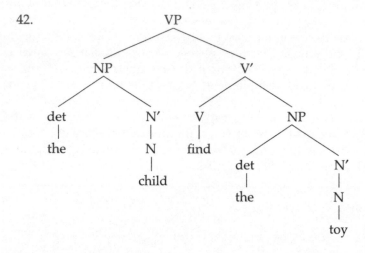

The inflectional aspect *-s* on the verb *find* is still missing. To capture
the insight mentioned in chapter 2 that this should be detached from
the verb, it is represented in a separate constituent called the **Inflection Phrase (IP)**. Like phrases with lexical heads, the IP has two internal levels: I", which includes I' and a specifier, and I' which includes
I and a complement. From this point on we will use I as the single-
letter abbreviation rather than INFL, to bring it in line with the other
categories. Though the head I is sometimes an actual word such as an
auxiliary *will* or *can*, it can also be an abstract element that includes the
features of tense (sometimes abbreviated to TNS) and agreement (AGR),
which are in fact realized by the PF component in the surface structure
as the inflections *-s, -ed*, and so on; in non-finite clauses it may also be
to. The inflectional elements of the sentence:

43.   The child finds the toy.

that need to be separated out are the present tense (rather than past) and the singular AGR (rather than plural), both indicated by the *-s* on *finds*. When these are syntactic features, they will be shown from now on within square brackets, i.e. [Present], [Past], [Singular] and [Plural]. So the IP of this sentence has within it a head I that includes the features [Present] and [Singular]. This head I has a complement, namely the VP.

44.

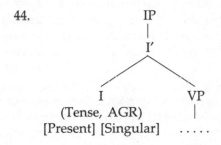

A fuller structure of the sentence is then:

45.

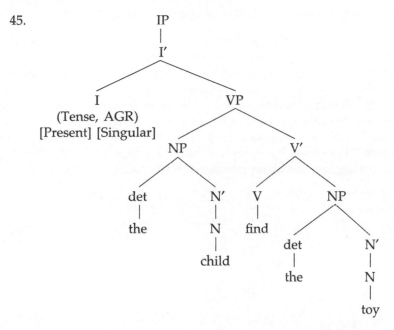

To sum up so far: a sentence consists of an IP (I″) that contains an element I′; this I′ contains an abstract element I and a VP that contains the rest of the sentence. The VP is the complement of the I. The IP conforms to the same X-bar scheme as the other phrases with IP (I″)

at the top level, I′ and a specifier at the mid-level, and I and a complement at the bottom level; chapter 6 will show how the NP specifier of VP moves to specifier of IP. One difference from other phrases is that the complement of the IP is compulsory; that is to say, *all* sentences must have VPs. The main difference between IP and the other phrases seen so far is that the head I is not necessarily a lexical item drawn from the lexicon, but is a conglomeration of the abstract features Tense and AGR that may or may not have surface realizations such as *-ed* and *-s*. **Lexical phrases** such as the VP and NP are built around lexical heads; **functional phrases** such as IP are built around functional heads, which may contain lexical material such as morphological endings but are not required to contain lexical material. The cell-like pattern of X-bar phrases of the lexical phrases is extended to functional phrases. Since the publication of *Barriers* (Chomsky, 1986b) increasing attention has been devoted to the functional phrases of the sentence.

But the phrase structure of the typical sentence is still not complete. Let us take as an example:

46.   They wondered whether she would pass.

How can we deal with one sentence *whether she would pass* embedded within the structure of another clause *they wondered*? In particular, how does the complementizer *whether* fit into the type of structure we have used? Another functional phrase needs to be introduced, called the **Complementizer Phrase** (CP). The head of the phrase, C, sometimes known as COMP, may be an actual complementizer such as *whether* or *that* in embedded sentences, or it may be an abstract element in other cases. The complement of C is the IP. So the embedded sentence *whether she would pass* has the structure:

47.

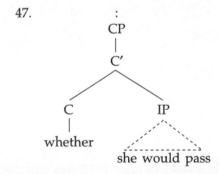

Again the regular X-bar structure extends to take care of the embedded sentence through CP, a second type of functional phrase with the usual levels of C″, C′ and C, and with possible specifiers and complements of its own.

The specifier positions of CP and IP remain to be described. These specifier positions prove to be immensely useful in dealing with syntactic movement in the sentence, as will be seen later. So far the CP seems redundant in main clauses since these do not have complementizers such as *whether* or *that*. As described earlier, sentences such as:

48.   Are you going to the concert?

have the S-structure form:

49.   are you *t* going to the concert?

representing movement from the D-structure:

50.   you are going to the concert

of *are*, representing present Tense and plural AGR. But what is the tree structure of the derived S-structure form? The auxiliary *are* has to fit into the phrase structure of the sentence rather than hang in mid-air. Elements in the sentence cannot be moved unless there is an empty place for them to move *to*. If all sentences have CPs and the head position is empty, the CP has a vacant place into which the auxiliary can be moved. The structure of questions in English requires an empty head of CP in the main sentence to which movement can take place. Thus, ignoring other movement in the sentence, the S-structure of:

51.   are you *t* going to the concert?

can be shown as:

52.

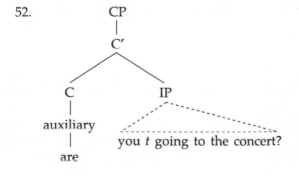

Later the role of the specifier of C in movement will be described.

The structure of the sentence is now essentially complete, even if it will have to be amplified further; it is a nesting of X-bar phrases within X-bar phrases, all with the same internal structure, going from the CP at the top to the lexical item or abstract category at the bottom.

X-bar Theory: Functional categories

Functional categories: I Inflection, C Complement; to be continued in later chapters

Parameter: the head parameter distinguishes languages that incorporate X-bar principle with complements (maximal bar categories) to the right or left of the head, i.e. as:
X' $\longrightarrow$ X complement(s)
or as:
X' $\longrightarrow$ complement(s) X

Extensions: many, chiefly in the new phrase types to be introduced in the next chapter

---

Levels of Structural Representation and Movement

Let us now try to relate this to the wider context of the levels of structural representation described in chapter 2, taking as an example the English sentence:

53.   Jane hated coffee.

In the principles and parameters model S-structure is the bridge linking the PF component, which deals with sounds, to the LF component, which deals with meanings.

The PF component describes how *Jane, hate* and *coffee* are pronounced, and whether -*ed* is realized as one of the regular endings /t/, /d/ and

/id/, or as an irregular past form such as *went* or *hit*. Such details are irrelevant so far as syntactic description is concerned; for S-structure it does not matter how *Jane* is pronounced or which form of [Past] is used; it is the presence of the word *Jane* and of the abstract element [Past] that needs to be taken into account, not the details of how [Past] is conveyed.

The component of Logical Form on the other hand acts as an interface between the S-structure and the semantic component; it puts the syntactic meaning of the sentence in an appropriate form so that a semantic representation for the sentence can eventually be found, giving the meanings of *Jane, hate* and *coffee*, the relationship between *Jane* and *coffee*, the meaning of [Past], and so on. The details of phonetic representation are unimportant so far as LF is concerned. The PF and LF components interpret S-structure by giving it different representations. They add nothing to the S-structure but 'interpret' it for their own ends.

Principles and parameters theory also makes use of a D-structure level at which properties of the sentence are stated that are obscured in the S-structure, as seen in chapter 2. The relationship between S-structure and D-structure is movement: S-structure equals D-structure plus movement. Questions with wh-movement, such as *what* or *who* questions, reflect the movement of a questioned constituent (a wh-phrase) to the front of the sentence; passives require NP movement from the object to subject position; and so on. To talk about movement at all implies movement *from* somewhere *to* somewhere; consequently, as well as S-structure, there must be an underlying form of the sentence, the D-structure, in which movement has not taken place. Chapter 6 deals with movement in detail, particularly with the involvement of the IP and CP. For this chapter we need to illustrate one type of movement to complete the analysis of a simple sentence.

There are still anomalies in the S-structures that are being generated. The sentence:

54.   The child finds the toy.

is actually being treated as if it were:

55.   -*s* the child find the toy

In other words, gathering together the inflectional aspects of the sentence into the IP has the side-effect of stranding them at the beginning of the sentence, seen in the repeated tree:

56.

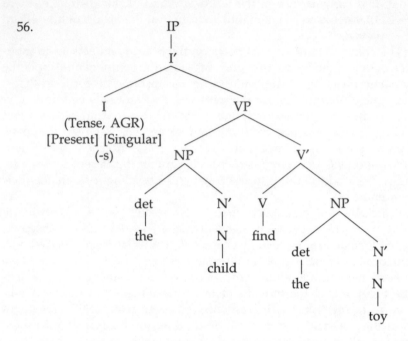

The I element occurs at the beginning of the sentence; the resulting forms of I, whether [Past] *-ed* or [Present] *-s*, are going to occur before the rest of the sentence. This is still some way from the S-structure of an ordinary English sentence where the *-s* and *-ed* endings are located after the Verb. Within current theory, this relies on two types of movement – movement of the subject and movement of the Verb. The subject NP moves from its position within the VP up to the empty specifier position of IP, leaving a trace *t*:

57.   *-s* the child find the toy

becomes:

58.   the child *-s t* find the toy

59.

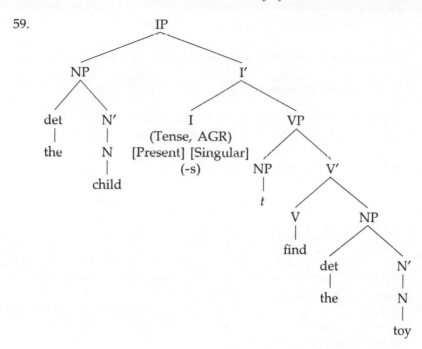

The I constituent is still, however, in front of the Verb *find*. Since the first days of Chomskyan theory, various solutions have been proposed to reverse the order of these two constituents; the current method is to raise the Verb head to the I head position. Discussion of this will, however, be postponed to the next chapter, as it needs a more complex analysis of phrases.

The S-structure sign that movement has taken place in the sentence is the presence of *t* (trace), which marks the location in S-structure from which something has been moved. This trace has no lexical form in the surface of the sentence:

60. The child finds the toy.

While present in the S-structure, it is, so to speak, 'invisible' in the actual sentence. There is, however, an odd exception to the trace's normal cloak of invisibility. The written question:

61. Who do you want to visit?

is ambiguous and could result in two answers:

62.   I want to visit Mr Jones.

– a visitor telling a nurse who he wants to visit in hospital, and:

63.   I want Mr Jones to visit.

– a patient saying who he wants to visit him in hospital. The original sentence could therefore have two S-structures:

64.   Who do you want to visit *t*?

and:

65.   Who do you want *t* to visit?

Who has moved from two different places in the D-structure, leaving a trace in different places in each S-structure. The PF component turns these into the same surface sentence.

Or does it? In American English, the pronunciation of *want to* in the two sentences is potentially different. Both can indeed be said with the full form *want to*:

66.   Who do you want to visit?

but only one can be said with the contracted form *wanna*:

67.   Who do you wanna visit?

The latter is only possible if the speaker intends the S-structure:

68.   Who do you want to visit *t*?

If an otherwise invisible *t* still separates *want* from *to* in the S-structure, *want to* cannot be reduced to *wanna*; in Chomsky's words, 'at the point in the PF component where the contraction rule ... applies, the trace of wh-movement is present so that "want" and "to" are not adjacent and the rule is blocked' (Chomsky, 1986a, p. 163). Hence:

69.   Who do you wanna visit?

is impossible with the S-structure:

70.   Who do you want *t* to visit?

in which the patient rather than the visitor is being discussed. Put another way, when *who* moves from object position, its trace does not affect the pronunciation of the sentence; when it moves from subject position, it leaves a trace that prevents *want t to* reducing to *wanna*. While too much should not be made of the pronunciation of a particular verb *want* in a particular construction *want to* in one form of English, it is nevertheless one small indication that the invisible *t* is actually there.

Let us briefly sum up this chapter. We started by describing X-bar theory as it applies to lexical categories, showing how these all conform to the same basic pattern:

71.

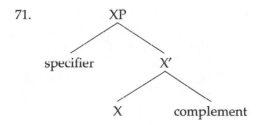

Of course, this pattern represents just one of the possible configurations allowed by the X-bar parameters: another possibility would be for the head to follow the complement, for example. However, in all languages an XP contains an X' and a possible specifier, and an X' contains an X and possible complements. The order of these elements is parameterized and hence may vary from one language to another.

The X-bar framework was then extended to the functional categories I(nflection) and C(omplementizer). The VP is taken to be the smallest representation of the clause, in that at D-structure it contains all the lexical elements which constitute a clause. The IP is built on top of this VP and contains the inflectional head (e.g. tense and agreement). CP in turn is built on top of IP and contains a head complementizer in embedded clauses and an empty head position in matrix clauses. Both IP and CP conform to the usual X-bar pattern. In order to achieve the correct surface order of elements, we assumed that the subject moves out of the VP into the specifier of the IP. In yes–no questions, where there is auxiliary inversion, the auxiliary can move to the vacant C position. Obviously there has to be a reason for these movements, which will be supplied in the following chapters. For now, however, we are only concerned with the description of the basic pattern that all the constituents of a sentence must conform to.

A short caveat needs to be made about the sentence trees that will be used from this point on. A full tree representation of the sentence is extremely complex in the current theory and may hinder readers rather than helping them to understand. We have so far simplified trees in two ways: one is the triangle convention that omits unnecessary detail in a phrase; the other is the omission of single-bar categories when these are not relevant to the structure in question. Virtually all the trees from this point will use these simplification techniques, plus others to be described later.

5

θ-Theory and Functional Categories

This chapter will discuss the following topics:

— Aspects of the lexical entry
— The Projection Principle and θ-Theory
— Grammatical functions
— Further types of functional phrase.

This chapter looks at the interaction of syntax and the lexicon via the Projection Principle and at the aspects of meaning covered in θ-theory; it goes on to the functional categories approach within the theory of X-bar syntax. The route in this book so far has led downward from the syntax to the lexicon. The next few sections go in the opposite direction upward from the lexicon to the syntax. Looked at from syntax, the VP (V″) for example has a head V′ which in turn has a head V that leads to a lexical entry for the particular Verb in question. Looked at from the lexicon, the lexical entry for a Verb affects first the V′ and then the VP: it projects the elements of the entry progressively onto the whole phrase.

Aspects of the Lexical Entry

We need then to elaborate the sort of information that is included in the lexical entry, expanding on the discussion of θ-theory in chapter 2. Earlier the lexicon was seen to be the place where information about individual words is stored – their pronunciation and meaning. But, as well as such phonological and semantic information, the lexicon also includes information about syntax, for instance whether a word is a Noun or a Verb. In particular the lexical entry describes how a word behaves syntactically in connection with other words and phrases. Take the Verb *deplore*, which can be used in sentences such as:

1.   Mary deplores violence.

but cannot be used in sentences such as:

2.   *Mary deplores.
3.   *Deplores violence.
4.   *Mary deplores violence that shade of pink.

What is it that we know about *deplore* that enables us to make these judgements of possible and impossible sentences? One aspect is certainly the knowledge that the act of deploring requires two entities, one to do the deploring, the other to be deplored. Other Verbs may only require a single entity, for example *cry*:

5.   Bill cried.

Other Verbs need more than two entities; for instance the Verb *show* requires three:

6.   Helen showed the policeman her licence.

Moreover it is not only Verbs that require a certain number of entities to be involved with certain relationships to each other. Nouns too can require such entities, as in:

7.   Hillary's conquest of Everest.

where the Noun *conquest* requires someone to act as conqueror and something to be conquered. Elements which say something about entities or their relationships are known as *predicates* and the entities concerned are known as *arguments*. A predicate then expresses the meaning relationship between arguments – the meaning relationship between the predicate *deplore* and the arguments *Mary* and *violence*, or between the predicate *conquest* and the arguments *Hillary* and *Everest*. Knowing how many arguments are related by a predicate is part of knowing what the predicate means. We don't know the meaning of *deplore* unless we know that it requires two arguments – someone who does the deploring and something that gets deplored. This aspect of meaning is called **argument structure**.

Knowing the argument structure of a predicate means knowing not just how many arguments are involved but also what kind. For example, in the sentence:

8.   Peter cooked spaghetti.

the Verb *cook* requires one argument involving the entity doing the cooking (*Peter*) and a second involving whatever is cooked (*spaghetti*). These semantic roles are called **thematic roles** or **θ-roles** for short. The perpetrator of an action is an **Agent** θ-role; the thing affected by the action is a **Patient** θ-role, and so on. These are two of the several possible θ-roles. Unfortunately there is no definitive list of θ-roles, different researchers tending to use their own lists. Here we will use a minimal number, as the actual existence of θ-roles is what is important rather than the differences between them.

The lexical entry for any predicate includes the θ-roles that its arguments bear. This is represented as a **θ-grid**. For example the lexical entry of the Verb *cook* is in part:

cook <Agent, Patient>

The θ-grid <Agent, Patient> tells us that the Verb *cook* takes two arguments, an Agent and a Patient. Different Verbs can be distinguished by their argument structures represented by θ-grids in the lexicon:

dance <Agent> (John danced)
give <Agent, Theme, Goal> (John gave the cheque to his friend)

(**Goal** is a further θ-role defined as 'intended end point of action', and **Theme** is 'thing moved by action'.) Thus the θ-grid of a predicate determines which θ-roles its arguments bear. Obviously there are restrictions on the arguments that may accompany a particular predicate: only certain types of argument can bear certain types of θ-role. For instance only sentient beings can normally bear the Agent role so the sentence:

9.   The apple ate John.

is odd outside a science fiction film. The predicate's ability to restrict the kind of arguments that accompany it is called **S-selection** (semantic selection). A predicate therefore s-selects a particular number of arguments bearing particular θ-roles.

To summarize, part of our lexical knowledge concerns the selectional properties of lexical items. These, represented in terms of θ-grids, tell us what kind of θ-roles the predicate's arguments will bear. In this way properties of lexical items influence the structure of the sentences in which they appear, because they restrict the kinds of elements which can, and must, accompany them.

Besides s-selection properties, it is often assumed that lexical items also have **c-selection** (category selection) properties. This is the ability to determine the type of complement that the lexical item may have. For example, take the verbs *ask* and *wonder*, both of which can have a question clause as their complement:

10.   Mary asked [what the time was].
11.   Mary wondered [what the time was].

However, only *ask* can take a complement that is an NP:

12.   Mary asked [the time].
13.   *Mary wondered [the time].

So it has been argued that the lexical entry for these verbs must also contain information about the category of complement that lexical item allows (Grimshaw, 1979). This has obvious connections with the traditional notion of 'subcategories of verbs'; some verbs take no complements (intransitive verbs such as *lurk*), some take a single NP complement (transitive verbs such as *see*), some take two NP complements (ditransitive verbs, such as *show*). These traditional subcategories of verbs can be seen as c-selecting either no complements, or a single NP complement, or two NP complements, respectively. C-selection is represented in the lexicon in terms of a **subcategorization frame**:

ask [__ CP/NP]
wonder: [__ CP]

This is a kind of representation of the syntactic context with the underlined gap indicating the position of the lexical item and the other elements inside the bracket being the complements that the lexical item c-selects. In the examples above the verb *ask* c-selects either a CP complement (*what the time was*) or an NP complement (*the time*) while the verb *wonder* c-selects only a CP complement.

Both c-selection and s-selection information is included in each lexical entry, the former in terms of a subcategorization frame, the latter in terms of a θ-grid. A more detailed lexical entry for the verb *cook* would be:

cook <Agent, Patient> [__ NP]

A major difference between c-selection and s-selection highlighted here is that, while c-selection deals only with complements, s-selection deals with all arguments including complements and the subject. Thus, while a lexical item both c-selects and s-selects its complements, it only s-selects its subject. We shall see below that there are other differences between complements and subjects that have led to the idea that they are different kinds of argument.

To a great extent, the category of the complement can be predicted from the θ-role that it bears. So, for example, Patients tend to be real-ized as NPs. But, if this is so, do we need to include both subcategor-ization frames and θ-grids in the lexicon? Couldn't we just include the θ-grid and work out the category of the complement from the θ-role that is given? One argument against this comes from the verbs *ask* and *wonder*: *ask* c-selects either an NP or a CP complement while *wonder* c-selects only a CP. However, *both* of these verbs s-select the same sort of complement: a question. So these verbs are not distinguished in terms of their s-selection properties, only in their c-selection properties. In order to distinguish these verbs, their c-selection properties must be included in their lexical entries. While this argument seems sound, Chomsky (1986a, pp. 88–90), basing himself on original work by Pesetsky (1982), has argued that if the difference between these kinds of verbs can be reduced to other lexical properties, then c-selection can be entirely reduced to s-selection and subcategorization frames may be eliminated from the lexicon.

The Projection Principle and θ-Theory

How does the kind of lexical information that we have been discuss-ing relate to the syntactic processes of X-bar theory? The crucial con-nection is through the concept of **projection**, mentioned briefly in chapters 1 and 2. A head Verb V, for example, projects to a V' and this in turn projects to a VP (V"). But X-bar principles are true of *all* cat-egories, not just of verbs; the head X projects to an X' and this projects to an X", whether it is an NP, a VP, or whatever. If the category that is inserted is a lexical Verb, then it will project all the lexical informa-tion for that V onto the VP. It is the lexical entry that tells us that an

---

S-selection and C-selection

predicate: a lexical item that says something about an entity or the relationships between entities

arguments: the entities which are related by a predicate

θ-roles: the semantic roles that arguments bear with respect to a predicate, e.g. Agent, Patient, etc.

θ-grid: part of a lexical entry of a predicate which states which θ-roles the arguments of the predicate will bear, e.g. Agent, Patient

subcategorization frame: part of a lexical entry which states the categorial status of the complements of a lexical element, e.g. [__ NP]

s-selection (semantic selection): the property of a lexical item by which it restricts the semantic kind of its arguments in accordance with the θ-roles given in the predicate's θ-grid that they must bear

c-selection (categorial selection): the property of a lexical item by which it determines the category of its complements as given in the lexical item's subcategorization frame. C-selection may reduce to s-selection in that it may be possible to predict the category of a complement from knowledge of which θ-roles the complement bears

---

item is a Verb. Once the head is initially inserted in the phrase, the rest of the lexical information will project further into the structure through the X-bar principles.

This process can be shown by building up a phrase from the bottom. The X-bar principles determine the general structure, i.e. that X″ consists of X′, and X′ consists of X:

14.   X″
      |
      X′
      |
      X

A lexical item such as *smile* can be inserted into this structure as an example of X:

15.   X″
      |
      X′
      |
      X
      |
      smile

The lexical entry for *smile* specifies that it happens to be a Verb and so this information from the lexicon will be projected to determine the category of X:

16.   X″
      |
      X′
      |
      V
      |
      smile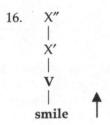

This information is in turn projected up to the next level in the structure, namely the single-bar, which is, naturally, a V′:

17.   X″
      |
      V′
      |
      V
      |
      smile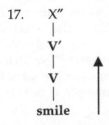

And finally it will be projected to the top of the phrase, determining that it is in fact a V″ (VP):

18.   V″ (VP)
      |
      V′
      |
      V
      |
      smile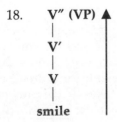

The subcategorization information from the lexical entry is also projected in the same way. Thus, if a Verb has a complement in its lexical entry, a position for a complement will appear in its projected VP, for example:

19.

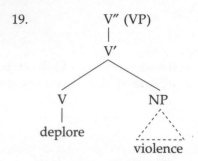

Although some languages allow elements to be moved about by transformations, it is a universal property of all languages that the information provided in the lexicon cannot be altered by such transformations. So, for example, if the lexicon states that a verb takes an NP complement, this complement cannot go missing through the operation of a transformation, i.e. just be deleted from the sentence. Similarly, complements cannot be added by transformations and their category cannot be changed by a transformation. The information in the lexical entry is sacrosanct: the sentence must be compatible with it. Thus lexical information is not only projected into the structure at some initial point in the derivation of a structure but is also projected throughout all levels of structural representation. The lexical entry controls not just the original use of the information but all subsequent uses. This is stated in the **Projection Principle** (Chomsky, 1981a, p. 29):

> **Representations at each syntactic level (i.e. LF, D- and S-structure) are projected from the lexicon, in that they observe the subcategorisation properties of lexical items**.

While the Projection Principle ensures that lexical information, once it is projected into the syntax, remains unchanged, lexical information also cannot be ignored. For example, it has already been shown that a sentence which has too many or too few arguments for a predicate is ungrammatical. We know that the verb *deplore* takes two arguments – an Agent and a Patient – and that *deplore* must appear with two arguments – no more, no less. Hence the following sentences are ungrammatical as they are not compatible with the arguments specified in the lexical entry:

20. *Mary deplores. (no Patient)
21. *Deplores violence. (no Agent)
22. *Mary deplores violence that shade of pink. (too many arguments)

One way of looking at this is that each θ-role that a predicate has in its θ-grid must be given to a single argument, and each argument that appears with a predicate must be given a single θ-role. In other words, there is a one-to-one relationship between arguments and θ-roles. This is stated in terms of a principle of long standing (see for instance Freidin, 1978), called the θ-**Criterion** (Chomsky, 1981a, p. 36):

Each argument bears one and only one θ-role, and each θ-role is assigned to one and only one argument.

Between them, the Projection Principle and the θ-Criterion ensure that lexical information is fed into the syntax, and, once it is there, is not altered or ignored.

Chomsky has, however, suggested some changes in the way that the θ-Criterion is to be viewed (Chomsky, 1986a, p. 97). One reason is that in its strongest form, given above, the θ-Criterion is not completely true; some arguments seem capable of having more than one θ-role. For example, in sentences like:

23. John left the room angry.

the subject *John* is related to two predicates *left the room* and *angry*: John is not only the one who left the room but also the one who is angry. This looks suspiciously like a violation of the θ-Criterion in that the same argument has two θ-roles. Attempts to patch up the θ-Criterion to accommodate data like these lead to complications elsewhere in the grammar: it may be simpler to relax the restrictions of the θ-Criterion.

UG theory is constantly changing in ways that make it more general and more explanatory; there is always pressure to reduce principles of the grammar such as the θ-Criterion to even more basic principles. A recurrent theme in Chomsky's writing is that human language seems to be constructed to avoid superfluous elements in sentence structure. There is no necessary reason why this should be the case: non-natural languages, such as mathematical systems, tolerate meaningless items in their constructs. The following arithmetical statement for example is perfectly acceptable:

24. $\forall x \; 2 + 2 = 4$

despite there being a superfluous universal quantifier ($\forall x$ means 'for all xs', i.e. where x is a variable that is superfluous to the meaning of $2 + 2 = 4$). But human language does not allow such superfluous elements; an equivalent sentence in human language is ungrammatical:

25.   *Every the man loves the woman.

meaning that the man loves the woman, with *every* superfluous to this meaning. Obviously in a human language the quantifier *every* cannot be simply viewed as meaningless and ignored. So Chomsky (1986a) proposed a principle, called **Full Interpretation** (FI), which states that every element that appears in a structure must be interpreted in some way, i.e. there are no superfluous elements in the structure of language.

FI obviously takes in part of the θ-Criterion; there can be no super-fluous arguments not related to any predicate and hence not given an interpretation in the sentence. We have already seen that the part of the θ-Criterion which states that arguments cannot bear more than one θ-role is too strong for the facts. It may therefore be that the whole of the θ-Criterion can be done away with.

Chomsky (1991c) has proposed a still more fundamental principle which may supersede FI: 'I think we can also perceive at least the outlines of certain still more general principles, which we might think of as "guidelines", in the sense that they are too vaguely formulated to merit the term "principles of UG". Some of these guidelines have a kind of "least effort" flavour to them, in the sense that they legislate against "superfluous elements" in representations and derivations' (Chomsky, 1991c, p. 418). He notes that the underlying point of FI is that language structures must be as economical as possible: the only things that can appear in a sentence are those which need to. Chomsky proposes that this **Principle of Economy** is relevant not only for the form and representation of structures but also for the processes that produce them. So, for example, languages always seem to use the minimum number of steps or processes to form a given structure that UG will allow; 'there can be no superfluous rule application, in a special sense, defined in terms of the difference between universal and language-specific rules' (Chomsky, 1991b, p. 43). Examples of how this works will be given in the discussion of movement in the next chapter. Thus the principle of FI is just one face of a more general and basic Principle of Economy. The Principle of Economy is so important that much of the developing framework called Minimalism is aimed at making this a central principle of the grammar, with some quite radical changes following from this (Chomsky, 1993), as we see in chapter 9.

Whatever the principle involved, the effect is still much the same: lexical information must be projected into the syntax and, once it is there, it cannot be altered or ignored. In what follows we shall adopt standard practice in referring to a set of phenomena using the name of the principle that originally accounted for them, though the principle itself may be outdated. Thus the term θ-Criterion will be used to refer to phenomena that are better captured by principles of Full Interpretation or Economy.

The θ-Criterion forms one part of the module of principles and parameters theory which is to do with the syntactic effects of θ-roles, known as **θ-Theory**. Another part of θ-theory concerns the process of how θ-roles get from the lexical entry of a predicate to the arguments that bear them. θ-roles are *transferred* from a predicate to its arguments by a process known as **θ-marking**. This could be interpreted in a number of ways. The usual assumption is that predicates are inserted into a structure along with their θ-roles which they then pass on to various arguments in the structure. The θ-criterion ensures that there is just the right number of arguments to bear the assigned θ-roles. This process is extremely constrained in that a predicate cannot assign its θ-roles to an argument in just any position in the sentence. In *Barriers*, Chomsky (1986b) proposes that θ-roles are assigned by predicates to their sisters: there is a sisterhood condition on the assignment of θ-roles. Thus, as complements are sisters to heads according to the principles of X-bar, a lexical head will θ-mark its complements straightforwardly, for example *deplore* θ-marks its NP complement *violence*. But this does not tell us how subjects are assigned their θ-roles. Recall that subjects are located in the specifier position of the VP and this, by definition, is *not* a sister of the head Verb:

The Projection Principle and the θ-Criterion

The Projection Principle: 'representations at each syntactic level (i.e. LF, and D- and S-structure) are projected from the lexicon, in that they observe the subcategorisation properties of lexical items' (Chomsky, 1981a, p. 29)

The θ-Criterion: 'each argument bears one and only one θ-role, and each θ-role is assigned to one and only one argument' (Chomsky, 1981a, p. 36)

Full Interpretation: 'every element of PF and LF, taken to be the interface of syntax with systems of language use, must receive an appropriate interpretation – must be licensed in the sense indicated.' (Chomsky, 1986a, p. 98).

The Principle of Economy: 'both derivations and representations are subject to a certain form of "least effort" condition and are required to be minimal in a fairly well-defined sense, with no superfluous steps in derivations and no superfluous symbols in representations' (Chomsky, 1991c, p. 447)

Gloss:

— **The Projection Principle** ensures that, once subcategorization information from the head's lexical entry is inserted into a structure, this is maintained throughout the derivation of that structure

— **The θ-Criterion** ensures that the θ-roles listed in a predicate's lexical entry are assigned each to a single argument and that no argument appears without bearing a single θ-role

— **Full Interpretation** (FI) captures the basic property of human language that there are no superfluous elements in structures, i.e. elements which fulfil no semantic, syntactic or phonological purpose.
The θ-Criterion may ultimately reduce to FI

— **The Principle of Economy** includes FI and states that all representations of structures and processes producing them must be as economical as the system allows

26.

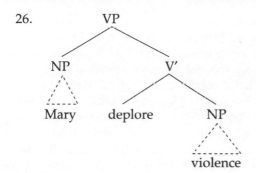

We have already mentioned that subjects are different kinds of argument from complements; while complements are c-selected and s-selected by their heads, subjects are only s-selected. Subjects are more distant from the head Verb than complements and this can be seen by the fact that it is not the head alone that determines which θ-roles a subject will bear: sometimes it is a combination of the head and the complement that determines the subject's θ-role. For example, in:

27. John broke the window.

John bears an Agent θ-role, being the person who perpetrated the action. However, changing the complement gets another possible θ-role assigned to the subject:

28. John broke his arm.

While it is possible to give this sentence an interpretation in which *John* is an Agent (where John deliberately breaks his own arm!), the more common interpretation is where *John* receives the Patient θ-role and he is viewed as the person to whom something happens, i.e. his arm gets broken. This interpretation is *not* available in the sentence in which the window gets broken, and so varying the complement of the Verb has an effect on which θ-roles can get assigned to the subject: in effect, the head Verb and the complement together seem to act as a single unit which θ-marks the subject. For this reason, complement arguments and subject arguments are viewed as different: complements are called **internal arguments** to indicate that they are included within a domain that only the head has direct control over; subjects are called **external arguments** to indicate that they lie outside this domain. Looking at the structure of the VP shows that it is the V' which forms the relevant domain: internal arguments are internal to the V' and external arguments are external to it. These observations help to unify the conditions on θ-marking. We have said that complements are θ-marked by the head under a sisterhood condition. Subjects are also θ-marked under the sisterhood condition, but it is the head and its complements that θ-mark the subject. In other words, the subject is θ-marked by the V' to which it is a sister. Other related terms are **direct** and **indirect** θ-marking: the former refers to the relationship between a head and its complements, as the head and this alone 'directly' determines the θ-role assigned to its complements; the latter refers to the relationship between the head and its subject, as the subject's θ-role is assigned 'indirectly' via the X'.

θ-Theory

'θ-theory is concerned with the assignment of thematic roles such as agent-of-action, etc.' (Chomsky, 1981a, pp. 5–6)

θ-*roles*:
Agent: the person or thing carrying out the action
   Mary bought a book
Patient: the person or thing affected by the action
   Mary bought *a book*
Goal: the recipient of the object of the action
   Mary gave *Peter* a book
Theme: thing which is moved by the action
   Mary gave Peter *a book*

internal arguments are sisters to the head X, i.e. complements
external arguments are sisters to the X', i.e. subjects

So far this book has taken the word order of a language to be determined by the X-bar parameters that dictate that heads either precede or follow their complements and that specifiers either precede or follow the X'. In the sentence:

29.   Mary read a novel.

this means that the head parameter setting for English of head-first has ensured that *a novel* comes after *read* and the subject-first setting has ensured that *Mary* comes before *read*.

However, the same facts can be dealt with under θ-theory. θ-roles tend to be assigned in a uniform direction: for English, internal θ-roles such as Patient are assigned to the right and external θ-roles such as the Agent to the left. So the sentence:

30. Mary read a novel.

reflects that the verb *read* has assigned the external θ-role Agent to the left of the V' and the internal θ-role Patient to the right of V. The direction in which θ-roles are assigned may be a parameter that varies from one language to another, as first suggested by Koopman (1984). Variation in word order may be caused by the θ-theory parameter setting for the direction of θ-role assignment, rather than the X-bar theory word order parameters.

The interesting question is: which fact determines the other? Does the X-bar setting lay down the direction of θ-role assignment or is it the other way round? On the one hand it may be that the way that X-bar parameters are set for English makes all internal arguments appear to the right of the head and all external arguments to its left and as a consequence they must be assigned their θ-roles in this position. On the other hand it could equally well be that English first assigns its internal θ-roles to the right and its external θ-role to the left and hence, as a spin-off, X-bar theory must generate the arguments in the relevant positions.

Koopman (1984) argued strongly that it is the θ-theory parameters that determine basic word order. A choice between the X-bar and the θ-theory solutions depends on issues that we have not introduced yet and so cannot pursue in detail. Suffice to say that the debate is still unresolved and that both suggestions have their strong points. Travis (1984) has suggested that both points may be valid: the θ-marking parameter determines the word order of arguments in relation to their predicates; the X-bar parameter acts as a default setting for determining the placements of non-arguments.

Grammatical Functions

Most theories of grammar have employed the notion of **grammatical functions** (GFs) such as subject and object of the sentence. X-bar theory defines these as particular configurations in the structure of the sentence rather than as having an independent status. In X-bar syntax the subject of the sentence at D-structure is the specifier of VP in the following configuration:

31.

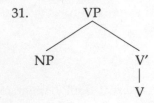

The GF subject is the NP (N″) immediately dominated by VP. The subject is defined in terms of this configuration. The GF object may be defined similarly as the NP (N″) dominated by V′, i.e. the complement of the Verb V, as seen in:

32.

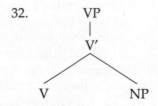

In Chomsky's words, 'We can now define the grammatical function *object* to be the NP of X′, and the grammatical function *subject* to be the NP of X″' (1986a, p. 161). Of course we are talking here of the D-structure position of the subject and we have said that this element moves to the specifier of IP at S-structure. However, note that this position is also immediately dominated by an X″ (the IP) and so this position can also be seen to be a 'subject' position according to the definition: the NP of X″.

The concept of object also extends to the GF object of Preposition, defined as the NP immediately dominated by P′, as in:

33.

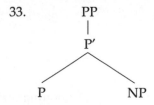

Here again the N″ is a 'sister' to the P. The grammatical functions of subject, object, and object of Preposition are combined in the D-structure tree for the sentence:

34. Her parents phoned the school on Friday.

35.

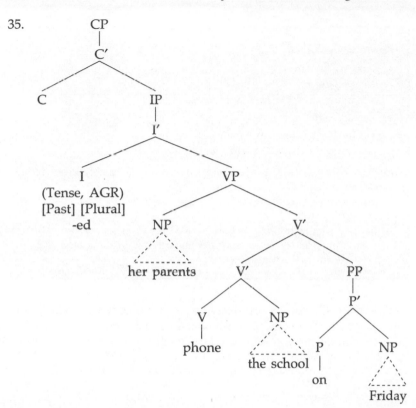

The GF subject is the NP *her parents* since it is the NP immediately dominated by VP; the GF object is the NP *the school* since it is the NP immediately dominated by V'; the NP *Friday* is a GF object of Preposition since it is the NP immediately dominated by P'. The definitions of grammatical functions in terms of configurations prove to be crucial to several aspects of principles and parameters theory.

We now need to return briefly to the movement relationship between D-structure and S-structure. The question:

36.   Who will Jim marry?

is in part a projection of the lexical entry for *marry*:

marry V, [__ NP]

which requires *marry* to be followed by an NP. However, how can it be grammatical when there is no NP after *marry* in this question? The Projection Principle requires an NP to be present at all syntactic levels to meet the specifications of the lexical entry, so the sentence would appear to violate the requirement that *marry* should have an NP

Grammatical Functions

Subject: the specifier in a phrase; the NP immediately dominated by VP at D-structure
Mike adores Belgian beer after work.

Object: the NP complement in a phrase; the NP immediately dominated by V' at D-structure
Mike adores *Belgian beer* after work.

Object of Preposition: the NP complement of a P; the NP immediately dominated by P' at D-structure
(Mike adores Belgian beer) after *work*.

Gloss: grammatical functions (GFs) are defined in terms of the structure of the sentence; there are no independent GFs in their own right (as there are in some other theories)

---

complement. Questions are derived by movement from the D-structure in which the element is present in a different location. For the moment the discussion will be concerned only with movement of the NP, not of the Verb. The D-structure is:

37.

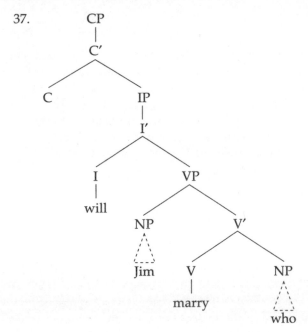

This satisfies the lexical entry for *marry* by supplying the missing NP *who* in the right place in the structure, i.e. the object position. Setting aside some details of movement, in the S-structure *who* comes at the beginning of the sentence within the CP but leaves a trace *t* where it was.

38.

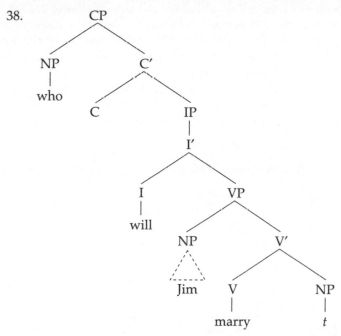

This now satisfies the projection of *marry* at S-structure by having the dummy element *t* in the correct place, standing for the moved NP. (The S-structure is still of course incomplete as it does not show the movement of the subject and of *will*.) *t* is a by-product of the Projection Principle; without a marker for the element that has been moved, the information projected from the lexical entry would not apply to S-structure. However, the Projection Principle does *not* apply to the PF component; while the specifications of lexical entries affect the sentence at all *syntactic* levels, they do not affect the phonetic representation. This S-structure therefore contains elements that do not appear in the actual sentence. NPs that appear in the S- or D-structure may in fact be 'empty', and so not appear in the surface; 'if some element is "understood" in a particular position, then it is *there* in syntactic representation, either as an overt category that is phonetically realised or as an empty category assigned no phonetic form' (Chomsky, 1986a, p. 84). The insistence of the Projection Principle that all specifications of the entry must be observed, combined with the notions of movement and traces, means that there are positions in D-structure and S-structure that are unfilled in the surface sentence.

GFs can now be linked to θ-theory. There are a set of positions in the structure in which we typically find arguments associated with GFs. The specifier of the VP is where the subject originates and so is the subject position par excellence. However, the subject usually moves out of this position into the specifier of the IP, as we see in the next chapter, and hence this too can be considered a subject position. The complements of verbs and prepositions are typical object positions. Collectively, all these positions are termed **A-positions** (argument positions), as they are the usual location for the arguments of a predicate. Let us take as an example the sentence:

39. Alec watched TV with Helen.

All the NPs, including the trace of the moved subject, occupy A-positions:

40.

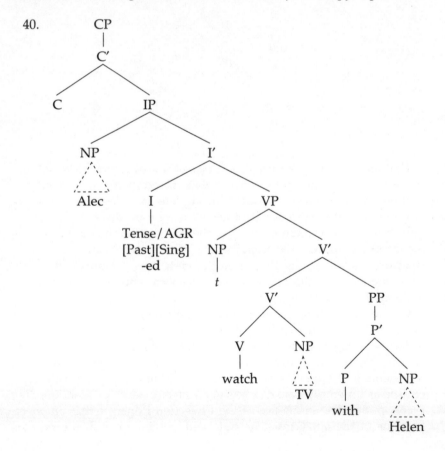

Alec is an NP in subject position originating in the specifier position in the VP to which the θ-role Agent can be assigned; *TV* is an NP in object position in the VP to which the θ-role Patient can be assigned; *Helen* is in object position in the PP. Each of the A-positions is then defined in terms of grammatical functions; an A-position is a GF position such as subject or object; a lexical entry can assign θ-roles only to those positions that conform to particular configurations of subject or object.

Positions that cannot take arguments are called **non-A-positions**, often symbolized as **Ā-position** and so often called **A-bar positions** (a completely distinct use of *bar* from that seen in 'X-bar-theory'). Two examples of non-A-positions are the specifier of CP, in this sentence unfilled, and the complement of I, filled by VP; whatever happens, no lexical entry can project arguments onto these positions. The distinction between A- and non-A-positions is crucial to the concept of movement to be dealt with in the next chapter.

Also relevant to movement is the concept of θ-**position**. A θ-position is one to which a θ-role is assigned. θ-positions are obviously restricted by the sisterhood condition placed on the process of θ-marking: θ-roles can only be assigned to sisters, both sister of a head for internal θ-roles and sister of X' for external θ-roles. Thus, in the above structure, the trace of the moved subject *t* is sister of V', the object *TV* is sister of V, and the object *Helen* is sister of P; all three are in θ-positions.

While all θ-positions are necessarily A-positions, not all A-positions are θ-positions: there are some A-positions that receive no θ-role. These always concern subject positions; thus some subject positions are A-positions, by definition, but are not θ-positions because no θ-role is assigned to them. When this is the case, one of two things can happen. One is that an element which originates in a θ-position at D-structure moves into the non-θ-marked subject position. For example, as we discussed above, the specifier of IP is a subject position and therefore an A-position. However, no θ-role is assigned to it: subjects usually originate in the specifier of VP where they receive their θ-roles. Usually subjects move from their original positions, inside VP, to the specifier of IP.

The second thing that can happen when there is a non-θ-marked subject position is that it is filled with a dummy 'expletive' element such as *it* or *there*. For instance, verbs such as *seem* do not have external θ-roles: no subject is specified in their lexical entry. Thus there is no element in the specifier of VP to move to the specifier of IP. Yet in these cases the specifier of IP must be filled, as in:

41.   There seems to be a fly in my soup.

or

42.   It seems that Sarah has left.

These expletive elements are indeed subjects, but they receive no θ-roles and hence are meaningless. This then is another example of an A-position which is not a θ-position.

Why do we need a grammatical subject when the Verb is not calling for a semantic subject? After all the same is not true of objects: when there is no semantic object, such as with intransitive verbs:

43.   The crowd disappeared.

there is no need to invoke a grammatical object. Chomsky (1981a) proposes that a (possibly language-specific) principle stipulates that all sentences must have subjects regardless of whether they are semantically required or not: 'in fact, the subject position *must* be filled by a pleonastic element in structures lacking a θ-marked subject. It seems, then, that the requirement that a clause have a subject position is independent of the Projection Principle' (Chomsky, 1982a, p. 10). Together, the Projection Principle and the requirement that clauses have subjects are called the **Extended Projection Principle**. Thus subjects are in principle required in a sentence independent of the actual lexical entry, whereas objects are only required if they are needed to bear the internal θ-roles assigned by a Verb or Preposition.

A-positions, θ-positions and the Extended Projection Principle

A-positions: the structural positions in which arguments are typically found: these include Spec of VP, Spec of IP and complement of V and P

Non-A-positions: the structural positions in which arguments are typically not found; these include Spec of CP and complement of I

θ-positions: the structural positions to which θ-roles are assigned. Because of the sisterhood condition on θ-marking, these are restricted to either sister of a lexical head or sister of an X′ projection of a lexical head

Extended Projection Principle: the principle that requires there to be a subject even if one is not needed semantically:
It seems that Sarah has left not **Seems that Sarah has left*

Further Types of Functional Phrase

The overall approach so far has extended the straightforward X-bar analysis of the lexical phrase to other types of phrase such as the IP and the CP. In recent years linguists have continued this trend by expanding the number of functional phrases, rather like physicists discovering new particles. The intention is to provide every functional category with its own phrase. This section introduces several of these new phrases, not all of which are fully accepted as yet. Many of the justifications for these phrases are in terms of movement, and so will emerge in the next chapter.

A starting point can be the IP (Inflection Phrase). As described so far, rather than having a single head, it consists anomalously of two features, AGR and Tense; it 'has the strange property of being "double-headed"' (Chomsky and Lasnik, 1993, p. 530). What would be more natural than to separate these two features by assigning each a phrase of its own? Pollock (1989) argued in favour of a separation between **AGRP (Agreement Phrase)** and **TP (Tense Phrase)**, both with the normal X-bar structure. This raises the further issue of whether TP dominates AGRP or vice versa, which has not been fully agreed as yet; Pollock (1989) has TP dominating AGRP and Chomsky (1991c) has AGRP dominating TP. Ouhalla (1991) indeed treats it as a parameter of variation between, for instance, a VSO language such as Berber, where AGR is inside Tense, and French, where AGR is outside Tense. Using Chomsky's order, the tree of the IP exploded into AGRP and TP appears as follows:

44.

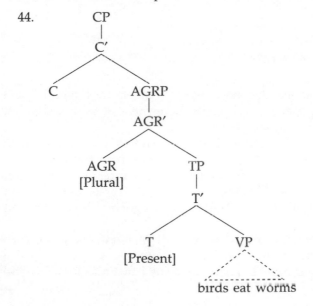

But even this does not cover all the possibilities in human languages. In some languages the Verb and the object agree as well as the Verb and subject; Chomsky (1991c) cites the agreement of French past participles with the clitic object in:

45.   Paul a   repeint   les chaises.
      Paul has paint + Singular the chairs
      Paul painted the chairs.

versus:

46.   Paul les   a   repeintes.
      Paul them has paint + Feminine Plural
      Paul has painted them.

where the plural of the Verb form *repeintes* reflects the plural object *les*. Hungarian provides a further example. In:

47.   Mutatom   a   süteményt
      show-1st sing def the cake-obj
      I am showing the cake.

the form of the Verb *mutatom* shows that the object is definite while in:

48.   Mutatok   egy süteményt
      show-1st sing indef a   cake-obj
      I am showing a cake.

the form of the Verb *mutatok* shows that it is indefinite. Spencer (1992) provides an additional example of the agreement of Verb and object in Chukchee, a Siberian language.

Hence two types of AGR need to be separated – agreement with subject and agreement with object – obviously potentially available in all languages. Chomsky (1991c) has AGR$_s$P (Agreement of Subject Phrase) dominate TP which dominates AGR$_o$P (Agreement of Object Phrase), on the argument that AGR$_s$ needs to govern the subject and so must be higher.

On the principle that every functional element needs its own phrase, the negative element in the sentence also needs to have a separate **NegP** (**Negation Phrase**), as argued in Pollock (1989) and

Chomsky (1991c). This has a head, i.e. in English *not*, a specifier and a complement. Ignoring for the moment the split AGRP, the D-structure of:

49.   John has not seen Bill.

is roughly:

50.

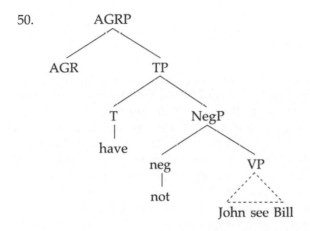

Again it is disputed whether NegP comes above or below TP (Newson, 1991).

The IP has then fissioned into several different phrases – AGR$_s$P, AGR$_o$P, TP, and NegP. Ouhalla (1991) and others expand this IP group still further by postulating Modal Phrases, Aspect Phrases, and Passive Phrases. The term IP or IP system nevertheless continues to be used as a shorthand for this group of phrases. Again the elaboration of different functional phrases creates problems for the representation of the sentence in tree form. Wherever possible we will keep the trees here as simple as possible by omitting phrases unnecessary to the point under discussion, in the same way that we have omitted unnecessary single-bar categories and used triangles within phrases.

Finally, to draw this list to a halt, a crucial new type of functional phrase that has been established outside the IP is the **DP (Determiner Phrase)**, first suggested in Abney (1987) and Fukui (1986). The functional items acting as determiners such as *the*, *a*, and *that* now get their own phrase. The phrase:

51.   that picture of Bill

has, according to Chomsky and Lasnik (1993), the structure:

52.

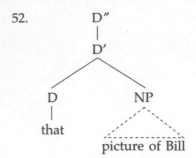

The NP *picture of Bill* is now the complement of the D. The reasons for preferring the DP analysis over NP put forward by Abney (1987) include making it conform to the usual X-bar scenario that non-heads in the sentence must be maximal phrases, accommodating determiners as heads of DP rather than as specifier of NP, and capturing the similarities that have often been referred to concerning 'NPs' and sentences: under the DP hypothesis noun phrases also have an inflectional/functional head, similar to the IP structure. In the DP analysis, pronouns are heads of DPs (and should now perhaps be called pro-determiners!), allowing *inter alia* a more plausible analysis of *I Claudius, We men,* and *You fool,* with the pronoun as head of the DP and the NP as its complement.

53.

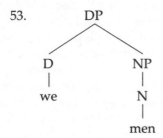

Similarly in:

54.   John's picture of Bill

the specifier of DP 'is filled by the "subject" of the DP, *John,* to which the affix POSS is adjoined by a phonological operation' (Chomsky and Lasnik, 1993, p. 533).

55.

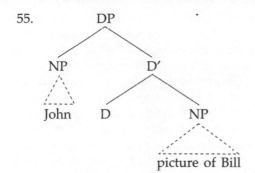

Lexical NPs are constituents within functional DPs.

Though the DP analysis is now widely accepted, it has not, however, been accommodated fully within all the principles or sub-theories of the principles and parameters theory. Hence it will not be possible to use DP throughout the rest of the book, logically necessary as this may be; like several other contemporary books, NP will be used for convenience where necessary.

Some Functional Categories		
	head	**possible lexical realizations in English**
CP	C	that, whether
AGRₛP	AGRₛ	-s
TP	T	-ed
NegP	Neg	not, n't
AGRₒP	AGRₒ	—
DP	D	he, the

The major differences between lexical and functional categories can now be summarized. The characteristics of functional categories summarized in the table on page 187 are based on Abney (1987, pp. 64–5) and Ouhalla (1991). Functional elements like C are closed, i.e. limited in number; it is virtually impossible for someone to invent a new functional element, as we see from the various unsuccessful attempts by people to create a non-gender-specific pronoun for English, for example *per* (Piercy, 1979). Lexical elements like N are usually open, i.e. unlimited in number; anybody can coin a new lexical item, as advertisers show every day. Abney (1987, p. 63), however, points out that prepositions are slightly anomalous: 'P seems to straddle the line between functional and thematic elements'; Newmeyer (1994) indeed postulates a parameter whether P is a lexical or functional category. Functional elements often depend phonologically on something else, i.e. they are clitics, lexical elements are not. Functional elements are unstressed in English; lexical elements may be stressed (though again until recently English prepositions have normally been unstressed). Functional heads select a very restricted range of complements; in most cases they only allow one type: C only has an AGRP complement, never a VP or NP, for example. Lexical heads often have a range of possible complement types. Moreover, functional heads do not assign θ-roles to their complements. Ouhalla (1991) therefore retains a role for c-selection as a property of functional categories while Chomsky (1986b) suggests it reduces to s-selection for lexical items at least. Functional categories often cannot be separated from their complements; lexical categories can. Lexical categories above all have an actual 'descriptive content'; they may refer to things: functional categories mark grammatical meaning, if they have a meaning at all, rather than a 'class of objects'. Abney (1987) points out that the last point is familiar in the grammatical tradition. In language teaching too the distinction between function words and structure words goes back several generations, capturing one important aspect of this distinction.

Ouhalla (1991) adds to this list the property that only functional categories have grammatical features such as number, person etc., and the major assumption that only functional categories have parameters. This is then a radical alteration to the theory, known as the **functional parameterization hypothesis**. Parameters do not, so to speak, belong to principles but to functional categories. In effect, what this means is that languages differ only in the properties they select for their functional categories: lexical categories are universal and uniform across all languages. For example the Verb *hit*, whatever its phonological form, will be transitive in all languages and hence universally takes an NP complement. However, T may take an AGR_oP complement in some languages (for example English) or it may take AGR_sP complement in others (for example Berber). Thus word order differences between languages may largely be due to differences in the c-selection properties of functional elements. There may then be two types of lexicon: one for lexical entries which contains Ns, Vs, As and Ps, each with a specification of its s-selection properties; one for entries which contain functional categories, each with the relevant setting for the appropriate parameters. This is an extension of the lexical parameterization hypothesis encountered in chapter 2: variation in language comes down to variation in the lexicon. There may be a difference between languages, not only in the actual values for parameters attached to lexical entries, but also in whether a functional category actually exists in a given language. Van Gelderen (1993), for instance, argues that English did not have a TP or AGR$_s$ before 1380 and that Dutch still does not have them.

The Contrast between Lexical and Functional Categories

functional phrases	lexical phrases
— closed class of heads	— open class of heads
— dependent phonologically	— phonologically independent
— usually unstressed	— potentially stressed
— have a single complement, not an argument	— have one or more complements
— inseparable complement	— separable complement
— no 'descriptive content', not linked to 'real' world	— descriptive content, linked to 'real' world
— have grammatical features	— do not have grammatical features
— linked to parameters	— not linked to parameters

It should be pointed out that the functional categories approach has met with a mixed reception from some morphologists. The main idea of functional categories is that each inflectional ending requires its own phrase – a TP is necessary to show past tense endings, an AGR$_S$ to show Verb agreement, and so on. But there are several problems with this. One is that a single inflectional form may actually show more than one type of information simultaneously. English present tense -s in fact shows both present tense and singular at the same time: a single inflection is then linked to two phrases. Joseph and Smirniotopoulos (1993) point to the case of Greek -ik- as in *plithikan* (they were washed) which indicates non-active voice, past tense, and perfective aspect at the same time, and hence would have to belong to three separate phrases simultaneously. Nor is it clear that postulating different phrases helps with the ordering of morphemes in the sentence. In English some forms also consist of replacements within the word rather than inflections – *run/ran*, *bite/bit*, etc. Again in Greek, Joseph and Smirniotopoulos (1993) point out that there is often no affix in the phrase; the perfect *plinun* (they have washed) differs from the imperfect *plenun* in its vowel, not in its affix. Chomsky's reaction to this is to claim that the relationship between overt morphology and actual functional heads is more abstract than assumed in these works.

For example, the actual form of a past tense verb may be determined in the lexicon, but the verb still has to move to the functional head position, not to pick up any morpheme, but to 'check' that it has the correct features. We shall expand on this in the discussion of Chomsky's Minimalist Programme in chapter 9. In general the goal of exploding the IP into as many phrases as there are affixes runs into trouble when it tries to deal with languages with highly complex morphology, such as Greek, rather than the sparse morphology of languages such as English and French. It has indeed been argued that the AGRP analysis is not necessary even for these languages. Assuming that the subject is internal to VP, Iatridou (1990) shows that the difference between English and French can be handled by allowing agreement of the subject within the VP when it is governed by a T that is [+Finite]. If an intervening phrase occurs between TP and VP, agreement cannot take place. When there is a NegP, the raising of verbs in French allows there to be a new agreement: the lack of verb raising in English prevents this relationship and triggers insertion of *do* and its agreement. For further discussion see Joseph and Smirniotopoulos (1993), Iatridou (1990), and Baker (1991).

To sum up, the complex phrase structure of human languages derives from a small number of X-bar principles with parameters of variation. D-structure 'is a "pure" representation of theta-structure, expressing theta relations through the medium of the X-bar theoretic conditions in accordance with the projection principle' (Chomsky, 1991c, p. 419). The central insight is that a sentence consists of phrases with a common structure, just as cells with different functions and locations in the body share the same structure. First comes a maximal phrase containing a related head of the same type as the phrase and a possible specifier; this head in turn consists of another head related to it and possible complements. In lexical phrases the latter head is a lexical category which links to a lexical entry with idiosyncratic properties that select which complements must occur in the phrase and how many semantic roles need to be associated with it. In functional phrases the head may or may not have lexical content. Language variation in X-bar syntax comes down to differences in the relative positions of complements and heads. Once the complex apparatus of X-bar syntax is established, the account of phrase structure is simple and all-embracing. The apparent diversity of different languages can be reduced to combinations within this UG system: 'there is a single computational system C_{HL} for human language and only limited lexical variety. Variation of language is essentially morphological in character' (Chomsky, 1995b, p. 388).

6

Movement and Case Theory

This chapter will discuss the following topics:

— NP-movement
— Wh-movement
— Subject-movement and Verb-movement
— Word order variation
— Case Theory
— The Case Filter
— Parameters of Case Theory.

This chapter looks at the nature of syntactic movement. Just as the development of X-bar syntax gradually eliminated the peculiarities of individual rules, so the general principle of movement has subsumed many separate rules previously known as transformations. Universal Grammar is seen once again as limiting the ways in which movement can take place, narrowing down the possible human languages.

The starting point is to consider that there may be no restrictions on movement at all: *any* part of the sentence could move *anywhere*. This can be stated as:

1. **Move α.**

where α stands for any category. 'The movement operation (henceforth Move α) is an invariant principle of computation, stating that a category can be moved to a target position' (Chomsky and Lasnik, 1993, p. 522). The theory of movement explores the restrictions that human languages actually place on movement. It is a property of UG that only certain elements may be moved, that they may only be moved to certain locations, and that they may not move more than a certain distance: 'Move α' is tightly constrained. Some of these restrictions apply uniformly to all human languages, some are parameterized and vary within limits from one language to another. Chapter 1 introduced the principle of structure-dependency, one of the consequences of which is that the elements which may be moved must be constituents of the sentence; structure-dependency prevents 'Move α' from applying to non-constituents. We will see in this chapter that the constituents that move are either maximal projections (XP) such as NP or are heads of phrases (X) such as N.

Chapter 2 sketched movement as the relationship between D-structure, at which all the thematic relationships are fully expressed, and S-structure, at which they are changed into a form that can act as a bridge between PF and LF. So the sentence:

2.   Where is the hospital?

has an underlying D-structure in which the elements are in the places projected from their lexical entries, i.e.:

3.   The hospital is where?

and an S-structure which preserves their original locations through traces (*t*):

4.   Where$_1$ is$_2$ the hospital t_2 t_1

Movement is one way of talking about this relationship. It can be seen as going in both directions, either deriving S-structure from D-structure or abstracting D-structure from S-structure. The sole purpose of D-structure is to show the original location of various elements in the sentence moved in S-structure, in particular to maintain the Projection Principle 'which expresses the idea that D-structure is a "pure" representation of thematically relevant GFs' (Chomsky, 1982a, p. 9).

The term 'movement' can be misleading as it conveys the idea that something actually 'moves' from one place to another. It should not be forgotten that the theory is always an I-language theory in which process plays no part; there is no time sequence in which X changes into Y, no real direction of movement. Instead movement is a way of expressing a relationship between one form and another *as if things moved*. An alternative way of expressing the relationship of D-structure to S-structure is via the concept of a **chain** that records the links that make up this relationship. Instead of relating the D-structure and S-structure of:

5. Where is the hospital?

through movement, the relationship can be seen as incorporating two chains. One chain:

6. (where, t_1)

links *where* to one place in the structure t_1. The second chain:

7. (is, t_2)

links *is* to another place in the structure t_2. 'Movement of an element α always leaves a trace and, in the simplest case, forms a *chain* (α, t) where α, the head of the chain, is the moved element and t is its trace' (Chomsky and Lasnik, 1993, p. 522).

NP-movement

While movement is a general relationship that applies throughout English and other languages, the specific example of the passive construction in English can be taken as a starting point. As was mentioned in chapter 1, the traditional analysis treats the passive as a form of movement in which, *inter alia*, the object of the active sentence is moved to be subject of the passive sentence;

8. The policemen chase the bank robbers.

becomes:

9. The bank robbers are chased by the policemen.

by exchanging *the policemen* and *the bank robbers*, and adding *are*, *-ed*, and *by*. Although the principles and parameters analysis relies on movement, it does not suppose switching elements in a sentence in this way. Instead the passive sentence is treated as having a D-structure in which the NP *the bank robbers* occurs after the Verb and then moves into subject position.

The Projection Principle requires lexical entries to project onto all syntactic levels. The Verb *defeat* has the entry:

10.   defeat V, [__ NP] <Agent, Patient>

It c-selects an NP and s-selects two θ-roles, Agent and Patient, as seen in:

11.   The Normans defeated the Saxons.

However, the passive sentence:

12.   The Saxons were defeated.

seems to contravene the Projection Principle by not having the required NP following the Verb *defeated*. To meet the requirements of the principle, the S-structure must supply the missing NP:

13.   The Saxons were defeated *t*.

The S-structure of the passive sentence is now satisfactory in that it incorporates the correct projection of the lexical entry in the form of an NP, even if only as a phonologically empty trace *t*.

The D-structure of the sentence locates the NP in its original position before movement takes place:

14.   were defeated the Saxons

The D-structure meets the specifications of the entry that *defeat* c-selects a following NP. But this D-structure is still deficient in that there is no subject A-position to fulfil the requirement of the Extended Projection Principle that there must always be a subject. Again the solution is to postulate an empty category *e* that occupies the missing position specified by the entry, yielding the D-structure:

15.   *e* were defeated the Saxons.

e can now be the missing subject. Note also that there is no subject to receive the external θ-role as the θ-criterion would demand. We discuss this issue later.

The following tree gives the D-structure for the sentence:

16.   The Saxons were defeated.

This chapter simplifies trees by sticking to NPs (rather than DPs), since these are used in most published discussion, and by using a single AGRP dominating TP (apart from one section).

17.

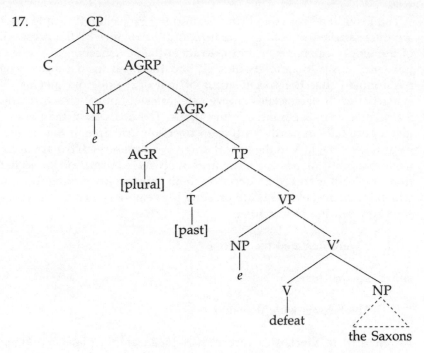

In the S-structure the NP *the Saxons* therefore moves to the specifier of AGRP position to get the S-structure:

18.

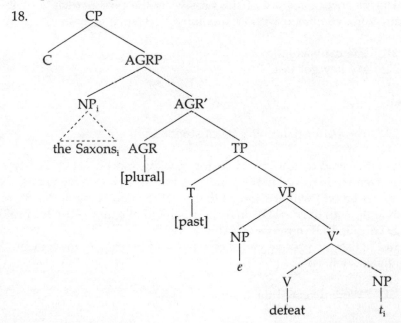

The Extended Projection Principle and the Projection Principle itself are thus satisfied at both D-structure and S-structure by the presence of the empty categories, *e* and *t*, to meet the specification of the lexical entry *defeat* for a following NP and the need for a subject. The requirement that the specification of a lexical entry be met at all syntactic levels necessitates empty categories at both D-structure and S-structure to indicate the missing items. The analysis of the passive given here falls in neatly with the Projection Principle in that movement allows the link to the lexical entry to be preserved; the apparent incompatibility of passive structures with the information projected from the Verb is solved by deriving them from an underlying form in which the correct elements are present. Movement is then the relationship between the D-structure:

19.   *e* were defeated the Saxons

and the S-structure:

20.   The Saxons were defeated *t*

An element in the D-structure moves to an empty place *e*, leaving behind it an empty category *t*. Movement cannot take place without an empty position into which the element can move.

The distinctive feature of the passive is the past participle of the main Verb, combined with an auxiliary Verb such as *be* or *get*, as in:

21.   The cat was killed.
22.   My key got lost.

and:

23.   The performance will be postponed.

This is referred to collectively as the 'passive morphology'. The type of movement involved in the passive is known as NP-movement since it moves an NP, with the trace *t* that is left behind being an NP-trace, although, with the new DP analysis, it should of course, strictly speaking, be called DP-movement (Abney, 1987).

In English the passive morphology is said to 'trigger' movement. A sentence such as:

24.   *Were defeated the Saxons.

is ungrammatical; the passive morphology forces the NP *the Saxons* to move. Passives in other languages need no movement; for example, according to Chomsky (1988, p. 119), in the Spanish sentence:

25. Ha sido   devorada la   oveja por el   lobo.
    (It has been devoured the sheep by the wolf)
    The sheep has been devoured by the wolf.

the object NP *la oveja* may stay in place after the Verb rather than having to move into preverbal subject position.

Some languages also permit impersonal passives in which the subject position receives an 'expletive' subject, as in German:

26. Es wurde getrunken.
    (it was drunk, i.e. drinking took place)

Indeed English also allows passives that have no NP-movement. For example, in the sentence:

27. It was thought that Abelard loved Heloise.

there is no object to move to the structural subject position. As with the German example given above, the subject position is filled with a pleonastic element *it*.

The triggering of movement in the passive has parameters of variation between languages. To quote Chomsky (1981a, p. 121): 'In the case of passive, languages tend to have devices for suppressing the subject, but these can work out in many ways, depending on how options are selected from the components of UG.'

Movement is also tied in with θ-theory. The θ-structure position of *the Saxons* is the Grammatical Function (GF) object. Hence it is an Argument position (A-position) and capable of receiving a θ-role. Movement takes *the Saxons* to the GF position of subject, also an A-position. So NP-movement shifts *the Saxons* from one A-position (the GF object) to another A-position (the GF subject): NP-movement is restricted to movement between A-positions. However, the position that the object is moved into not only has to be empty of any lexical element, but it must also be free of any θ-role that would otherwise be assigned to it. This is because, if the object NP were to move from its original position, which is already assigned a θ-role by the verb, to the subject position, which has another θ-role, the chain formed by the movement would end up with two θ-roles and hence be in violation of the θ-criterion. Note that, although the Principle of Full Interpretation, which supersedes the θ-criterion, allows arguments to bear more than one θ-role, these must be assigned at D-structure, and an argument is *not* allowed to pick up extra θ-roles as it moves. This must follow from other constraints on movement, but what these are is not exactly obvious. It is questions such as these that have led to the current developments in Chomsky's thinking, i.e. the Minimalist Programme, dealt with in chapter 9.

So it is not just that NP-movement can only move an NP into a position that is empty of lexical content, but also that the position must be free of thematic content: i.e. there must be no θ-role assigned to the subject position. This, however, raises a problem: the verb *defeat* usually assigns a θ-role to its subject and so this should prevent the subject position from being moved into. The solution to this problem is indicated in the quote by Chomsky given above: 'languages . . . have devices for suppressing the subject' (Chomsky, 1981a, p. 121). Thus not only does the passive morpheme trigger movement of the object to the subject position (in a way that we will discuss later), but also it 'absorbs' the subject's θ-role, leaving the subject position free to be moved into by the object. One of the simplest ways of looking at this phenomenon is presented in Jaeggli (1986) who suggests that the passive morpheme acts like a kind of argument which needs to be assigned a θ-role. Given that verbs subcategorize for complements, the appearance of an object is obligatory and hence the object θ-role must be assigned to the object. So the only θ-role available to the passive morpheme is the subject θ-role and hence it is this that is 'absorbed', i.e. assigned to the passive morpheme.

Before developing movement more generally, let us consolidate the analysis of the passive by including 'full' passives with a *by* phrase, as in:

28.   The battle was won by the Normans.

The D-structure is:

29.   *e* was won the battle by the Normans

The NP *the battle* is in the A-position of GF object and has the θ-role Patient: the GF subject is filled by *e* and is prevented by the passive morphology from receiving the Agent role. An Agent role, possibly passed on from the passive morpheme, has been assigned to a PP *by the Normans*, which acts as an Adjunct in the VP. The passive morphology triggers movement to the empty A-position at the beginning of the sentence, yielding the S-structure:

30.　The battle was won *t* by the Normans.

While the examples given so far all involve the θ-role Patient, it is also possible for the passive to involve other θ-roles, as in:

31.　The witness was sent a summons.

where the subject *the witness* is a Goal.

But, as always within principles and parameters theory, a construction such as the passive is treated as the interaction of various principles rather than as a single 'rule'. Hence the concept of NP-movement applies not just to passives but also to phenomena such as the 'raising' that occurs with sentences with *seem*. A sentence such as:

32.　They seem to be competent.

is analysed as having a D-structure in which *they* occurs in the subject position of the infinitival complement clause and as such receives its θ-role from the predicate *be competent*:

33.　*e* seem they to be competent

with *they* moving to the subject position in the S-structure:

34.　They seem *t* to be competent

leaving a trace behind. Like the passive, the raising of NPs to subject position with Verbs such as *seem* depends upon the fact that an Agent θ-role is not assigned at D-structure to the external subject position by such Verbs, so that movement can take place to a position that is not already θ-marked.

The passive is not a rule of its own; nor are raising Verbs such as *seem* odd exceptions: 'movement is never determined by specific rule, but rather results from the interaction of other factors' (Chomsky, 1986b, p. 5). Instead such constructions are examples of the general principle of movement Move α where α is in this case NP. The restrictions on NP-movement apply to all languages, subject to parametric variation and to the difference in lexical entries.

Let us go back briefly to the idea of a chain. The relationship between the D-structure and the S-structure of:

35.   The Saxons were defeated.

is the chain:

36.   (the Saxons, *t*)

This chain has a single link. However, the passive sentence:

37.   The book was said to be lost.

has an S-structure:

38.   The book was said *t'* to be lost *t*

The NP *the book* comes from the object position of the VP headed by *lose* via the VP headed by *say*. This means a chain with two links:

39.   (the book, *t'*, *t*)

One link is between *the book* and *t'*, one between *t'* and *t*. To sum up, a chain 'is the S-structure reflection of a "history of movement", consisting of the positions through which an element has moved from the A-position it occupied at D-structure' (Chomsky, 1986a, p. 95). NP-movement involves a link between an A-position in D-structure and an empty A-position that has neither contained an actual NP nor had a θ-role assigned to it. These are known as **A-chains** – movement from θ-marked A-positions in D-structure to non-θ-marked A-positions.

NP-movement

Principle of movement: Move α (i.e. move any element anywhere)
In NP-movement α = NPs (strictly speaking DPs), which move from θ-marked A-positions to non-θ-marked A-positions, leaving an NP-trace

Gloss: a typical case of movement is the English passive. A passive sentence such as *The mouse was killed* derives from the D-structure *e was killed the mouse* by movement of the NP *the mouse* to the empty specifier of AGRP leaving trace *t* behind in the S-structure *the mouse was killed t*

Chain: an alternative way of expressing movement is as a chain consisting of links between a moved element α and its trace *t* (α, *t*)

Wh-movement

A second type of movement, known as wh-movement, concerns the movement of wh-phrases. A wh-phrase is one that contains a wh-word; these include the item *how* as well as words starting with *wh* such as *who* and *which*; 'we may think of *wh* as a feature that appears in the surface form within a word . . . but is abstractly associated with the NP of which this noun is the head (or the PP containing this NP)' (Chomsky, 1986a, p. 69). Under the X-bar analysis of chapter 4 either the wh-word is the head of a phrase:

40. Where did you go?

or it is the head of a DP containing an NP:

41. Which person did you mean?

Two areas of English that have traditionally been seen as involving wh-movement are questions and relative clauses, both of which contain wh-phrases. Let us start with an example question:

42. Who did he see?

with the D-structure as follows, continuing for the moment to avoid the problem of *did*:

43. He past see who

The lexical entry for *see* is:

44. see V, [__ NP] <Experiencer, Source>

The θ-role Experiencer is assigned to the GF subject *he*, the θ-role Source to the GF object *who*. Since both the object and subject positions are filled, there is no A-position in the D-structure to which *who* can move. One difference between NP-movement and wh-movement must be that wh-movement moves the wh-phrase into a non-A-position rather than into an A-position.

The resulting S-structure after movement, omitting details of *did*, is:

45. who he past see *t*

The wh-phrase *who* has moved from the object position to the front of the sentence, leaving a trace *t* behind it; this type of trace is consequently a wh-trace, also known as a variable. But what exactly is the non-A-position to which *who* has moved? There must be an empty position in the D-structure at the beginning of the sentence. The structure of CP that was introduced in chapter 4 now proves its usefulness, in particular the empty specifier position. Wh-movement takes a wh-phrase from an A-position and moves it to the specifier of CP, which is otherwise unfilled. The abbreviated D-structure of:

46. he past see who

can be seen in the following tree, which shows the empty specifier position:

47.

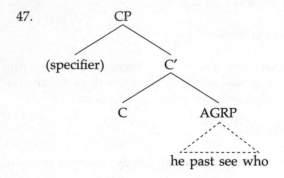

The S-structure after movement is then:

48.

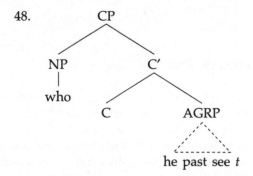

The wh-phrase *who* has moved into the vacant specifier position. As the specifier of CP is not an A-position, θ-roles cannot be assigned to it; wh-movement goes from an A-position, where it gets its θ-role, to a non-A-position, where it does not pick up an extra θ-role, thus conforming to the θ-criterion that each argument has only one θ-role. The principle 'Move α' is constrained in that movement can be either to an empty A-position (NP-movement) or to a non-A-position (wh-movement); it cannot be to an A-position that is already filled and has a θ-role. As with NP-movement, there may be several steps, as in:

49.   What did he believe he saw?

which has the S-structure:

50.   What he past believe *t'* he past see *t*

The original location of *what* is the object A-position of the embedded VP. It moves first to the specifier of CP within the embedded clause, a non-A-position. From there it moves to specifier of CP in the main clause, a further non-A-position.

As was said in the discussion of NP-movement, within principles and parameters theory movements are assumed to be motivated: there are reasons why things move from one position to another. Thus, for the passive, the passive morphology 'triggers' movement in a way that we will discuss towards the end of this chapter. But what 'triggers' wh-movement? One suggestion is that the complementizer system contains an abstract interrogative feature that forces wh-elements to move to it, rather like Verbs moving to AGR to pick up agreement features (see next section). Evidence for this can be seen in the fact that complementizers themselves are differentiated in terms of whether they are interrogative or not: *whether* is an interrogative complementizer in:

51.   I wonder whether there will be sausages on the menu.

and *that* is a declarative complementizer in:

52.   I think that there will be sausages on the menu.

This can be handled through an abstract feature [±Wh], to be included in the lexical entry of all complementizers: *whether* is categorized [+Wh] and *that* is categorized [−Wh]. Furthermore, if the empty complementizer can be either [+Wh] or [−Wh], depending on whether it introduces an interrogative or declarative clause, the C-system will always be headed by a [+Wh] or a [−Wh] element.

But how does this make wh-items move to the specifier of CP? To explain this, we need to introduce two mechanisms. The first may be called the **Wh-Criterion**, after Rizzi (1991), which states:

all [+Wh] complementizers must contain a [+Wh] element

(This is not in fact Rizzi's own formulation of the Wh-Criterion, but is more similar to a principle proposed by Aoun et al. (1981).) While this is obviously satisfied when there is a [+Wh] complementizer such as *whether* in head position, it does raise the problem of how the Wh-Criterion can be satisfied by wh-movement, which moves a wh-word into the *specifier* of CP, not the head position. This is where the second mechanism comes in, namely **specifier–head agreement**, abbreviated to spec/head agreement. This accounts for a set of phenomena where there is agreement between the head of a phrase X and the element which occupies the specifier of that phrase, specifier of XP. For example, the subject of a finite clause sits in the specifier position of AGRP and it 'agrees' with the head AGR in that they must have the same nominal features of person, number and gender. If this relationship between specifier and head is universal and so applicable to all phrases, the specifier of the CP will also agree with the head C in that both will share the [±Wh] feature. Now, if a wh-item moves into a [+Wh] specifier of CP, this will be enough to satisfy the Wh-Criterion as, although the complementizer position itself may not contain a [+Wh] element, the specifier with which it agrees *does* contain such an element. So the Wh-Criterion is satisfied either by the head complementizer of the CP having [+Wh] or by the [+Wh] of the specifier of CP migrating to the head via spec/head agreement.

The Wh-Criterion accounts for the ungrammaticality of examples such as:

53.   *who$_i$ do you wonder John likes t_i

Here the verb *wonder* subcategorizes for a CP complement whose head carries the [+Wh] feature – *I wonder whether* . . . , *I wonder who* . . . , etc. If this CP does not contain a [+Wh] element, the Wh-Criterion will be violated. Note that if we assume that the wh-phrase moves through the lower CP leaving a trace behind, as we have been, it seems that this trace does not satisfy the Wh-Criterion. Perhaps this indicates that wh-traces do not have the [±Wh] feature.

There may also be a complementary principle to the Wh-Criterion that states that a [+Wh] element cannot occupy a [−Wh] position. This accounts for the ungrammaticality of the following sentence:

54. *I think who$_i$ John kissed.

Here the verb *think* subcategorizes for a [−Wh] CP complement and thus a [+Wh] element is not allowed to stay in this C-system, though of course it can move further up to the highest CP:

55. who$_i$ do I think John kissed t_i

The Wh-Criterion is obviously parameterized in some way since not all languages have to move wh-items to the specifier of CP; Chinese and Japanese, for example, do not move wh-items at all at S-structure. It may be that these languages have Wh-movement at LF, in which case the parameter concerns the level of representation at which the Wh-Criterion applies, whether S-structure or LF.

Wh-movement also applies to the wh-phrase in relative clauses. Take the sentence:

56. The student who the examiner failed was Tom.

The D-structure is:

57. The student [the examiner failed who] was Tom.

Who is the GF object, an A-position. It moves to the specifier of CP to get the S-structure.

58. The student [who the examiner failed t] was Tom.

Relative clauses behave like questions in that movement starts from a θ-marked A-position and goes to a position that is not θ-marked.

There are nevertheless some peculiarities to relative clauses in English. On the one hand the wh-word may be omitted from the surface sentence when it moves out of object position:

59. The student the examiner failed was Tom.

On the other hand, as well as wh-words such as *who* and *what*, English also has *that* in relative clauses:

60.   The student that the examiner failed was Tom.

This is in fact the complementizer *that* characteristic of embedded CPs as in:

61.   I said [that he was right].

So *that* is an example of the actual C category, i.e. the head, as in the abbreviated tree of the relative clause:

62.

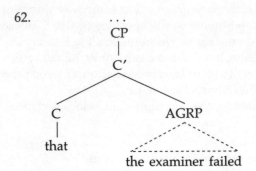

However, in English the sentence may *not* contain both a wh-word and *that*:

63.   *The student who that the examiner failed was Tom.

One of them, or both of them, have to be left out. One way of handling this is through the **Doubly Filled COMP Filter** (Chomsky and Lasnik, 1977, p. 450), which can be paraphrased as:

The C-system may not contain both an overt wh-element and an overt complementizer.

Filters such as this prevent otherwise grammatical sentences from occurring; they are restrictions on output that exclude certain sentences. The Doubly Filled COMP Filter is not universal; some languages permit both wh-words and complementizers to occur together, as in Dutch:

64. Ik vroeg him *wie of*   hij had gezien.
(I asked him whowhether he had seen)

where both *wie* and *of* are in the C-system (van Riemsdijk and Williams, 1986, p. 161). The presence of this filter is a parameter of UG. Its presence in English explains why *who* and *that* cannot be combined; its absence in Dutch permits the juxtaposition of *wie* and *of*. An interesting issue arises here concerning the learnability of such filters. Obviously children have to learn whether or not their language has the Doubly Filled COMP Filter on the basis of positive evidence. But there can be no positive evidence that a language has the filter as its job is precisely to filter out certain structures: a language which has the filter will differ from one that does not only by the *absence* of certain structures, and this fact cannot be expressed by positive data. If we assume that possession of the filter is the unmarked parameter setting, i.e. that children assume this setting initially, the presence of the structures that the filter filters out will act as positive evidence that the filter is inoperable. The child can then discard the filter, accepting the marked setting of the parameter. Thus the English setting for the parameter is unmarked and the Dutch setting is marked: Dutch children need positive evidence to set the value for the parameter away from the unmarked position, i.e. structures containing *wie of*.

This section finishes with a reminds that wh-movement is a relationship that can be expressed equally as a chain. The movement in the sentence:

65. Who did he see?

with the partial S-structure:

66. Who did he see *t*

can be seen as a chain:

67. (who, *t*)

in which *who* is linked to *t*. Wh-movement involves movement from an A-position to specifier of C, a non-A-position. These are known as **non-A-chains** because they end in non-A-positions.

Wh-movement

Principle of movement: Move α (i.e. move any element anywhere)
In wh-movement, α = a wh-phrase, which moves from an A-position to
   the non-A-position of specifier of CP, leaving wh-trace (variable)
The Wh-Criterion: All [+Wh] complementizers must contain a [+Wh]
   element
The Doubly Filled COMP Filter:
The C-system may not contain both a wh-element and a complementizer

Gloss:

— questions such as *What did the cat kill?* involve wh-movement of the
   wh-phrase *what* from the D-structure *the cat past kill what* to the specifier position of CP, yielding the S-structure *what did the cat kill t*
— relative clauses, such as *(the mouse) which the cat killed*, derive from
   D-structures, such as *(the mouse) the cat killed which* by movement of
   the *which* to the specifier of CP, yielding the S-structure *(the mouse)*
   which the cat killed t

Subject-movement and Verb-movement

Chapter 4 outlined two types of movement that are necessary to generate the structure of virtually all English sentences, namely subject-
movement and Verb-movement. We will recap these briefly before
looking at some of their implications.

First the subject of the sentence. In the version of principles and
parameters theory presented here, the subject of the sentence is introduced as the specifier of VP. For those familiar with earlier versions
of the theory, this is a major change from its former position as specifier
of the IP (the *Barriers* analysis) or from still earlier versions where it
was the NP of S (sentence). Reasons for this analysis are presented in
Koopman and Sportiche (1991).

The sentence:

68.   Susan likes tomatoes.

has the following D-structure, eliminating redundant single-bar categories and using a single AGRP for convenience (as AGR_o does not
occur overtly in English):

69.

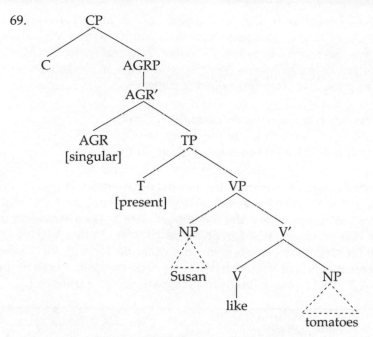

In the S-structure the subject *Susan* moves by NP-movement to become the specifier of the AGRP:

70.

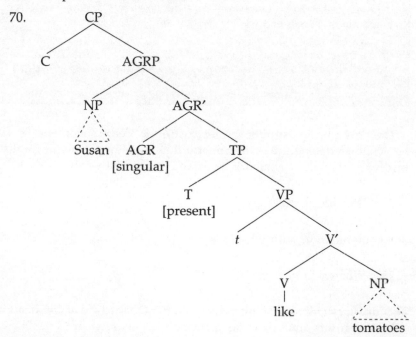

Subject-movement is in fact a parameter of variation between languages. According to Koopman and Sportiche (1991), in Welsh and Irish the subject remains in the VP rather than raising to the AGRP. Catalan, for example, allows Verb–subject order in declarative sentences in particular contexts, as in the sentence:

71. ha   ficat les sabates a l'armari   l'Oriol
    (has put the shoes   in the closet the Oriol)
    it was Oriol who has put the shoes in the closet

Earlier this was seen as part of the pro-drop parameter. It may, however, reflect the fact that Catalan subjects do not raise and are relatively free to move within the VP (Bonet, 1990). The discussion of passive and wh-movement earlier in the chapter cheated slightly by not mentioning subject-movement; for example each of the chains in passive movement should have more than one link, because the subject NP has to pass through intermediate subject positions.

Subject-movement

Subject-movement involves the subject NP of the VP moving to the specifier of AGRP, compulsory in some languages such as English, optional in Welsh and Irish

Gloss: the subject *Max* in the sentence *Max will play the drums* starts as specifier of VP and moves, leaving a trace in S-structure *Max will t play the drums*

The next step in forming the S-structure is Verb-movement. So far no acknowledgement has been made that some questions in English involve inversion of auxiliary Verb and subject either on its own:

72. Will Judith pass?

or in combination with wh-movement:

73. When will you leave?

The auxiliary *will* may be introduced in the D-structure as the head of TP (though this analysis is far from agreed), as seen in:

74.

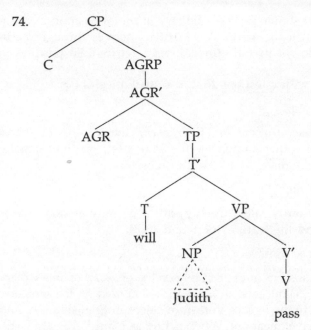

As always the subject NP *Judith* moves to the specifier of AGRP. The auxiliary also moves; first to the head of AGRP, then to the head of CP, thus producing the order:

75.   Will Judith pass?

76.

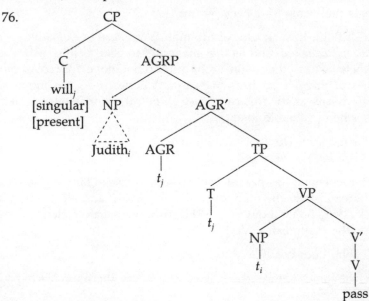

In English tense is shown on the auxiliary in initial position in questions rather than on the Verb. The auxiliary moves through Verb-movement, first to get its inflection, then to get its final position in front of the subject.

What happens with questions that *lack* auxiliaries? Take:

77.   John saw him.

There is no auxiliary present in TP to 'carry' the features of T and AGR. Unlike some other languages, the Verb itself may not usually move in modern English, i.e. we do not have:

78.   *Saw John him?

The English solution is called **do-support**; a dummy auxiliary *do* is introduced to carry the features of T and AGR:

79.   Did John see him?

Hence inversion questions in English rely on the presence of an auxiliary in the D-structure; failing this, an auxiliary is imposed on the sentence.

The exceptions to the lack of Verb-movement in English are *be* and *have* with 'possessive' meaning. When acting as main Verbs, they still behave like auxiliaries in being able to move to the C position, as in:

80.   Have you many children?

and:

81.   Is the Prime Minister a wimp?

In British English, such uses of the main Verb *have* as causative (*Have the maid make the bed*) and as that meaning 'to bear a child' (*Mary had twins*) behave like other main Verbs and do not move. Moreover other varieties of English, such as Standard American, do not move any main Verb *have* at all. This can cause some communication problems, as enshrined in the old joke:

82.   American: Do you have children?
      Briton: Not very often.

Verb-movement has parametric variants between languages, which were indeed partly the motivation for the AGRP and NegP analyses. Pollock (1989) pointed out that, in English, the negative element must precede the main lexical Verb as in:

83.   John does not like Mary.

where *not* comes before *like*. It may not follow the main Verb, as in:

84. *John likes not Mary.

However, in French the negative element *pas* must follow the inflected Verb, as in:

85. Jean n'aime pas Marie.

where *pas* follows *aime*. This difference between English and French can be expressed in terms of Verb-movement, according to Chomsky's 1991 version of Pollock's proposal: in English the Verb cannot move across the AGR_oP; in French it can (Chomsky, 1991c). Both English and French have similar D-structures; many differences in their S-structure arise from a single parameter of movement. The partial D-structure for:

86. Jean n'aime pas Marie.

is then:

87.

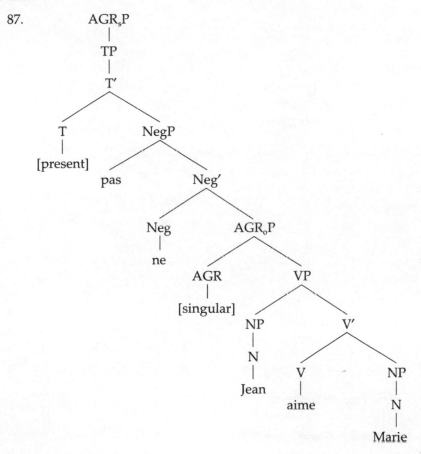

The subject *Jean* moves to the specifier of AGR$_s$P; the Verb *aime* moves first to the head position of AGR$_o$P, then to the head position of NegP picking up the *ne*, and to the head position of TP, picking up *present*; and finally it ends up before the negative element *pas* (but attached to the negative element *ne*):

88.

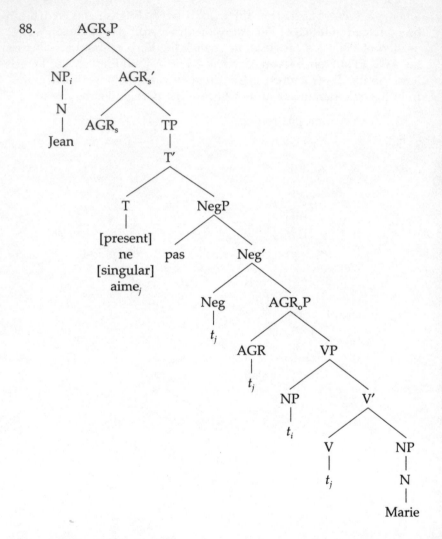

The English sentence:

89. John doesn't like Mary.

has to all intents and purposes the same D-structure as the French sentence. But the Verb *like* is prevented from moving across AGR_o and so stays in place after the negative element *not*. What prevents Verb-movement in English has to do with the 'strength' of AGR_o: a strong AGR_o allows a Verb to pass through it and still be able to assign a θ-role to its complement, a weak AGR_o does not permit this. In English AGR_o is weak which means that, if a lexical Verb were to move into it, the Verb would not be able to assign its θ-roles. In French AGR_o is transparent and does allow a lexical Verb moved into it to assign its θ-roles. This explains why English auxiliaries are allowed to move into AGR_o: it does not matter if AGR_o is strong or weak as they do not assign θ-roles. Pollock (1989) proposes that the reason why English *have* and *be* are able to move is that they too do not assign θ-roles.

The setting for the AGR_o parameter thus leads to several differences between the two languages in addition to negation:

— Main Verbs cannot come at the beginning of the sentence in English questions, with the exception of *have* and *be*, as we saw above:

90.   *Likes he Mary?

but they can in French:

91.   Aime-t-il Marie?
      (Likes he Mary)
      Does he like Mary?

— Adverbs cannot come after the Verb in English (as the Verb cannot move into the head position of AGRP because of the weakness of AGR_o):

92.   John *often* kisses Mary.

versus:

93.   Jean embrasse *souvent* Marie.
      (John kisses   often   Mary)
      John often kisses Mary.

where the Verb has moved in front of *souvent*.

— The quantifier *all* precedes the Verb in English while *tout* follows it in French:

94.   My friends *all* love Mary.

versus:

95.   Mes amis   aiment *tous* Marie.
       (My friends like   all   Mary)
       All my friends like Mary.

Thus a difference in parameter setting has widespread consequences for the grammar of a language.

Verb-movement differs from NP-movement and wh-movement in two ways; first it involves the movement of the head of the phrase (X) rather than of the maximal phrase (X''); secondly it goes to the head position of another phrase rather than to the specifier position: for these reasons it is known as **head-movement**. Movement has to take place in a series of steps rather than all at once – for example in:

96.   Jean n'aime pas Marie.
       John does not like Mary

aime moves from V to Neg to T to AGR_s rather than going all the way at once. The reason for this is the **Head Movement Constraint** (Chomsky, 1986b, p. 71), which claims that a zero-level category can only move to a position that governs its maximal projection, i.e. it may only move a short distance at a time.

There is still one snag with the analysis of Verb-movement so far as English is concerned: how do the tense and number features get attached to the Verb in the sentence if there is *no* auxiliary and no question or negation to introduce *do*? In other words, given the D-structure:

97.   Susan -s like tomatoes.

how does the -*s* get attached to the end of *like* to yield an S-structure with *likes*?

98.   Susan likes tomatoes.

The rather *ad hoc* standard analysis is that the features of Tense and Number lower onto the Verb to get attached to its right. Lightfoot and Hornstein (1994) regard Verb-lowering as the default setting for language acquisition; the child therefore needs evidence to reset the parameter for languages like French that move the Verb to AGR. However, in the Minimalist approach, Chomsky (1993) and Chomsky and Lasnik (1993) assume that English has Verb-movement at LF rather than in syntax, just as Japanese has wh-movement at LF; 'French-type and English-type languages now look alike at LF' (Chomsky, 1993, p. 28). This leads to the assumption that movement to the inflectional nodes is not really to 'pick up' the actual inflections, but that inflected verbs are inserted into the V position from the lexicon and movement to the inflectional nodes is to *check* that the verb has the right features. We will discuss these ideas more in chapter 9.

Verb-movement

Verb-movement involves moving the head V of the VP, first to head of AGR_oP, then to TP, then to head of AGR_sP

The AGR_oP parameter: in languages like English V cannot cross AGR_oP; in French it can
John doesn't like Mary   *John likes not Mary
*Jean aime ne Marie   Jean n'aime pas Marie

Do-support: in English a dummy auxiliary *do* is introduced to carry the features of T and AGR when no other auxiliary is available to do this: Do you like plums?

Head Movement Constraint: a zero-level category can only move to a position that governs its maximal projection, i.e. in a series of steps up the maximal projections in the tree

---

Word Order Variation

The concept of head-movement applied to Verbs allows us to approach some of the major word order differences between languages, namely how they differ in terms of the order of Subject (S), Verb (V) and Object (O). Some languages, like English, are SVO:

99.   The drummer hit the cymbal
          S   V   O

Others, such as Japanese, are SOV:

100.   Shikisha-ga boo-o furu
            S   O   V
        conductor baton waves
        (The conductor waves the baton)

Still others like Welsh, are VSO:

101. Lladdodd y ddraig   y   dyn
       V   S   O
      killed   the dragon the man
      (The dragon killed the man)

All the possible combinations of S, V and O occur in the world's languages, though with different frequencies; Tomlin (1986) established that 45 per cent of languages are SOV, 42 per cent SVO, 9 per cent VSO and 3 per cent VOS; less than 1 per cent are OVS and OSV – all by extreme coincidence occurring in the Amazon basin, though from unrelated language families.

At first sight the existence of languages where the subject intervenes between the Verb and the object, such as a VSO language, appears to cause problems for some of the structural claims made so far. In particular the Verb and the object have been claimed to form one constituent, V', and the subject to form another constituent, VP, with this constituent, as we see in the following SVO structure:

102.

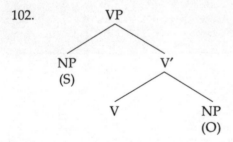

But, if this is so, the subject cannot come between the verb and the object without forming an unacceptable tree which has 'crossing branches'. The tree for a VSO language would be:

103.

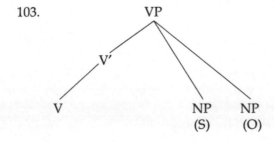

The way out of this dilemma is to assume that the Verb and object start off adjacent in such languages and that the Verb moves out of the VP over the subject, yielding a surface word order where the subject comes between the Verb and object. For example, a possible analysis of the Welsh sentence:

104. Lladdodd y ddraig y dyn.

is that the underlying word order inside the VP is SVO:

105.

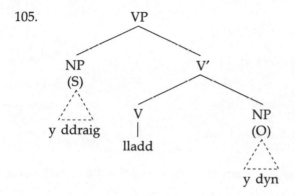

The Verb then moves out of the VP to the inflectional nodes, thus deriving the VSO word order:

106.

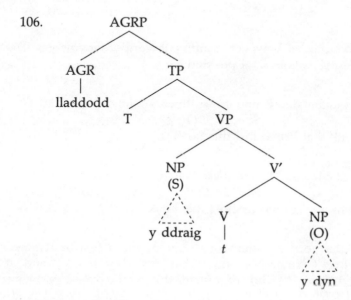

A second tricky problem can be solved through the notion of Verb-movement. This concerns languages such as German which have different word orders in main and subordinate clauses. In German main clauses, the finite Verb always sits in the second position following either a subject, an object or an adverb:

107.   Bruno verlor dieses Buch
      S   V   O
      Bruno lost this book

108.   Dieses Buch verlor Bruno
      O   V   S
      this book, Bruno lost

109.   Heute verlor Bruno dieses Buch
      Adv V   S   O
      today Bruno lost this book

When there is an auxiliary Verb, it is finite and the main Verb comes in the final position:

110.   Bruno hat dieses Buch verloren
      S   aux   O   V

In subordinate clauses, however, a different word order emerges. The finite verb always sits in final position:

111.   Ich glaube, daß Bruno dieses Buch verlor
                    S   O   V
      I think that Bruno lost this book

112.   Ich glaube, daß Bruno dieses Buch verloren hat
                    S   O   V   aux
      I think that Bruno has lost this book.

From the surface order of the words, one might at first be tempted to assume that German sometimes has a Verb-initial VP and at others a Verb-final VP. But, of course, this would cause problems with the all-or-none notion of parameters, which assumes that languages are *either* head-initial *or* head-final but not *both* on different occasions.

An analysis which overcomes this problem dates back to Bach (1962) and Bierwisch (1963), though it has been elaborated on in subsequent work, for example Thiersch (1978) and Haider (1986). This assumes that the finite Verb in German originates in the VP-final position and then moves to the complementizer position, if this position is free. Thus, in main clauses, where there is no complementizer, the finite Verb will move to the front of the clause. This, of course, does not account for why the Verb appears in the *second* position, but this is easily rectified by the assumption that some other element – subject, object or Adverb – must move to the specifier of CP. Thus, the underlying structure for the sentence:

113.   Bruno verlor dieses Buch.

would be:

114.

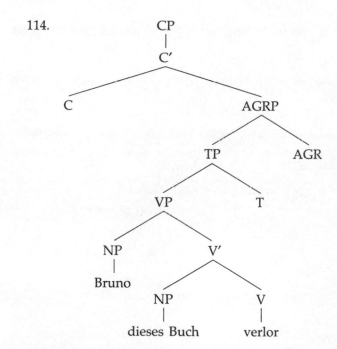

The Verb would then move to C, via T and AGR:

115.

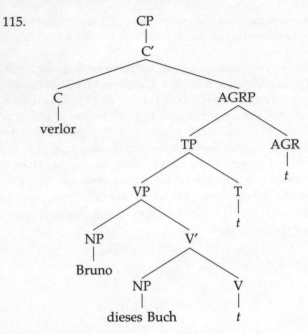

The subject then moves to the specifier of CP, to produce the observed surface order:

116.

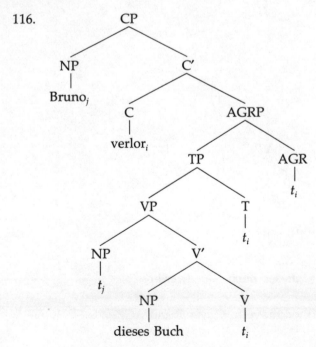

When there is an auxiliary Verb, this will be the element that moves.

However, when the complementizer position is filled, as is the case in subordinate clauses, the finite Verb will not be able to move to C and hence will stay in the inflectional nodes and in final position:

117.

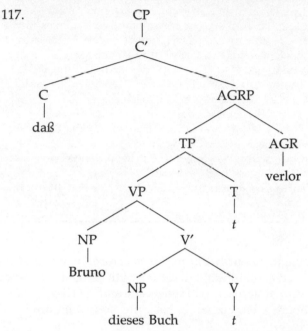

This phenomenon of the Verb moving to the second (complementizer) position is often referred to as **Verb-Second** or **V2** for short. Most Germanic languages are V2, though not all are underlyingly SOV like German. (English is exceptional in being a true SVO, not V2 with underlying SOV.) Some, such as Danish, are SVO (Vikner, 1995). The important point concerning V2 phenomena is that in main clauses the finite Verb is always in the complementizer position following some other element in the specifier of CP. Thus Verb-movement, this time to C, plays a large role in the analysis of the word order of such languages.

It must be pointed out at this stage that it is by no means clear that a combination of X-bar theory, in the form presented here, and the theory of movement can account for all the word order phenomena found in the world's languages. In particular, there are languages, such as Hungarian, in which the order of S, V and O is relatively free. Often these are referred to as **non-configurational** languages in contrast to **configurational** languages, such as English and German, where the word order is more rigid. It is a matter of current debate whether languages such as Hungarian are underlyingly configurational and so

---

Verb-Second (V2)

V2 languages move the finite Verb to the complementizer position when this position is free, i.e. in main clauses, but not in subordinate clauses. Some other element, such as subject, object or Adverb, moves to the initial CP specifier position hence placing the finite Verb in the second position. This phenomenon is most obvious in languages such as German which are underlying SOV. The Verb, moving out of the VP, may leave the object behind and if the subject is moved to the initial position we derive SVO surface word order in main clauses:

    underlying: Bruno diesen Buch verlor (Bruno this book lost)
    surface: Bruno verlor diesen Buch (subject-initial) (Bruno lost this book)

When C is filled, say with a complementizer in subordinate clauses, the Verb must stay in the inflectional nodes and hence appear finally:

    Ich glaube, daß Bruno diesen Buch verlor (I think that Bruno this book lost)

---

able to move elements about freely in the structure, or whether they are underlyingly non-configurational; see Horvath (1985) for an underlyingly configurational account of Hungarian and É. Kiss (1987) for counter-arguments that Hungarian is basically non-configurational.

Case Theory

Within principles and parameters theory, there always has to be a reason for movement. Passive movement, for example, is 'triggered' by passive morphology, as we saw earlier. But this looks like an *ad hoc* solution specific to passives, rather than the general principles the theory is always looking for. A better explanation is found in the module called **Case Theory**. Case Theory is related to the traditional syntactic ideas of case, which saw the relationship between elements in a sentence as being shown by their morphology as well as by word order. In the Arabic sentence:

118.   kataba zaydun al-maktu:ba
        (wrote Zayd   a letter)
        Zayd wrote a letter

the subject *zaydun* is in the Nominative case -*un* while the object *al-maktu:ba* is in the Accusative case -*a*. Latin is also a familiar example; the Noun *amor* (love) is the subject of the sentence in the Nominative case:

119. amor vincit omnia
      Love conquers all.

However, *amorem* is the object of a sentence in the Accusative case, while *amoris* is in a possessive relationship, shown by the Genitive case.

In languages such as German and Finnish, case figures prominently. Case in English is confined to the Genitive -*s* in NPs (*John's book*), and to the pronoun system, where there is a greater range: *they, them, their,* and so on. Thus in the sentence:

120. She rides a bicycle.

she can be said to be in the Nominative. In:

121. She disliked him.

him is in the Accusative. And in:

122. Her piano-playing was amazing.

her is in the Genitive. These examples show that case is still part of English, even if it manifests itself in the surface of the sentence in a comparatively small number of instances.

But Case Theory in principles and parameters theory goes beyond morphological endings of Nouns. It deals not just with the case forms visible in the surface structure but with 'abstract' Case, by convention given a capital letter to show its technical use. Abstract Case is an important element in the syntax even when it does not appear in the surface; the fact that *Helen* is not overtly Nominative or Accusative does not mean that it does not have abstract Case. 'In some languages, Case is morphologically realised, in others not, but we assume that it is assigned in a uniform way whether morphologically realised or not' (Chomsky, 1986a, p. 74). Case Theory is the module that assigns abstract Case to NPs and, by so doing, provides a principled explanation for various aspects of movement.

Let us start with the example:

123. She dislikes him.

In this sentence the subject *she* is in Nominative Case (contrasting with *her* and *hers*) and the object *him* is in Accusative Case (contrasting with *he* and *his*). In English it is the structural position in which the NP is located that determines its Case: subjects usually have Nominative Case and objects have Accusative Case. Case Theory assumes that Cases are similar to θ-roles in certain respects: θ-roles are assigned by certain θ-role assigners (predicates), to certain elements (arguments), under a certain structural restriction (sisterhood); Case is also assigned by elements to certain other elements under particular structural restrictions.

What are the Case assigners? Given that objects are always objects of something, an object with Accusative Case cannot exist without an element that takes an object – a Verb or a Preposition. So it is Verbs and Prepositions that assign Accusative Case. Nominative Case, however, is restricted to the subject positions of finite clauses. While the sentence:

124.   I think she hit him.

is grammatical, the sentence:

125.   *I tried she to hit him.

is not. One difference between finite and non-finite sentences is the appearance of the agreement element: Verbs in finite clauses are inflected for agreement and Verbs in non-finite clauses are not. The infinitival clause also apparently has a 'tense' element: i.e. *to*, as this element shows the lack of tense. In terms of features, the infinitival marker *to* can be classified as a [–tense] element and the finite tense element as [+tense]. But if non-finite clauses have no AGR element, only a tense, they should be analysed as T(ense)Ps, not as AGRPs. The difference between a finite and a non-finite clause is represented in the following trees:

126.   **Finite clause**

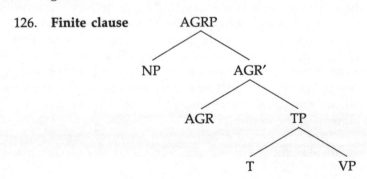

127. **Non-finite clause**

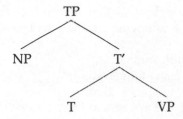

One major difference between these two structures is that the subject of the finite clause is in the specifier of AGRP, while the subject of the non-finite clause is in the specifier of the TP. Given these assumptions, the Nominative subject only appears along with an AGR head; therefore it is AGR that assigns Nominative Case. These ideas are represented in the following tree:

128.

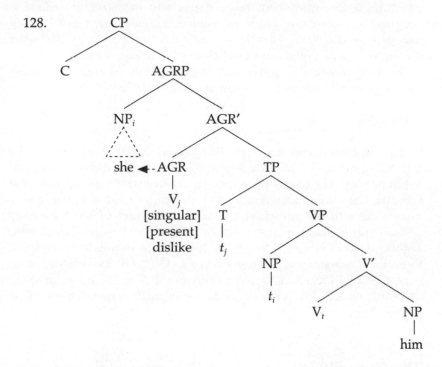

Case Theory distinguishes Cases that are assigned to NPs by virtue of the positions that they occupy at S-structure, known as **'structural'** **Case**, and those that are associated with particular arguments of predicates, known as **'inherent'** **Case**. Nominative and Accusative are obviously structural Cases as they are assigned to the structural positions 'specifier of AGR' and 'complement of V' respectively; it is the structural configuration that determines the Case. Inherent case can be seen in the following German sentence:

129. Sie hilft ihm.
      She helps him (Dative)

The object of *hilft* appears in Dative Case rather than Accusative and, unlike the structural Cases, the Dative is retained by an object in the passive construction:

130. Ihm wird geholfen.
      him is helped

For this reason, it is assumed that inherent Case is assigned at D-structure, before movement takes place, whereas structural Case is assigned at S-structure, after movement takes place; Case is then assigned by the Verb, i.e. the lexical entry for *helfen* specifies that it assigns Dative to the argument that it θ-marks internally.

The assignment of Genitive Case is a contentious area. In English the Genitive element occupies the specifier position of the NP:

131. Barry's book.

If the Genitive Case functions like other Cases, there should be something inside the NP to assign it to the specifier of NP. However, opinions vary. The theory presented in Chomsky (1981a) suggests that Genitive Case is not assigned by any particular Case assigner, but is associated with the particular position of specifier of NP. Chomsky (1986a) argues that Genitive Case is inherent and is associated with arguments of Nouns, and hence the head Noun should be considered to be the Case assigner. Under Abney's (1987) DP hypothesis, however, Genitive Case is assigned to the specifier of DP by an abstract determiner head. We will not try to distinguish between these alternatives here.

The Case Filter

Perhaps the most important aspect of Case Theory is not what Cases are assigned to which position but the principle that forces Case to be assigned. This is called the **Case Filter** (Chomsky, 1986a, p. 74):

Case Theory: Case Assignment

'Case Theory deals with assignment of abstract Case and its morphological realisation' (Chomsky, 1981a, p. 6)

Case is assigned to all NPs by Case assigners, either structurally or inherently:

— Nominative is assigned by AGR in S-structure to the GF subject:
He disappeared.
— Accusative is assigned by V in S-structure to the GF object:
I liked *him*.
— Accusative (Oblique) is assigned by P to the GF object of Preposition in D-structure:
She gave the book to *him*.
— Genitive is assigned by the structure $_{NP}$ [NP __] in D-structure:
Barry's book
— in languages with 'inherent' Case, Cases are assigned at D-structure by assigners such as the Verb

---

Every phonetically realised NP must be assigned (abstract) *Case*

The Case Filter can be approached through infinitival constructions. In the sentence:

132. I was sorry [to have to leave].

the complement of the Adjective *sorry* is an infinitival clause, headed by the tense element *to*. However, this clause has no overt subject (a construction to be discussed in the next chapter). If, however, an overt subject occurs in this clause, the result is ungrammatical:

133. *I was sorry [I/me/myself to have to leave].

Why is an overt subject not allowed here? Note that the answer cannot be that an overt subject is not allowed in the complement clause of a predicate like *sorry* for semantic reasons, as there can be an overt subject if the complement clause is finite:

134. I was sorry [I had to leave].

The answer is that, as pointed out earlier, infinitival clauses do not have an AGR element and hence are only TPs rather than AGRPs. As it is AGR that assigns Nominative Case to the subject, there is no element to assign Case to the infinitival subject. But why should this result in ungrammaticality, unless there is some reason why the subject must be assigned Case? This, then, is the consequence of the Case Filter: every NP must receive a Case otherwise the sentence that contains the non-Case-marked NP will be 'filtered out' as ungrammatical.

Before exploring the importance of the Case Filter, we should mention that not all overt subjects of infinitival clauses violate the Case Filter, as can be seen in:

135.   I believe him to be intelligent.

and in:

136.   We were anxious for him to leave.

If these sentences violated the Case Filter, they would be ungrammatical: the fact that they are grammatical shows that their infinitival subjects must somehow satisfy the Case Filter. As there is no AGR in these infinitival clauses and, as we have seen, T does not assign Case, the Case that is assigned to these subjects does not come from within the infinitival clause itself. It is usually assumed that the Case assigner in these cases is the governing Verb (e.g. *believe*) and the complementizer (*for*). Indeed when the subject of the infinitival clause is allowed to be overt, it appears, not in the Nominative, but in the Accusative Case. This supports the assumption that the Case comes from the Verb and complementizer as, assuming that the complementizer has prepositional features (it is a prepositional complementizer), it is Verbs and Prepositions that assign Accusative Case. (As an aside one might point out that this explains why *Me* is the answer to the question *Who's that?*, rather than *I*.) However, English is exceptional in allowing overt subjects of infinitival clauses and, as we have seen, not all English infinitival clauses can have overt subjects. For this reason, these constructions are usually called **Exceptional Case Marking** (ECM) constructions. We will discuss these in more detail in the next chapter. In chapter 9 we will see that recent treatment of this phenomenon deals with it in a less exceptional way.

To come back to the Case Filter, this has a large part to play in the motivation of NP-movement. In the passive we saw that the passive morphology 'triggers' the movement of the object to subject position. So the following D-structure:

137.   *e* will be dismissed the miners

is transformed into the S-structure:

138.   the miners will be dismissed *t*

by the movement of the object to subject position. This is obviously not satisfactory as it does not say what the nature of the triggering process is. We also said that the passive morphology 'absorbs' the external θ-role by in effect taking this θ-role for itself. Suppose the same is true for the Case that the Verb has to assign to its object: the Accusative Case now gets given to the passive morpheme and not to the object. If this is so, then the object will be sitting in a Caseless position and hence will be in violation of the Case Filter. Now, given that structural Cases are assigned at S-structure, there is a way to salvage the passive construction: if the object moves to a position where it can get Case at S-structure, then the Case Filter will be satisfied. Obviously, the subject position *is* a position to which Case is assigned and hence this gives a more principled account of why objects move to subject position in passive constructions: in effect, the Case Filter forces NP-movement from a Caseless position to a Case-marked position.

Moreover, this account of the passive escapes from the construction-specific mechanism of claiming that the passive morphology or some other element triggers the movement of the object, as the Case Filter is a more general principle that is needed for other reasons as well. In fact, the Case Filter plays a role not only in the passive construction, but also in all other constructions that involve NP-movement. For example, in 'raising' constructions with verbs like *seem*, the subject of a complement clause is moved to the subject position of the raising verb. So, the D-structure:

139.   *e* seems John to be intelligent

is transformed into the S-structure:

140.   John seems *t* to be intelligent

The moved NP is the subject of an infinitival clause at D-structure: obviously a non-Case-marked position. The Case Filter will therefore rule out this structure should the NP stay in this position. Thus the subject will be forced to move into the subject position of the finite clause, where it will be assigned Nominative Case by AGR. Again, then, the Case Filter plays an important part in motivating the movement of NPs. Finally, the Case Filter also explains why the subject, which starts off as the specifier of VP, moves to the specifier of AGRP. So far, nothing has been said about why the subject has to move from its original position inside the VP: why, for instance, the correct word order for English declarative clauses is not:

141.   Will John kiss Mary.

rather than:

142.   John will *t* kiss Mary.

The fact that the specifier position of the VP is a non-Case-marked position means that the subject moves out of the VP in order to get Case and to comply with the Case Filter. This will indeed be the root cause of all other instances of NP-movement.

The Case Filter is a general principle that has consequences for many aspects of language. Yet it is still a filter on what is and is not allowed and as such it retains a degree of arbitrary stipulation rather than of explanation. Ideally, all such stipulative fiats would be reduced to even more basic processes. A way of effecting this for the Case Filter suggested in Chomsky (1986a) is through the notion of **visibility**. The arguments of θ-theory need to be marked out to make them 'visible' so that they can be θ-marked. Assigning Case to an NP argument precisely makes them visible. Under these assumptions, the Case Filter now falls within the Principle of Full Interpretation, which states that all elements must be appropriately interpreted: if an NP is not Case-marked, it will be invisible to θ-theory and hence will not get a θ-role and be in violation of Full Interpretation.

Case Theory: the Case Filter

Case Filter: 'Every phonetically realised NP must be assigned (abstract) Case' (Chomsky, 1986a, p. 74)

Gloss: this therefore eliminates as possible surface structures any sentence with an NP that has not received abstract Case, thus motivating NP-movement such as the passive to avoid NPs occurring in Caseless positions

Visibility: assigning Case to an NP makes it 'visible' so it can be θ-marked, making the Case Filter fall within the Principle of Full Interpretation

Parameters of Case Theory

This final section considers the parameters of Case Theory. The most obvious differences between languages with regard to case phenomena are which cases a language makes use of and which elements they go with. So, while English distinguishes three cases (Nominative, Accusative and Genitive) on its pronouns, German distinguishes four cases (Nominative, Accusative, Genitive and Dative) on its determiners, adjectives and nouns, and Chinese distinguishes no cases on any of its elements. However, these differences are obviously a matter of morphological case rather than abstract Case. As far as the latter is concerned, all languages are very similar. In fact, the only differences may be lexical: some verbs in languages such as German may assign inherent Cases to their objects while others, such as English, have no verbs which assign inherent Case.

Another difference is between languages that allow exceptional Case marking structures and those that do not. The former will obviously allow infinitival clauses with overt subject such as:

143.   I want Mary to sing.

In the latter, these types of sentence will be impossible. However, again, it may be that this is not caused by a parameter of the Case Theory, but is due to lexical differences in the relevant languages. Without anticipating the analysis of ECM structures in the next chapter, it is difficult to say what these differences are. For now we can say that it boils down to differences in the types of complements that certain verbs take.

Case Theory then presents very few parametric differences between languages, mostly arising from lexical differences. There are a few phenomena, however, that may be seen as parameters of the Case Theory. Some languages, such as English, demand that the Case assigner be 'adjacent' to the NP that it assigns Case to. For example, an NP complement cannot be split from its Case-assigning head:

144.   *I liked very much him.

though it is possible to split other kinds of complements from Verbs:

145.   I banged very loudly on the door.

The principle that Case assigners must be next to their Case assignees is known as the **Case Adjacency Principle** and was introduced by Stowell (1981). However, some languages *do* allow the object to be separated from the Verb, as in this French example:

146.   J'aime beaucoup   la   France.
       I love very much (the) France

which shows that the Case Adjacency Principle is not operative in all languages and hence can be seen as a parameterized part of Case Theory.

Another variation between languages is the direction in which Case is assigned within the sentence. Head-initial languages like English obviously assign Cases *from* Verbs *to* objects in a rightward direction (i.e. V $\rightarrow$ O) and head-final languages, like Japanese, assign Case to the left (i.e. O $\leftarrow$ V). 'It is plausible to assume that the direction of Case-marking for lexical categories is uniform and, in the unmarked case, corresponds to the head parameter of X-bar theory' (Chomsky, 1986a, p. 193). As implied in this quote, however, it is possible to have a 'marked' situation in which the direction of Case-marking is opposite to the position fixed by the X-bar parameters. Koopman (1984), for instance, analyses Chinese as essentially a head-final language (i.e. OV), but NP complements of Verbs sit to the right of the Verb (VO):

147.   Zhangsan zuotian   zai xuexiao kanjian-le Lisi
       S   ADV   PP   V   O
       Zhangsan yesterday at school   see -ASP Lisi
       Zhangsan saw Lisi at school yesterday.

Koopman claims that this is because Case is assigned rightwards in Chinese and hence the object (*Lisi*) has to move from a position in front of the Verb (*kanjian-le*) to one following it, giving a surface SVO order different from the underlying SOV. So there is a parameter of Case Theory which determines the direction of Case assignment.

This chapter has spelled out the relationship between the level of the sentence at which the semantic θ-roles of the lexical phrases are expressed and the level at which they get a representation which can be interpreted by the PF and LF components. At the moment this is put in terms of two levels of the T-model, namely D-structure and S-structure, linked by movement ('Move α') or chains ('Form-chain'). Chomsky's current 'minimalist' work departs from the notion of two

Case Theory: parametric variation

(1) **Adjacency**: some languages such as English require Case assigners to be adjacent to the NP that receives Case
I liked him very much *versus* *I liked very much him
Others, such as French, have no such requirement
J'aime beaucoup la France (I like very much France)

(2) **Direction**: some languages such as English require Case assigners to be to the left of their NPs; others such as Chinese require them to be to the right
Zhangsan zuotian   zai xuexiao kanjian-le Lisi
   S   ADV   PP   V   O

Zhangsan yesterday at school   see-ASP Lisi
Zhangsan saw Lisi at school yesterday

(3) **Exceptional Case Marking**: the lexical subject of infinitival clauses in English exceptionally has Accusative Case, for example:
I want them to go.
(extended in chapter 7)

definite levels of D-structure and S-structure without abandoning the idea of a chain relationship (Chomsky, 1993; 1995b).

The logic of the chapter was to start from the broadest possibility for human language and then see how this could be narrowed down. The widest definition of movement is 'Move α' – move anything at all – which was seen to be limited in several ways. However, Lasnik and Saito (1984) have argued that even this starting point is too specific. 'Move α' implies that the only relationship between D- and S-structure is movement. Some syntactic analysis may require deletion of items from the sentence; this cannot be accommodated within 'Move α'. It may be better to use a formulation that does not prejudge the issue, say, ' "Affect-α" (do anything to anything: delete, insert, move)' (Chomsky, 1986a, p. 74). As always, the theory is searching for the greatest generalization compatible with the facts of language, as we shall see in chapter 9.

7

Government and Other Developments

This chapter will discuss the following topics:

— C-command and government
— Government and Case Theory
— Control structures
— Binding Theory
— Binding Theory and empty categories
— The boundedness of movement and proper government
— Relativized Minimality.

This chapter provides a more formal account of several aspects of principles and parameters theory that have already been mentioned informally: Case assignment, empty categories, binding and constraints on movement, all of which make use of the central notion of government. The chapter starts by providing a more formal definition of government and then goes on to give an account of the role that government plays in these areas; it then develops the central contemporary notion of Relativized Minimality. Since it is thus getting close to areas in which research is currently taking place, the presentation inevitably only sketches some of these developments rather than treating them in full depth.

C-command and Government

The source of the word 'government' can be found in the familiar terms of traditional grammar. A typical statement might be that made by William Cobbett in 1819: 'Nouns are governed, as it is called, by verbs and prepositions; that is to say, these latter sorts of words cause nouns to be in such or such a case; and there must be a concord or agreement between the nouns and the other words, which along with nouns, compose a sentence' (Cobbett, 1819, p. 67). The major differences between this and current theoretical approaches is that nowadays government is defined in terms of structural configuration and is a general relationship rather than one affecting only Nouns. This section presents the configurational definition of government, later sections developing its uses.

So far this book has relied on a small number of simple configurational relationships that hold between elements in a structure, namely dominance (what comes below a particular item on the tree) and sisterhood (what comes alongside it). There are a number of structural relationships, however, that require a slightly more complex configuration. One of the most basic of these, and the one on which government is based, is **c-command** (= constituent command). This relationship has roots that go as far back as Langacker (1966) who used a notion of command in his analysis of pronominalization. Ten years later Reinhart (1976), who was also mainly interested in pronominalization and anaphora, developed the idea into a form which has had a lasting impact.

To see what this relationship entails, let us consider some of the pronominalization facts it was originally intended to account for. In the sentence:

1. Ben's father didn't trust him.

the pronoun *him* is ambiguous in that it can refer either to *Ben* or to someone else not mentioned in the sentence, as we saw in chapter 2. However, it is clear that *him* cannot refer to *Ben's father*. C-command provides the relevant structural relationship to explain these facts. Personal pronouns, called **pronominals** within Binding Theory, cannot be c-commanded by an antecedent which is within the same clause as themselves. In the above sentence *him* is not c-commanded by *Ben* but is by *Ben's father*, so only the former can be a possible antecedent for the pronominal. To see how the relevant structural relation can be defined, consider the tree diagram of this sentence (with some unnecessary detail pruned out):

2.

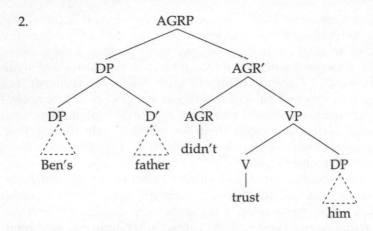

The relationships to focus on are those between the three DPs in the tree, in particular the difference between the relation that holds between the subject DP *Ben's father* and the object DP *him*, and the relation between the genitive DP *Ben's* and the object *him*. It is easy to see that, in the first case, the phrase immediately containing the subject *Ben's father* (i.e. the whole AGRP *Ben's father didn't trust him*) also contains the object *him*. However, in the second case, the phrase immediately containing the genitive DP *Ben's* (i.e. the subject DP *Ben's father*) does not contain the object *him*. C-command is then the configuration where both elements are contained in the phrase immediately dominating one of them.

The more formal definition presented by Chomsky is as follows:

C-Command
α c-commands β iff α does not dominate β and every γ that dominates α dominates β. (Chomsky, 1986b, p. 8)

While this may look difficult, the general idea is simple enough (with 'iff' meaning 'if and only if'). Firstly, consider the role of γ in this definition. This variable defines the domain that c-command operates within: if γ is an XP, the c-command domain for an element α will be the first XP which contains it, i.e. is above it. The element α will c-command any other element contained in its domain that it itself does not contain: 'α c-commands every element of its domain that is not contained within α' (Chomsky, 1986a, p. 162). For example, in a tree like:

3.

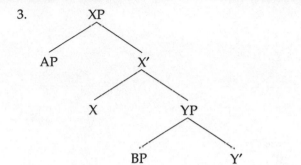

The element X c-commands AP, YP and everything inside YP, because all of these are contained inside XP, the first maximal projection dominating X, as we see in:

4.

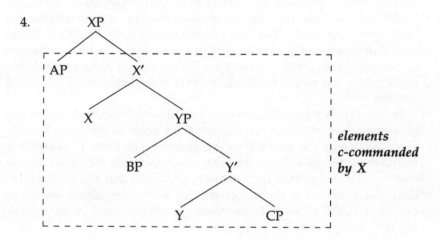

Y, on the other hand, c-commands only BP and CP, not AP and X, as these are not contained in YP, the c-command domain for Y.

5.

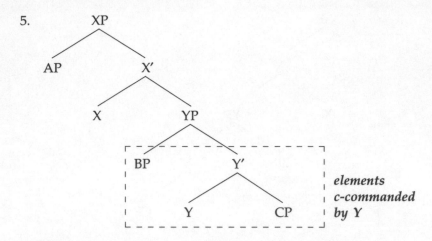

The reason why the domain is stated in terms of a variable γ and not, for example, XP, is that there are a number of different ways of defining c-command that have been proposed. It may even be that different versions are needed for different tasks. Reinhart (1976), for example, has the c-command domain determined by the 'first branching node'. For our purposes, the best definition (introduced in Aoun and Sportiche (1983)) uses XP to define the domain. Chomsky (1986a) has 're-christened' this notion **m-command**, because of the use of the maximal projection to define the c-command domain.

In tree (2) on page 236 above, repeated with modifications in tree (6) below, the domain of the subject *Ben's father* is everything inside the AGRP, and the domain of the genitive DP *Ben's* is everything inside the subject DP. Thus the subject c-commands the object *him*, as this is contained within its domain (i.e. AGRP), but the genitive DP does not c-command the object, as this is not contained within its domain (i.e. the subject). These relations are indicated in the following tree (omitting many irrelevant details):

6.

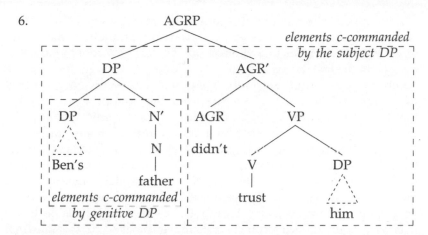

Briefly returning to pronominalization, we should remark that the subject is clearly not a valid antecedent for the object because the subject c-commands the object and both are within the same clause. The genitive DP, on the other hand, despite being in the same clause as the object, does not c-command it and therefore is available as a possible antecedent.

C-command

'α c-commands β iff α does not dominate β and every γ [XP] that dominates α dominates β' (Chomsky, 1986b, p. 8)

Gloss: c-command is a structural configuration used in various parts of principles and parameters theory to express a relationship between elements with one element being 'superior to' but not dominating other elements which are c-commanded by it. When it is defined in terms of maximal projections, it may be termed 'm-command'.

Example: Ben doesn't trust him
The domain of the subject *Ben* is the whole clause and hence it c-commands the object *him*. For this reason, the pronominal *him* cannot take the subject of its own clause as its antecedent as it cannot be c-commanded by an antecedent within the same clause, according to the Binding Theory.

Government is a version of c-command, with two types of restrictions. Firstly, while any element can c-command another, the ability to govern is restricted to a limited number of 'governors', basically, the set of lexical heads (i.e. N, V, A and P), though there are a number of exceptions. Secondly, government is restricted compared to c-command in that it is limited from the bottom as well as the top. From our discussion of c-command, it can be seen that any element is capable of c-commanding only those elements inside the maximal projection that contains that element: an element cannot c-command anything which lies above this maximal projection and so the relation is limited from the top. Government sets a limit at the bottom as well. So, for example, while a head is capable of governing its complements, it cannot govern very far inside them: it is as though the government relation is blocked at the maximal projection of the complement and can go no further. Government has both a floor and a ceiling through which the relationship cannot penetrate.

As a starting point, the formal definition of government can be given in the following way:

Government
α governs β if and only if
  (1) α is a governor (e.g. N, V, P, A, etc.)
  (2) α and β mutually c-command each other

Clause (1) of the definition states that only certain elements are eligible to govern – the familiar small group. Clause (2) is what sets the upper and lower limits of government. C-command is a relationship between an element and other elements at the same structural level or below but not elements higher in a tree. Saying that the governor and the governee must c-command each other is another way of stating that they must both be at the same structural level: neither higher than the other. For example, in the sentence:

7.   John supposed [that Bill would be late].

the Verb *suppose* c-commands its CP complement [*that Bill would be late*] and everything inside it. But it is only the CP node itself that c-commands the Verb: the Verb is too high for any element inside the CP to c-command it, as can be seen with the aid of the tree for this sentence, again with many details omitted:

8.

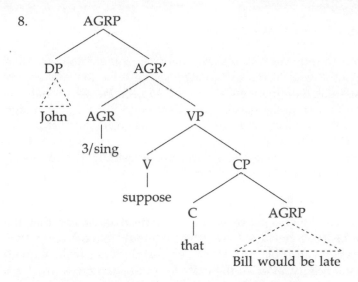

Out of the CP and all it contains, only the CP node has the VP as its c-command domain: the c-command domain of the complementizer *that* is the CP, not the VP, and anything inside AGRP has at most AGRP as its c-command domain.

The following sections build on this definition of government to demonstrate the need for this relationship.

Government

α governs β if and only if
  (1) α is a governor (e.g. N, V, P, A, etc.)
  (2) α and β mutually c-command each other

Gloss: government is a more restricted version of c-command in that only certain elements are allowed to govern (lexical heads) and these can only govern as far as their complements, but no further.

Example: The magician threw the knives at his assistant
The Verb *threw*, the Preposition *at* and the Nouns *magician*, *knives* and *assistant* are lexical heads and hence potential governors. However, as there is no complement of any of the Nouns, these do not govern anything. The Verb governs its object *the knives* and the Preposition governs its object *his assistant*.

Government and Case Theory

The previous chapter discussed Case Theory in some detail, claiming that Prepositions and Verbs assign Accusative Case to their objects and AGR assigns Nominative Case to the subject. However, half the picture is still missing: the reasons *why* Verbs and Prepositions assign Case only to their objects and not, say, to the subject, and *why* AGR assigns Case only to its own subject and not, say, to the subject of another clause or to an object of a Verb or Preposition. The following sentence shows the issue more clearly:

9.   *him AGR hit he

The reason why this sentence is ungrammatical is clearly that the subject *him* bears Accusative Case when it should have Nominative, and vice versa for the object *he*. However, this does not really explain the ungrammaticality; after all there are two Case assignors (the Verb and AGR) and two DPs which need Case. What we have to say is that AGR *always* assigns its Case to its subject and *never* to an object, and Verbs *always* assign Case to their objects and *never* to the subject of their own clause. But the question is, why should this be so?

Chomsky's answer is that Case is assigned under the restrictions of government (Chomsky, 1981a), the **Case Assignment Principle**. Thus, an element can only assign Case to a DP that it governs. To see what the government possibilities are for certain elements, consider the following tree, as usual omitting irrelevant detail:

10.

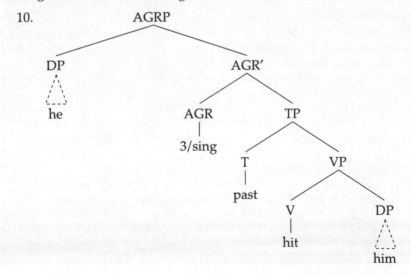

AGR governs the subject and the TP. However, as the TP does not need Case, the only element that AGR will ever assign Case to is the subject and hence only the subject will receive Nominative Case. The Verb, on the other hand, governs only its complement as nothing else lies within its c-command domain (the VP). Thus, the Verb can assign Accusative Case only to its object.

Inevitably there are several slight complications to this picture. One is raised by the assumption that subjects start off inside the VP and so are originally governed by the Verb. Presumably, they move to the specifier of AGR in order to be assigned Nominative Case: but why do they not get Case-marked by the Verb in their original position? One possible solution is the rightwards direction of Case assignment in English, as discussed in the last chapter: the Accusative Case can only be assigned to the right of the Verb; however, the specifier position is to the left. Of course, Nominative Case is assigned leftwards in English so the actual solution to this problem is a little more complicated. Stowell (1981) suggests that government is unidirectional for any element, such that if an element governs something to its right it cannot govern another to its left, and vice versa. In chapter 9, we present another theory that avoids this problem altogether by claiming that Case is not assigned under government, but that Case features are 'checked' in the specifier–head relationship.

A second complication comes from the observation that AGR is a Case assigner and therefore also a governor. The list of governors has therefore to be extended to include AGR.

A third complication is raised by clauses which have Accusative subjects: Exceptional Case Marking (ECM) structures, so called precisely because it is normal to assign Nominative Case to the subject. We find ECM clauses either as the complement of certain verbs, such as *believe*, as in the following:

11.   No one believed [him to be very talented]

or as the complement of certain adjectives, such as *anxious*:

12.   They were anxious [for her to believe their story]

or in subject position:

13.   [for me to win a prize] would be unlikely

Notice that in the last two examples the ECM clauses were introduced by a complementizer, and in fact they would be ungrammatical without it:

14. *they were anxious [her to believe their story]
15. *[me to win a prize] would be unlikely

This indicates, at least in these examples, that this complementizer plays an important role in the formation of these structures. The nature of this role is indicated by the fact that ECM clauses are always non-finite and, as we have seen, it is the finite inflection that assigns Nominative Case to the subject. The non-finite inflection is not a governor and hence is not able to assign any Case at all to its subject. Given the obligatory status of the complementizer in these examples, it is reasonable to assume that it is this element that assigns the Accusative Case to the subject. However, this assumption is problematic as the Accusative subject is not the complement of the complementizer, but is in the specifier of its complement.

On the assumptions we have made so far, the complementizer should not govern and therefore Case-mark the subject. To handle this, we will have to make an extension to the notion of government. Suppose we assume that if an element governs a category, then it also governs the specifier of that category. This will allow the complementizer to govern the subject of its complement clause.

It is important to convince ourselves before we proceed that this extension to the notion of government does not raise problems for the more straightforward cases we have already considered. For example, under normal circumstances, we would not want to allow the Verb to be able to assign Accusative Case to the subject of its complement clause, otherwise sentences such as:

16. *The doctor thinks [me is ill].

might be grammatical. Indeed this is impossible even with the extension to government we have now proposed. The reason for this is that the Verb takes a CP complement and the subject sits in the specifier of an AGRP inside the CP. So while the Verb governs the CP and its specifier, it still does not govern the subject and therefore it cannot Case-mark the subject. But this now brings us back to the first example we considered:

17. No one believed [him to be very talented].

Why is the subject of this clause allowed to appear in these? ECM constructions are limited to the complements of certain Verbs and thus the relevant features of these clauses that allows them to have overt subjects looks to have something to do with the selectional properties of these Verbs. The second observation is that these clauses seem incapable of having complementizers:

18.   *No one believed [for him to be very talented].

which is odd because we have supposed all clauses are CPs and hence they all should be able to have overt complementizers. Furthermore, in other ECM constructions, the complementizer is obligatory, as we showed above. The solution to all these puzzles is to assume that these clauses are not CPs at all, but are simply TPs. This obviously accounts for why a complementizer cannot appear: if there is no CP, there is no complementizer position. It also accounts for why we can have an Accusative subject. If there is no CP, the subject is in the specifier position of a TP complement of the Verb and hence, under the extension to government we introduced above, the subject is governed by the Verb. All we need to say is that certain Verbs, such as *believe*, can select for a TP complement, the rest falls out from general principles.

To summarize briefly, the assumption that Case is assigned under government accounts for the fact that Nominative Case is assigned to the subject of a finite clause and nowhere else, as the subject is the only DP position that AGR governs. That Accusative Case is assigned mainly to objects of Verbs and Prepositions is also accounted for as these tend to govern only their objects. In the case of ECM structures, where there is no CP to prevent government of the subject from outside the clause, the Verb will indeed be able to assign Accusative Case to the subject.

Control Structures

A second major role that government plays in the theory is to determine the distribution of certain empty elements. This section concentrates on just one of these elements, usually called **PRO**, sometimes called 'big pro' to contrast with *pro* (alias 'little pro'). PRO is restricted to the subject position in non-finite clauses.

In sentences such as:

19.   I wanted Sally to go.

> **Government and Case Theory**
>
> *The Case Assignment Principle*: Case is assigned under government
> This principle enables us to explain why certain Cases are assigned
> to certain positions in a structure. In particular, Nominative Case will
> only be assigned to the subject position of a finite clause because this
> is the only position that AGR, the assigner of this Case, governs.
> Similarly, Accusative Case will mainly be assigned to the objects of
> Verbs and Prepositions as this is the only position governed by these
> elements. Exceptionally, however, a subject of a non-finite clause
> will receive Accusative Case from either the complementizer *for* or
> from a Verb which is able to select a TP complement instead of a
> CP:
>   No one believed [him to be very talented]

it is obvious that the complement of the Verb *want* is a clause. In
particular it is an infinitival clause headed by the T element *to* with the
structure:

20.

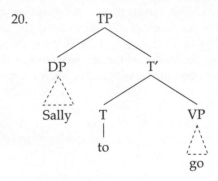

The assumption is that the absence of the whole AGR system leads to
infinitival clauses lacking an agreement element and also that, as *to* is
not a governor, the subject of this clause receives its Case from outside
the TP.

In sentences such as:

21.   I wanted to go.

by the same arguments, the complement of the Verb *want* must also be an infinitival clause: it is headed by the infinitival T and hence, by the principles of X-bar, there must be a TP. However, this clause seems to lack a subject and so its structure seems to be:

22.

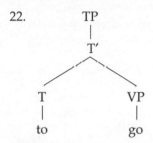

Yet there are reasons to believe that there really is a subject to this clause, but that it is 'invisible'. Put more technically, there is an element in the subject position of this infinitival clause which has both syntactic and semantic properties, but which lacks a phonological form and hence is not visible in the phonetic representation of the sentence. It is precisely the fact that this element has syntactic and semantic properties that speak for its existence: how could it have these properties if it did not exist? For example, in:

23. I want to leave.

it is obvious that someone will be doing the leaving, i.e. *me*. But if there were no subject of the Verb *leave*, why doesn't the sentence mean 'I want someone else to leave'? Why can the sentence only be interpreted as referring to the speaker? Note that, while current versions of θ-theory do indeed allow an argument to be assigned two θ-roles from different predicates (unlike previous versions which adopted the θ-Criterion), the subject of the matrix clause is not in a position where it can be thematically related to the Verb *leave* as it sits in an entirely different clause. Moreover, this cannot be treated as a case of raising where the main clause subject originates in the lower clause since the main clause subject position is not semantically empty and hence not available to be moved into.

The conclusion is that there must be an independent subject of the infinitival clause which behaves like a pronoun in that it takes its reference from, and hence is co-indexed with, the subject of the higher clause. This subject is another empty category, PRO:

24.

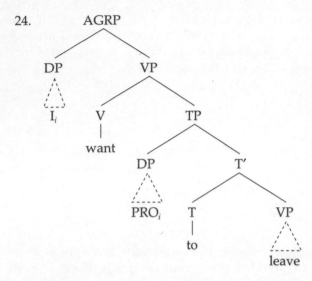

The referential properties of PRO will be considered in a later section of this chapter. For now we are interested in the factors which determine its extremely restricted distribution: PRO can only appear in the subject position of non-finite clauses; it is banned from all object positions and from the subject position of finite clauses. For example, the following sentences are all ungrammatical:

25.   *I_i think that PRO_i will go
26.   *I_i like PRO_i
27.   *I_i sent it to PRO_i

Government plays a large part in determining the conditions for the distribution of PRO in that PRO is unable to appear in governed positions. The subject position of a tensed clause is governed by AGR and the object positions of VP and PP are governed by the heads of those phrases. It is only the subject of the non-finite clause that is ungoverned. Thus the following principle holds of PRO (Chomsky, 1986a, p. 183):

PRO is ungoverned

Now, if this is true, we would predict that PRO should also be banned from infinitival subject position where that position is governed from outside the clause, i.e. in ECM constructions. The fact that this prediction is confirmed goes a long way to add support for the assumptions made here:

28. *I$_i$ believe PRO$_i$ to be intelligent

Overall, then, the notion of government helps to account for the restricted distribution of this empty subject; these observations add independent motivation for the assumptions that are made about government.

It is worth briefly mentioning that the verb *want* is rather odd with respect to control facts. As we have seen, it can appear with an overt subject in its infinitival complement:

29. I want Sally to leave.

suggesting that this is an ECM construction. However, *want* can also take an infinitival complement with a PRO subject:

30. I want PRO to leave

suggesting that this is not an ECM construction. The standard account of these facts dating back to Chomsky (1981a, p. 69) is to assume that the infinitival complement of *want* is a CP, but that there is a phonologically empty prepositional complementizer which assigns Case to the subject:

31. I want [$_{CP}$ e$_p$ [$_{AGRP}$ Sally to leave]]

Obviously, this complementizer must be optional, as it cannot be present when the subject is PRO:

32. I want [$_{CP}$ [$_{AGRP}$ PRO to leave]]

If the complementizer were present here, it would govern PRO and the sentence would be ungrammatical.

Control

Control structures are those in which the 'empty' subject PRO appears, for example *I wanted to go* is seen as having the structure *I wanted PRO to go*. The distribution of this element is restricted by the principle:
  PRO is ungoverned
For this reason PRO can only appear in the subject of a non-finite clause as there is no governor for this position.

Binding Theory

A third use of the notion of government is in Binding Theory, which, as we have seen in chapter 2, is concerned with the referential properties of elements such as pronouns. The beginning of this chapter introduced the notion that pronominals must not have a c-commanding antecedent within the same clause. Hence, the following sentence is ungrammatical, co-reference being indicated as usual by co-indexation:

33.   *Bill$_i$ likes him$_i$

However, exactly the opposite applies to reflexive pronouns, which *must* have a c-commanding antecedent within the same clause:

34.   Bill$_i$ likes himself$_i$
35.   *Bill$_i$ likes himself$_j$

It also appears that referring expressions such as names can never have c-commanding antecedents anywhere in the sentence:

36.   *He$_i$ thinks Bill likes John$_i$

These observations are accounted for by the three basic principles of the Binding Theory (Chomsky, 1986a, p. 166):

A   an anaphor is bound in a local domain
B   a pronominal is free in a local domain
C   an r-expression is free

Let us build on the discussion in chapter 2. The reflexive pronouns such as *herself* and *themselves* are **anaphors** and as such are governed by principle A. The term **bound** used in this principle simply refers to the conjunction of c-command and co-indexing. Thus binding can be defined as:

α binds β if and only if
  (1) α c-commands β and
  (2) α and β are co-indexed

In principle B, which refers to pronominals such as *them*, the term **free** simply means not bound. In principle C, the term r-expression refers to elements such as names and other 'referential' Noun phrases.

Up to this point, the 'local domain' referred to in principles A and B of the Binding Theory has been equated with the smallest clause containing the relevant pronoun. However, there are instances where an anaphor can take its antecedent from outside the clause that contains it and where pronominals are prevented from having a c-commanding antecedent in the next highest clause. Consider the following sentences:

37.   John$_i$ believed himself$_i$ to be the winner
38.   *John$_i$ considers him$_i$ to be the best candidate

These cases make apparent the importance of government in Binding Theory. In both of the above sentences the pronoun sits in the subject position of an infinitival clause. As these are overt subjects, they must be Case-marked and hence governed from outside this clause. If the local domain for a pronoun is the smallest clause containing the governor of the pronoun, and therefore the pronoun itself as well, the reason why the non-finite clause does not act as the local domain for these pronouns is that this clause does not contain the pronoun's governor.

Because of the importance of the governor in the definition of the local domain, this is termed the governing category: 'we take the local domain for an anaphor or pronominal α . . . to be the minimal governing category of α, where a governing category is a maximal projection containing both a subject [hence, it is a clause] and a lexical category governing α (hence, containing α)' (Chomsky, 1986a, p. 169). Though there is more to Binding Theory than presented here, we will not go into these issues here as further complications arise that do not directly concern government.

Binding Theory and Empty Categories

At this point, let us stop to consider why government is important in so many parts of the grammar. One possible answer might be that some of the apparently different phenomena reviewed so far are only different on the surface and in fact may be derived from the same underlying principles which are based on the notion of government.

But what have the phenomena that we have looked at got in common with each other? It turns out that the principles governing the distribution of PRO can be reduced to those of the Binding Theory

---

Binding Theory

α binds β if and only if
  (1) α c-commands β and
  (2) α and β are co-indexed

The Binding Principles:
  A an anaphor is bound in a local domain
  B a pronominal is free in a local domain
  C an r-expression is free (Chomsky, 1986a, p. 166)

Gloss: Binding is a structural relationship which governs the co-reference properties of elements in a sentence. Different elements behave differently with respect to binding and these are dealt with by the Binding Principles. Anaphors are elements such as reflexive pronouns, pronominals are personal pronouns and r-expressions are referential Noun phrases. There is a locality restriction on the binding relationships concerning anaphors and pronominals and the relevant local domain is defined by the inclusion of the governor of pronoun. The local domain of the pronoun is known as its governing category.

Examples: John$_i$ likes himself$_i$
Here the reflexive is an anaphor and hence must be bound in its governing category. It is c-commanded by and co-indexed with the subject and hence it is bound by this element. Its governor is AGR and therefore its governing category is the matrix clause, this being the clause containing the governor. Thus the sentence is grammatical.
    *John$_i$ believes him$_i$ to be intelligent
The personal pronoun is a pronominal which must therefore be free in its governing category. It is bound by the subject of the matrix clause. However, as the pronoun is the subject of an exceptional clause, its governor is the matrix Verb and hence its governing category is the matrix clause. As the pronoun is bound in its governing category, the sentence is ungrammatical.

---

and that this reduction shows why government plays a role in determining the distribution of PRO. To motivate these ideas let us first examine the behaviour of other empty categories.

Some of the earliest work on the behaviour of anaphors noted that there seems to be a connection between the restrictions placed on anaphor behaviour and those placed on certain types of movement. In particular, two positions within the same clause can be related not only through movement, with a DP moving from one position to the other, but also by reference of an anaphor:

39. John$_i$ was admired t_i
40. John$_i$ admired himself$_i$

However, two positions cannot be related by these processes over a clause boundary:

41. *John$_i$ was thought Mary admires t_i
42. *John$_i$ thinks Mary admires himself$_i$

The one exception to this is where the moved DP originates in the subject of a non-finite clause and, as we have seen, this is the position of the anaphor:

43. John$_i$ was thought t_i to like Mary
44. John$_i$ considered himself$_i$ to be intelligent

It is mysterious why there should be this parallel in the behaviour of elements which appear to have little in common, especially as the behaviour of anaphors is governed by principle A of the Binding Theory. To capture the similarities between anaphor binding and DP-movement, we will have to claim that both are in some way subject to the same restrictions: i.e. principle A. One piece of evidence is that a trace of a moved DP always has an antecedent, namely the moved DP itself. Hence there is some similarity between a trace and an anaphor. If we were to go further and claim that DP-traces are anaphors and hence must be bound by the moved DP within a local domain, we can see why there is a similarity between DP-movement and anaphor binding: DP-movement is restricted to moving a DP only to positions from which it is possible to bind its own trace.

Further support for this line of reasoning can be found in the observation that it is not only DP-traces that behave like the elements that are restricted by the principles of the Binding Theory. The traces left behind by wh-movement behave similarly to r-expressions. The relevant phenomenon here is known as **the strong crossover effect**, where it seems that it is impossible to move a wh-item over the top of an antecedent:

45. *who$_i$ did he$_i$ say Mary likes t_i

Of course this sentence is fine if the trace is not bound by *he*, but with this indexing the sentence is ungrammatical. Thus, it appears that the trace of a wh-element cannot be bound by any element other than the wh-element itself. In other words, the wh-trace must be free from virtually everything, which is similar to the restrictions placed on r-expressions by principle C. This fact can be explained if wh-traces are r-expressions, though we will have to say a little more to account for the fact that overt r-expressions cannot be bound by anything whereas a wh-trace is bound by the wh-element. A suggestion made in Chomsky (1981a) makes use of the observation that a moved wh-element always sits in an A-bar position (i.e. a non-argument position), whereas the overt elements that Binding Theory is concerned with always sit in A-positions. This makes it possible to differentiate between two different sorts of binding: **A-binding**, which concerns binding from A-positions, and **A-bar-binding**, which concerns binding from non-A-bar positions. Once this distinction has been made, it follows that wh-traces and r-expressions behave exactly alike with respect to A-binding: both must be A-free, i.e. free from all elements in A-positions.

Finally, in this brief survey of empty categories and their relationship with Binding Theory, we can observe that the missing subject *pro* in null-subject languages behaves exactly like a pronominal with respect to the Binding Theory: this element is interpreted as a personal pronoun, and can be exchanged with one, though for pragmatic reasons null-subject languages do not normally make use of an overt subject when a null subject can be used.

So the overt elements that conform to the Binding Theory have empty equivalents: a DP-trace is the same as an anaphor, a wh-trace as an r-expression, and *pro* as a pronominal. But how does the empty element PRO behave with respect to the Binding Theory? Sometimes, PRO behaves like an anaphor in that it requires a local antecedent. In fact, there is one particular case where PRO can be exchanged for a reflexive pronoun with no consequence for the interpretation of the sentence, seen in:

46.   John wants [PRO/himself to win]

where the sentence works equally well with PRO and with *himself*. However, there are other instances where PRO behaves more like a pronominal. When PRO is non-controlled, it does not have an antecedent and seems to be able to be free, in other words behave like a pronominal. While in these cases PRO can again be exchanged for a pronoun, this time it is the pronominal *one* which is used (though for reasons to do with Case theory the *for* complementizer must accompany the overt subject):

47. PRO to leave would be a mistake
48. For one to leave would be a mistake

Thus, PRO appears to behave *both* like a pronominal *and* like an anaphor and for this reason is often referred to as a pronominal anaphor.

But this leads to a paradox. Anaphors must be *bound* in their governing categories, pronominals must be *free* in theirs. So a pronominal anaphor is both bound and free in its governing category, an oxymoron on a par with *married bachelor*. However, there is one way to avoid the contradiction: PRO can be subject to both principles A and B of the Binding Theory if it *never* has a governing category. An analogy may help to make this clear. Suppose the government of some country were to make a law that all the citizens of the country have to wear hats if it is raining. Now this government have not told the people what they should do if it isn't raining and hence when it isn't raining they can either wear hats or not without breaking the law. Suppose that the government in typical fashion makes another law, without retracting the first, which says that the wearing of hats is forbidden when it is raining. Still the government have not said what the people should do when it *isn't* raining. The unfortunate citizens of this country are in trouble because if it rains they will break the law if they wear a hat and break it if they don't. But, and this is the important point, everyone can live perfectly legally wearing hats or not as long as it never rains. Principles A and B only state what anaphors and pronominals must do *if* they have a governing category and make no predictions about what such elements must do if they do not have one. So something can conform to both principles at the same time if it does not have a governing category. A further legal-type example is Colin MacInnes's anecdote of the stranger who saw the notice on the London Underground *Dogs must be carried* and went out to buy a dog so that he could travel on the Underground; if you haven't got a dog (or a governing category), the principles don't apply.

The question now arises of how an element can avoid having a governing category. This is the central role of government in unifying Binding Theory and the principle that PRO must be ungoverned. Recall that the governing category is partly defined by the presence of a governor in that it may be defined as the smallest clause which contains both the pronoun and its governor. Therefore, an element will fail to have a governing category whenever it fails to be governed; the fact that PRO must be ungoverned is derived from the assumption that it is a pronominal anaphor which therefore must not have a governing category.

Binding Theory and control

PRO is a pronominal anaphor and hence must be bound *and* free in its governing category. Hence it cannot have a governing category, in order to avoid this contradiction. The only way for an element not to have a governing category is for it not to have a governor. Thus PRO is ungoverned.

Finally, let us sum up with the following table what has been said about the relationship between overt and empty elements. Here we make use of the features [+/−anaphor], [+/−pronominal] to distinguish the elements that the Binding Theory is concerned with.

The relationship of overt and empty categories

overt	empty	anaphor	pronominal
reflexive pronouns	NP-trace	+	−
personal pronouns	*pro*	−	+
r-expressions	wh-trace	−	−
—	PRO	+	+

As we can see, most categories have both an overt and an empty element. The one exception to this is the lack of an overt element which is [+anaphor, +pronominal]: a pronominal anaphor. This, however, is to be expected given that the only way for a pronominal anaphor not to be a contradiction is for it to avoid having a governing category and the only means of doing this is to be ungoverned. As we have seen in the previous chapter, overt NPs must be governed as they must be Case-marked in order to satisfy the Case Filter and Case is assigned under government. Thus it is impossible for any language to have an overt pronominal anaphor that does not violate some principle of UG.

The Boundedness of Movement and Proper Government

This section introduces two notions that have not always been linked in the theory, though they are in the treatment we give below. Both are to do with restrictions placed on movement and both are concerned with movement as a strictly local process.

The notion of **bounding** goes back to early observations, for example Ross (1967), that movements are not possible out of certain constructions, consequently known as 'Islands' by analogy to a person marooned on an island. Ross noted that wh-movement is possible out of the complement clause of a Verb, as in:

49.   who$_i$ did Mary think [John saw t_i]

But it is not possible to move a wh-item out of a relative clause:

50.   *who$_i$ did Mary see [the man [who$_j$ t_j knows t_i]]

Such sentences suggest that movement is always to a 'local' position and that apparent 'long distance' movements are really the result of a series of local movements. So the reason why movement is allowed out of a Verb complement clause is that the specifier of the complement CP is vacant to be moved into and out of again as the wh-item moves to the higher CP-specifier. The analysis of such sentences is something like:

51.   who$_i$ did Mary think [$_{CP}$ t_i [$_{IP}$ John saw t_i]]

As indicated by the intermediate trace in the specifier of the lower CP, the movement from object of *see* to the specifier of the matrix CP takes place in two smaller steps. However, in the case of the relative clause, the CP-specifier position of this clause is already filled by the relative wh-element and hence is not vacant to be moved into. Subsequently movement out of a relative clause will be too long and hence the sentence will be ungrammatical. Of course, the important questions are: how long is *too* long and what determines this?

The second notion, called **proper government**, concerns the asymmetry between movement from subject and object positions. The central case concerns the impossibility of moving a wh-element out of a subject position when there is a *that*-complementizer:

52.   *who$_i$ did Mary think that t_i saw Bill

This restriction does not apply to the movement of objects:

53.   who$_i$ did Mary think that Bill saw t_i

This phenomenon was originally called the **that-trace effect** because descriptively it seems that a trace cannot occur after a complementizer *that*; movements which are possible from object positions are not always possible from subject positions and hence there is an asymmetry in the behaviour of elements in these positions.

To see what these phenomena have in common means investigating each one a little more closely. We will then outline Chomsky's 1986 'barriers' proposal, which essentially tries to unify the phenomena under the single notion of barrier.

Bounding

The basic idea to be captured by bounding theory is that no movement can move an element too far. This requires a principle of some kind to limit movement in the required way. One way of handling this is the theory of **Subjacency** proposed by Chomsky (1973). This works by defining certain nodes in a tree as 'hurdles' to be leapt over by a moving item. While it is possible to leap over one hurdle at a time, what is not possible and what therefore acts to prevent movement over long distances is leaping over two or more hurdles in one leap, impossible even for Colin Jackson. To put this into more formal language, nodes which are hurdles are called **bounding nodes**. The Principle of Subjacency is thus:

> **No movement can move an element over more than one bounding node at a time.**

Obviously, this principle accounts for the fact that all movements are local. However, it is the stipulation of what nodes count as bounding nodes that will provide us with a description of how far is *too* far.

When Subjacency was first proposed, the bounding nodes were claimed to be NP and S, though it has since been proposed that there is some parametric variation of bounding nodes between languages. Interpreted in terms of current theory, this means taking DP and AGRP (TP?) as the bounding nodes (for English). Let us demonstrate how this theory works through a few examples. Movement can take place from the complement clause of a Verb, as in:

54.   who$_i$ did [$_{AGRP}$ Mary think [$_{CP}$ [$_{AGRP}$ John saw t_i]]]

If this movement were to take place in one step, it would jump *both* AGRP hurdles and hence be a violation of the Subjacency Principle.

However, as the specifier of the lower CP is empty, the wh-element can use this as a stopping-off point, thus splitting the movement into two parts, both of which jump only one AGRP:

55.   who$_i$ did [$_{AGRP}$ Mary think [$_{CP}$ t_i [$_{AGRP}$ John saw t_i]]]

Thus, this sentence does not violate Subjacency and is grammatical. Now consider another sentence:

56.   * who$_i$ did [$_{AGRP}$ John ask [$_{CP}$ when$_j$ [$_{AGRP}$ t_i fixed the car t_j]]

This time the intermediate CP-specifier is already filled by another wh-element and hence is not available to be used in the move to the matrix CP. So the movement necessarily crosses two AGRPs and violates Subjacency.

The final sentence to consider demonstrates the need to take DP as a bounding node:

57. *who$_i$ did [$_{AGRP}$ John believe [$_{DP}$ the statement [$_{CP}$ t_i that [$_{AGRP}$ Bill hit t_i]]]]

In this sentence the lower CP-specifier is again open to be moved into and hence we can assume that the wh-element makes use of it. For this reason, why the sentence is ungrammatical is not because the movement crosses over two AGRPs. However, it nevertheless *is* ungrammatical and therefore must violate Subjacency by other means. The only difference between this sentence and the grammatical:

58.   who$_i$ did [$_{AGRP}$ John believe [$_{CP}$ t_i that [$_{AGRP}$ Bill hit t_i]]]

is that the subordinate clause in the ungrammatical structure is a complement of a Noun and hence appears inside a DP. It is the appearance of the DP that makes the difference. This is explained by treating DP as a bounding node, as movement out of the Noun-complement clause will now cross the two bounding nodes DP and AGRP.

The Principle of Subjacency has an extremely long history as a central part of bounding theory in comparison to most grammatical principles that have been proposed. However, it is not without its problems and more recently some linguists have attempted to account for the data with other principles. For example, one problem with Subjacency is that it does not have much to say about certain movements which none the less seem to be restricted in a similar way. One such movement is that of heads, which is also a strictly local movement. Basically, head movement is restricted to moving a head into the next head position up the tree. So an auxiliary verb can be moved into an inflectional node:

59. John has$_i$ t_i seen Mary

or an auxiliary in an inflectional node to C:

60. has$_i$ John t_i t_i seen Mary

But what is not allowed is moving an auxiliary into C directly from its original position, i.e. over the top of another auxiliary in the inflectional node:

61. *have$_i$ John will t_i seen Mary

Obviously, Subjacency is not violated here as the auxiliary moves over only one bounding node: AGRP. However, the sentence is still ungrammatical. This restriction is usually termed the **Head Movement Constraint** (HMC) (Travis, 1984). Later in this chapter we shall look at a way of unifying the boundedness phenomena with which Subjacency is concerned with other movement restrictions such as the HMC.

Proper government

We noted earlier that there is a basic subject–object asymmetry in movement possibilities from within finite embedded clauses introduced by a *that* complementizer. It seems that the movement of object wh-elements is relatively free and is allowed whether or not a *that* is present. On the other hand subject wh-elements can only be extracted when *that* is not present.

One thing that separates object position from subject position is that objects are the objects of lexical heads and so are governed by these. Subjects, of course, may also be governed, but only by AGR, which

---

Bounding and Subjacency

The Principle of Subjacency: no movement can move an element over more than one bounding node. Bounding nodes are AGRP and DP.

Gloss: bounding theory is concerned with the locality restrictions on movement: why movement cannot be over too long a distance. One way to do this is to suppose that certain nodes in a tree are hurdles of which no more than one may be leapt at a time.

Examples: who$_i$ did [$_{AGRP}$ John think [$_{CP}$ t_i that [$_{AGRP}$ Mary saw t_i]]]
Here the wh-element is moved into the matrix C-specifier position in two short hops: one from its original position to the lower C-specifier and one from the lower C-specifier to the higher one. As each of these movements crosses only one bounding node (both AGRPs), the sentence is grammatical.
  *who$_i$ did [$_{AGRP}$ John wonder [$_{CP}$ what$_j$ [$_{AGRP}$ t_i bought t_j]]]
Here, as the lower C-specifier position is already filled by *what*, the wh-element *who* has to move directly into the matrix C-specifier. This movement crosses two bounding nodes, hence Subjacency is violated and the sentence is ungrammatical.

---

is a functional category rather than a lexical one. The sole exception to this is in Exceptional Case Marking structures where there is no complementizer position and hence the question of whether the exceptional subject can move in the presence of a complementizer is simply not applicable. This observation has led to the claim that traces are licensed by being governed by lexical heads, but not by functional heads: thus a trace can always be left in an object position, but traces in subject position must be licensed in some other more restricted way.

The idea that traces are licensed by being governed by lexical heads is known as the **Empty Category Principle** (ECP). This is normally stated in terms of the notion of proper government, where government by a lexical element is one way in which something can be properly governed:

62. **The Empty Category Principle**
    an empty category must be properly governed
      α properly governs β if and only if
        (1) α governs β and
        (2) α is lexical

Returning to the cases of movement from subject position, as this position is not governed by a lexical head, the question is what properly governs traces here? Chomsky (1981a) assumed that the notion of a governor is extended in this case to include elements which are co-indexed with the governee and that this extension of governor is also relevant for proper government. Thus a trace will be properly governed, in this instance, if it is governed by an element that it is co-indexed with, i.e. the moved element or one of the other traces left behind by the moved element. This relationship is often called **antecedent government** and is contrasted with **head government**.

This clearly helps us to account for the *that-trace* phenomenon. In the absence of a *that* complementizer, the trace in the specifier of CP properly governs a trace in subject position. However, when there is a complementizer present, this must interfere with the process of antecedent government, thus making the original trace non-properly governed and in violation of the ECP. Intuitively we can view the situation from the notion that government should be a unique relationship such that if one element governs another, then the governed element should not also be governed by anything else. The appearance of the complementizer blocks antecedent government because it adds a nearer potential governor (the complementizer) but, as this is not a proper governor, the original trace will violate the ECP.

This can be made clearer with some diagrams:

63.

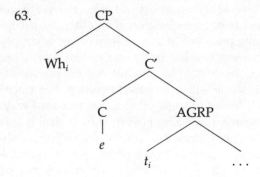

Here, the trace is in a subject position, and hence is not head-governed. The only way for it to be licensed by proper government therefore is for it to be antecedent-governed by the wh-item (or its trace) in the CP-specifier position. As the complementizer position is empty, there is no nearer governor and hence the trace is properly governed and the ECP is satisfied. However, if there is a complementizer:

64.

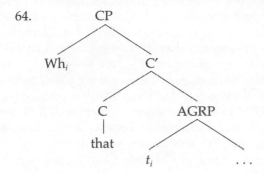

the complementizer is a nearer governor and so the trace is not ante-cedent-governed. Moreover, as the complementizer is not a lexical item, the trace is not head-governed either. For these reasons, the trace is not properly governed and so is in violation of the ECP.

Proper Government

The Empty Category Principle (ECP): an empty category must be properly governed
α properly governs β if and only if
   (1) α governs β and
   (2) α is lexical or an antecedent

Gloss: empty categories are 'licensed' by being governed by either a lexical head or by an antecedent. Thus, traces in object position are always licensed as they are always governed by the head they are an object of. Traces in subject position are never head-governed and there-fore must be antecedent-governed. This gives rise to the *that*-trace effect as antecedent government is blocked by the presence of an overt complementizer.

Barriers

We now turn to Chomsky's proposal to unify notions involved with the various constraints on movement discussed above (Chomsky, 1986b). Chomsky's barriers theory is extremely complex and has re-percussions for the analysis of many different phenomena, sometimes in quite radical ways. The partial picture of this theory presented here is not particularly harmful for the reader who wants to know about current developments in syntactic theory, as the importance of the barriers framework lies not with the particular analysis that Chomsky presented but in the line of research that it spawned. Much of this subsequent research was aimed at improving and simplifying the barriers framework. The barriers framework was also proposed before Pollock put forward the articulated INFL analysis which separated the inflectional elements AGRP, TP, etc., discussed in chapter 5. It is not exactly clear how Pollock's proposals affect Chomsky's, and here is not the place to investigate this. For this reason, we will here remain faithful to the original formulations in Chomsky (1986b) and use IP instead of AGRP and TP, etc.

From the way they are presented here, it may appear that Subjacency is completely different from the ECP. Subjacency is a direct constraint on movement allowing movement over one, but not more than one, bounding node. The ECP restricts the relationship that must exist between a trace and its antecedent in some cases, thus restricting the movement indirectly.

However, clearly both *do* limit movement; in some cases there is an overlap in what they restrict: a Subjacency violation by an element moved from a subject position is also an ECP violation as, if an element is moved too far, it is not able to govern its trace. The redundancy that this gives rise to is one reason why a unified approach seems reasonable.

Chomsky (1986b) tries to unify bounding theory and the ECP under the notion of a **barrier**. In short, movement over such a barrier should lead to ungrammaticality and barriers block government. Take the following abstract structure:

65. $\ldots \alpha \ldots [\gamma \ldots \beta \ldots]$

α and β are two positions in a tree which may be linked in one of a number of ways, by movement for example, in which case α is the moved element and β is its trace, or by government, in which case α is the governor and β is the governee. This structure will be grammatical if no node of the tree that lies between them, i.e. γ, is a barrier and will be ungrammatical if γ is a barrier.

But what counts as a barrier? The first thing to note is that there is no single node that can universally be associated with a barrier. To demonstrate this we can compare movement out of a complement clause, which is possible:

66.   Who$_i$ did you think [t_i that [Mary went out with t_i]]

to movement out of an adjunct clause, which is not possible:

67.   *who$_i$ were you so drunk [t$_i$ that [Mary went out with t$_i$]]

Given that both of these movements are from similar structures, essentially CPs, we cannot say that these are inherently barriers. Rather, structures become barriers by virtue of the positions they occupy. In particular, structures that are complements of lexical elements are *not* barriers, whereas structures that are not complements of lexical elements *are* barriers. To account for this difference Chomsky (1986b, p. 14) proposes the definition of a **Blocking Category** making use of the notion **L-marking**, which is simply θ-marking by a lexical head:

γ is a Blocking Category for β if and only if γ is not L-marked and γ dominates β

However, not every Blocking Category constitutes a barrier, as can be seen by the following:

68.   who$_i$ did [$_{IP}$ Mary see t$_i$]

Obviously IP is not L-marked as it is the complement of a functional category C, not of a lexical category. Thus, according to the definition, IP is a Blocking Category. However it is not a barrier as, if it were, this sentence would be a Subjacency violation. To account for this, Chomsky assumes that IP is defective in that it is the only Blocking Category that is not a barrier. Thus, his definition of a **barrier** is:

γ is a barrier for β if and only if γ is a Blocking Category for β, γ ≠ IP
(p. 14)

However, further complications arise from the fact that although an element can always move over IP into CP and an element can always move out of a complement CP, no element can move over both of these categories in one go, as the familiar wh-islands examples demonstrate:

69.   *who$_i$ did you wonder [$_{CP}$ what$_j$ [$_{IP}$ t$_i$ bought t$_j$]]

Here the offending movement from out of the complement clause into the matrix CP-specifier jumps over both the IP and the CP. However,

IP is not a barrier because it is defective and CP is not a barrier because it is L-marked. So there should be no problem as no barrier is crossed, but the sentence is still ungrammatical. To overcome this, Chomsky proposes a second way for a category to be a barrier – by inheritance. That is to say, a category can become a barrier for an element if the category dominates a Blocking Category of that element. Thus, although in the above sentence the CP is not a barrier in its own right, it inherits barrierhood from the dominating IP which is a Blocking Category for the wh-element. Of course, if the intermediate C-specifier were vacant to be moved into, CP would not inherit barrierhood as the IP is not a Blocking Category for an element which is in the specifier of CP. To see this more clearly, consider the relevant structures:

70.

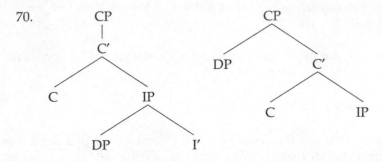

In the left-hand structure IP is a Blocking Category for the DP because it dominates it. Therefore CP inherits barrierhood and, if we were to try to move the DP directly from this position over the CP, there would be a violation of some principle. On the other hand, in the right-hand structure IP is not a barrier for DP as it does not dominate it. Therefore CP does not inherit barrierhood and, if it is not a barrier in its own right, movement will be possible from this position.

Finally let us consider how the ECP effects are handled in the barriers framework. Obviously, a barrier blocks government and therefore an element will only be governed if there is no intervening barrier between it and its governor. As there is no barrier between a head and its object, the object will always be governed. Thus a trace in an object position will always be properly governed as before. The interesting case is the *that*-trace effect. Subjects can only be licensed by antecedent government as they are not head-governed. Thus, movement of a subject will only be possible if it does not cross a barrier which blocks antecedent government. The movement of a subject into the CP-specifier crosses only IP, which is not a barrier as it is defective. However, this movement is not allowed when there is an overt complementizer. Chomsky assumes that the presence of the complementizer causes a barrier to come into existence. In particular, it is the C′ bar that is the barrier:

71.

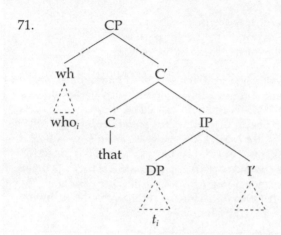

To handle this, Chomsky introduced the **Minimality Condition**, which formalizes the intuitive notion we referred to previously that government is a unique relationship and if an element is governed by one thing it will not be governed by another. The observation is the same as before: the complementizer is a more minimal governor of the subject than the wh-element in the C-specifier. However, the assumption is that this fact causes the node immediately dominating the nearest governor, in this case the C′, to become a barrier. Thus, this is another way that a node can become a barrier, though of course this will only be relevant to government and not to bounding.

This section has only touched on part of Chomsky's analysis and other parts have not been mentioned (such as why VP is not a barrier, though it is not L-marked). However, the general gist of the analysis is enough for present purposes. Though the barriers framework is probably too complex and convoluted to have lasting impact of its own, it was nevertheless an important step in the development of the theory because it led to much work along the same lines which tried to improve on and simplify the framework, for example the work of Rizzi whose idea of Relativized Minimality, to be discussed below, can be seen as a progression from Chomsky's barriers framework.

Barriers

γ is a Blocking Category for β if and only if γ is not L-marked and γ
    dominates β
γ is a barrier for β if and only if.
    (1) γ is a Blocking Category for β, γ ≠ IP;
    (2) γ dominates a Blocking Category for β or
    (3) γ immediately dominates the governor of β

Gloss: a barrier is a node on a tree that serves to block the syntactic
    processes of movement and government and as such unifies bound-
    ing theory and the ECP. A node is defined as a barrier by virtue of its
    position in a sentence. Specifically, anything, with the exception of IP,
    will be a barrier if it is not L-marked – assigned a θ-role by a lexical
    category – and it dominates the element that the barrier is defined for.
    Other nodes will also become barriers for an element if they dominate
    non-L-marked nodes dominating that element or if they dominate the
    nearest governor of that element. This last addition to the definition
    of the barrier is known as the Minimality Condition.

Relativized Minimality

The final section of this chapter briefly introduces Rizzi's (1990)
Relativized Minimality framework as this is an important extension to
Chomsky's work on barriers. While Relativized Minimality does not
completely replace the notion of a barrier, it complements it in a way
that enables the whole theory to be simplified.

Relativized Minimality is expressed in terms of government, though,
like the barriers framework, it attempts to unify bounding and ECP
phenomena. Essentially the whole framework is based on an observation already mentioned a number of times in this chapter, namely that
government should be a unique relationship between two elements
such that if one governs the other then no other element will be able
to govern it. However, the unique feature of Relativized Minimality is
that the notion of what counts as a governor is 'relativized' to what is
being governed; no type of government interferes with any other type,
quite unlike the barriers framework.

What are the reasons why Rizzi considers 'minimality' to be relative to what is being governed? One problem that we encountered

with Subjacency is that it says nothing about why head movement is restricted and so a separate principle, the Head Movement Constraint, had to be proposed to account for why a head cannot be moved too far, i.e. over the top of another head:

72. *have$_i$ Mary will t_i gone

In fact, the HMC has a number of things in common with other restrictions on movement: just as a head cannot be moved over the top of another head, a wh-item cannot be moved over the top of another wh-item, as can be seen in the familiar wh-islands:

73. *who$_j$ did you ask what$_j$ t_i fixed t_j

and an argument such as a subject cannot be moved over the top of an argument position, as can be seen in ungrammatical sentences involving 'super raising':

74. *John$_i$ seems it to be likely t_i to win

However, heads *can* be moved over arguments, arguments over heads, and wh-words over heads and arguments. It seems that what blocks each type of movement is relevant only to that type and not to others.

This is where Relativized Minimality comes in. Starting with HMC effects, if the trace of a moved head is assumed to be properly governed, as the ECP demands, and a proper governor for the trace of a head can also only be a head, head movement is restricted to positions where the moved head is able to govern its own trace. Given that other heads are 'potential' governors for the trace of a head, and as such will block antecedent government if they are nearer to the trace than the moved head, head movement will be restricted to the next head position up the tree to prevent antecedent government from being blocked. This can be seen clearly in the following tree:

75.

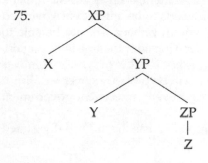

If Z moves to Y, there is no other head nearer to the trace of Z in ZP to block antecedent government and hence the movement will be grammatical. But if Z moves instead to X, then Y will be a nearer governor of the trace in ZP, thus blocking government from X. As Y is not the antecedent of the trace, the trace will not be antecedent-governed and therefore it will violate the ECP.

Exactly the same is true of A(argument)-movements, such as raising and passivization. If the trace of a moved argument has to be governed by an antecedent in an A-position, then A-movement will be restricted to the next A-position up the tree to prevent another element in an A-position governing and therefore blocking antecedent government of the trace. Again, consider the following tree:

76.

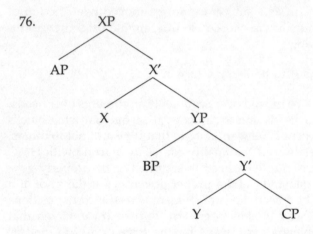

Assuming that AP, BP and CP are A-positions, CP can move to BP without there being another A-position preventing antecedent government of the trace left behind. However, if CP moves to AP, BP will be a nearer governor, hence blocking antecedent government.

Finally, consider the case of A-bar movement, such as wh-movement. Assuming that the trace of a wh-item needs to be antecedent-governed by an element in an A-bar position, wh-movement will not be able to move a wh-item over the top of another. Consider the tree above again, but this time AP and BP are A-bar positions. If CP (a wh-item) moves to BP, everything is fine and the trace will be properly governed. But if CP moves to AP, BP will intervene to prevent antecedent government and the ECP will be violated.

The principle of Relativized Minimality can be informally stated thus:

Relativized Minimality
An element will minimally govern its trace if there is no other
'typical potential governor' that is closer to the trace.

Obviously, this now relies on the notion of a 'typical potential governor', which is where the relativization comes in: a typical potential governor for a head will be a governing head; a typical potential governor for an element in an A-chain will be a governor in an A-position, and a typical potential governor for an element in an A-bar-chain will be a governor in an A-bar position.

To see how this simplifies the barriers framework, consider the notion of CP becoming a barrier by inheritance. Recall that IP is not a barrier because it is 'defective' in some way. However, it is still impossible to move out of an IP and past the CP in one movement (as demonstrated by wh-islands) even if the CP is not a barrier because it is L-marked. Chomsky dealt with this by assuming that the CP inherits its barrier status by dominating a Blocking Category: IP. But this makes the whole theory very complicated as there is more than one way that a node can become a barrier: either by being a Blocking Category (not for IP, though), or by dominating a Blocking Category. Relativized Minimality, however, gets rid of the need for this complication, as the data that necessitate it (e.g. wh-islands) are now dealt with by Relativized Minimality: a wh-item cannot move out of both an IP and a CP in one go as it would be moving over the top of a typical potential governor: the specifier of CP.

Another way that Chomsky (1986b) proposed that an element can become a barrier is through the minimality condition: recall that C′ becomes a barrier when C is overt to account for the *that*-trace phenomenon. Relativized Minimality also gets rid of the need for this complexity, though some additions are needed to allow *that*-trace phenomena to be accounted for in Rizzi's theory. The problem is that in Rizzi's framework, a head, such as a complementizer, should not be able to interfere with antecedent government other than through another head: *that*-trace phenomena, however, obviously concern A-bar-movement, not head movement. Thus Rizzi is forced to reject the idea that ungrammaticalities such as those in:

77.   *who$_i$ do you think t_i that t_i left

are caused by the original trace not being antecedent-governed by the trace in the lower CP. To handle this, Rizzi assumes that the ECP is satisfied only if **both** antecedent government and head government are satisfied. With *that*-trace phenomena, the original trace is anteced-ent-governed but it is not properly licensed because the complementizer is not a lexical element and therefore does not count as a proper head governor.

When the complementizer is not there, however, because of specifier–head agreement between the specifier of CP (the intermediate trace) and the empty head, the empty complementizer becomes a proper head governor for the original trace and hence the structure is saved from the ECP.

While this has done no more than outline the important points, Relativized Minimality can be seen to unify a set of phenomena (wh-islands, super raising and HMC violations) that seem to have a number of things in common, and, because of the overlap between Relativized Minimality and the *Barriers* framework, the latter can be made sim-pler: all that remains, in fact, is the definition of a barrier as a non-L-marked element.

Relativized Minimality

An element will minimally govern its trace if there is no other 'typical potential governor' that is closer to the trace.
typical potential governors:
   — a governor in an A-position (for an element in an A-chain)
   — a governor in an A-bar position (for an element in an A-bar chain)

Gloss: government varies according to what is being governed.

8

Topics in Language Acquisition

This chapter will discuss the following topics:

— The acquisition of functional phrases
— Alternative explanations of children's null-subject sentences
— Access to Universal Grammar in second language acquisition
— Maturation and Universal Grammar
— Binding parameters and acquisition of Binding Theory.

This chapter follows up some of the ways in which the UG model of language acquisition has developed within principles and parameters theory. The aim is not to provide a complete coverage of current work. The first edition of this book grumbled in 1988 that applications of principles and parameters theory to first language acquisition had hardly been tackled. Almost the opposite complaint can be made now: a plethora of research has been carried out in the intervening years, making it necessary to select which research to include; opponents of the principles and parameters approach now confront a mass of accumulated evidence in both L1 and L2. More comprehensive introductions are Goodluck (1991) for the L1 area, and Cook (1993, chapters 8 and 9) for the L2 area; more theoretical surveys can be found in Atkinson (1992) for L1 and Towell and Hawkins (1994) for L2. The purpose of this chapter is to raise some issues based to a greater or lesser extent on current principles and parameters theory; inevitably this involves pursuing a more individual line than in earlier chapters, reflecting the interests of the two authors. It should perhaps be pointed out that Chomsky himself has contributed little to the recent study of language acquisition, unlike the major effect of his ideas reported in chapter 3, confining himself to a few gnomic utterances on the importance of the lexicon to acquisition; for example, 'language acquisition is in essence a matter of determining lexical idiosyncrasies' (Chomsky, 1991c, p. 44).

The Acquisition of Functional Phrases

Chapter 5 introduced the contrast between lexical and functional categories. Lexical phrases such as NP and VP have a substantive head such as N or V that always figures as a word or phrase in the lexicon; they s-select sisters for θ-roles. Functional phrases may have either lexical heads such as *that* or inflectional heads such as *-s*; these are either realized lexically as morphemes or may be absent; they c-select compulsory complements, such as the AGRP complement for CP. If we accept the functional parameterization hypothesis, parameters of variation are associated with functional categories, for instance a value for the pro-drop parameter in the AGRP and a value for the wh-movement parameter in the CP. Thus functional and lexical phrases have two distinct types of syntactic system, one based on lexical properties, one on functional properties.

At early stages of language acquisition, English children produce sentences like:

1.   Here book.

and:

2.   Slug coming.

In adult terms, the child's sentences seem to leave out certain grammatical morphemes; the child does not convey singular or plural agreement on either the Noun or the Verb. For some time it was felt that such sentences represented a semantic stage of language acquisition (Gleitman, 1982); the child expresses certain ideas through the choice and sequence of vocabulary rather than through syntax.

Interpreted in terms of principles and parameters theory, at this stage the child appears to know lexical phrases but not functional phrases. We can predict what the effects of missing functional categories will be on the child's language:

(1) VP. The child would know the VP with the subject included as specifier, i.e. a so-called 'small clause'. However, as the child's grammar does not have any functional phrases, there is nowhere outside this VP for the subject or Verb to move to.

(2) NP. The child would know lexical NPs but not DPs. Hence, if pronouns are heads of DPs, the child would produce pronoun-less sentences or misanalyse pronouns as Ns.

(3) TP. Since the child lacks a TP, Verbs would not be able to move into it to be marked for tense; hence children's sentences should lack tense markings as in:

3. Daddy sleep.
   (Daddy is sleeping)

(4) AGRP. If AGRP were also missing, Verbs would not be able to move into it to be marked for agreement with the subject and the subject would not move to the AGR-specifier position to receive Case.

(5) CP. Without a CP, English children would lack wh-questions and inversion questions, as in:

4. Help jelly.
   (Can you help me to some jelly?)

German children should lack the Verb-second construction since there would be nowhere for the Verb to move to, restricting them to SOV sentences, as in an example from Clahsen and Muysken (1986):

5. Ich Schaufel haben.
   (I shovel have)

This is ungrammatical in adult German as the Verb has not moved to second position, to get the SVO:

6. Ich haben Schaufel.

if not the grammatical adult form:

7. Ich habe die Schaufel.

(6) DP. Without a DP, children should lack determiners, as in:

8. Look plane.

and:

9. Pretty car.

Also assuming that it is DP that requires Case, not NP, without DP the Case Filter would have nothing to operate on.

Thus the acquisition of inflections has become inextricably connected with, first the acquisition of the functional phrases to which the inflections are heads, second the notion of Verb movement that moves Verbs into these phrases by head movement.

One plausible explanation is therefore that, to start off, L1 children know only lexical phrases, i.e. the projections of the four main lexical categories N, V, etc.; they have to acquire functional phrases such as IP and DP. This possibility was first mooted in Radford (1986) and presented in an expanded version based on a large corpus in Radford (1990). The basic claim is that up to the age of 24 months (±4 months) children lack functional phrases. The sole phrasal category is the VP; as this is the domain within which θ-role assignment of semantic roles takes place, the child's speech will indeed give the illusion of a semantic stage; 'the early child grammars of English are lexical-thematic systems in which thematic argument structures are directly mapped into lexical syntactic structures' (Radford, 1990, p. 263). The entire structure of a child's sentence such as:

10. Slug coming.

is then:

11.

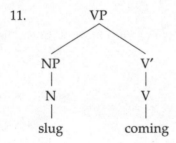

Apart from this type of structure, the child needs to know that in English internal θ-roles are assigned to the right and external θ-roles are assigned to the left, so that subjects come before Verbs and objects come after them.

Radford's main evidence is the lack of inflectional elements in children's speech. Radford (1990) uses a DP analysis but has a single IP with an 'I-system'. He claims, *inter alia*, that:
— lack of articles indicates children have no DPs, as in:

12. Paula good girl.

— lack of question inversion means they have no CPs, as in:

13. Daddy go.
(where does Daddy go?)

— lack of Nominative Case shows they have no Case system, since Nominative must be assigned to the subject in S-structure after movement to AGRP, as in:

14. Me got bean.

— lack of modals, finite inflections (-s, -ed), infinitival *to*, etc., shows they have no IP as in:

15. Want have drink.

Radford's account unites current syntax with data from actual children and needs careful refuting by others who want to pursue alternatives, as we shall see. The view expressed in Cook (1990a) is that this position relies too heavily on the *absence* of forms in children's speech rather than on their *presence*; it is based on what children leave out of their sentences rather than on what they put in. For example, chapters 4 to 7 in Radford (1990) are titled *Absence of...*, respectively, *Determiner System, Complementizer System, Inflection System*, and *Case System*. Providing a list of the books that are in the room at the moment is easy; compiling a list of the books that are not in the room would end up with the British Museum catalogue. Evidence of absence is ambiguous since almost anything can be absent; as Sartre (1957) points out, the number of things that are not true vastly exceeds the number of things that are. Hence 'what doesn't occur in children's speech should only support ideas already vouched for by observational data or by other types of evidence, such as comprehension tests' (Cook, 1990a). Furthermore, since children's early language is so sparse, 'it would be hard to imagine evidence for functional categories below that MLU [1.5–1.9] [Mean Length of Utterance], given the bias towards content words and the lack of evidence from ordering' (de Villiers, 1992, p. 441).

The missing functional categories proposal suggests that children's first grammars differ from adults' grammars in lacking the superstructure of functional phrases. According to Radford (1990), these functional categories emerge at roughly the same time in the children's speech. There are, however, several researchers who deny that early speech is devoid of functional categories. Meisel and Müller (1992) find early examples of Verb-second in children learning German, for example:

16.   Kaput is der.
      (broken is it)

and:

17.   Da fährt die Caroline.
      (there goes Caroline)

They argue that these children have both an AGRP and a TP, and use TP as a place into which to move the finite Verb; they do not, however, have a CP.

An alternative view is that the functional categories are present but not fully visible in the child's speech for one reason or another. The overall choice is between a **discontinuity** model in which adult and early child grammars bear little relationship to each other, and a **continuity** model in which adult grammars are natural developments of early child grammars; in earlier days this was put as a choice between tadpoles changing into frogs by metamorphosis and frogs growing into bigger and better frogs without abrupt change (Gleitman, 1982). Clearly there are sub-alternatives within these positions; it is possible for example to combine a missing functional categories analysis with the view that these actually emerge in a particular sequence in acquisition; thus some of the apparent counter-examples might simply reflect the emergence of the first functional category, namely the IP, before other phrases such as the CP. Déprez and Pierce (1993) for example argue for the emergence of Verb movement to I before Verb movement to C in children learning Swedish: Verb-second follows the acquisition of finite Verb inflections.

Déprez and Pierce (1993) extend the dispute to the NegP analysis of negation. The early work of Klima and Bellugi (1966) drew up stages for the L1 acquisition of negation using the analysis of negation then current. At the first of their stages, children's negative sentences were seen as having the structure Negation + Nucleus (i.e. the rest of the sentence), as in:

18.   No the sun shining.

and:

19. No a boy bed.

The negative element *no* occurs at the beginning of the sentence rather than in its adult sentence-medial position. Déprez and Pierce (1993) argue that in NegP terms the children have not moved the subject NP out of the VP: 'the subject NP can be case-marked VP-internally and is therefore licensed to remain in VP-internal position' (p. 34). But the children nevertheless have a NegP from which they can hang the negative element:

20.

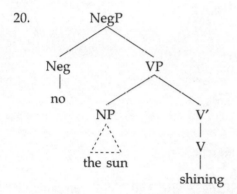

Instead of lacking all functional categories, children possess at least one part of the IP system, the NegP. English children have to learn, not the actual existence of NegP, but the necessity for subject movement across it. Déprez and Pierce (1993) apply similar arguments to children acquiring negation in French: in French, unlike English, the Verb has to move to I, as we saw in chapter 6. Typical sentences from French-speaking children are:

21. Pas la   poupée dormir.
    (not the doll   sleep)

and:

22. Elle a   pas la bouche.
    (she has not a mouth)

The negative element *pas* only occurs at the beginning of the sentence when there is a non-finite Verb; otherwise it occurs after finite Verbs.

The claim is that the children move the finite Verb to precede the *pas*, as is necessary in French because of the setting for the AGR parameter discussed in chapter 6. Again this is only possible if there is the necessary structure to bear the Verb, i.e. the S-structure:

23.

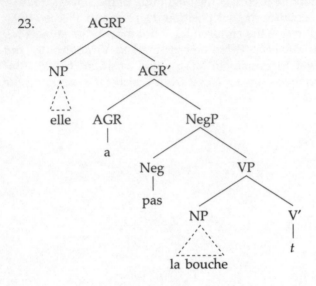

Thus French children too need the AGRP and NegP components of the I-system. In general Déprez and Pierce (1993) conclude that children's grammars differ from adults', not because they lack functional phrases or movement, but because they allow the subject NP to remain inside the VP. Children at the earliest stage of syntax know that English differs from French in Verb movement. Since parameters are always associated with functional heads, children must *ipso facto* know functional categories.

An elegant counter-attack on the missing functional categories analysis has been mounted by Wexler (1994). Wexler finds sentences in early child language from several different languages that imply Verb movement of different kinds. To take two of his test cases:

(1) *French negation.* Drawing on the work of Déprez and Pierce (1993), Wexler sees the crucial difference between the child's:

24.   Pas manger la   poupée.
      (not eat   the doll)

where the negative *pas* occurs before the Verb, and:

25. Est pas mort.
    is not dead

where the *pas* follows the Verb, as whether the Verb is finite, and so
has inflections, or non-finite. When the Verb is non-finite, as with the
infinitive *manger*, it does not move in front of the negative element *pas*;
when the Verb is finite, as with the 3rd person singular *est*, it does
move.

(2) *German Verb-second*. In the child's sentence:

26. Ich der fos hab'n.
    I   the frog have

the Verb *hab'n* occurs in final position, incorrectly for adult German.
In:

27. Mein Hubsache had Tiere   din.
    my   helicopter has animals in it.

the Verb *had* occurs in Verb-second position. In other words movement to Verb-second takes place when the Verb is finite (*had*) but not
when the Verb is non-finite (*hab'n*).

Children are therefore capable of Verb movement for negation and
for Verb-second purposes when the Verb is finite, but not when it is
non-finite. Children do not lack the functional categories necessary to
provide landing sites for the movement to take place; they simply do
not move Verbs when the Verb is non-finite. One possible explanation
is that the children have a grammar in which the T (tense) element
is optional; all the oddities in their Verb movement amount to sometimes raising the Verb, and consequently gaining inflections, sometimes not raising it, and so ending up with an uninflected non-finite
phrase.

So what about English? To take the third person inflection -*s*, English children sometimes leave it out, as in:

28. Pig go in.

sometimes put it in, as in:

29. Here's Teddy.

This looks like a different phenomenon from that in other languages.
But English is peculiar in that the non-finite infinitive form of the Verb

is identical with the uninflected base form, for example the infinitive *sleep* is the same as the base *sleep*. In other languages the infinitive has a form of its own; while the infinitive of the English Verb *sleep* is *sleep*, in French it is *dormir (dorm+ir)*, German *schlafen (schlaf+en)*, and so on. So there is no way of telling in English if the child is producing an uninflected Verb stem *go* or an infinitive *go*. Wexler's solution is then to claim that the English child is behaving like other children in vacillating between a sentence with T including an inflected Verb and a sentence without T including an infinitive, only we cannot tell from the surface of the sentence which is happening. This would also be seen in the children's tendency to miss out *to* as in:

30.   Want have drink.

since this is indeed the head of TP. English children therefore also have functional phrases so that they can move the Verb to get inflection; like other children at first they do not feel this is a compulsory aspect of the sentence. This clear and lucid argument by Wexler indeed demolishes some of the support for missing functional categories; it does not of course say anything about missing DPs.

Some L2 researchers have also been attracted by the functional categories analysis. There had already been extensive arguments about Verb movement in L2 German. Clahsen and Muysken (1986) had claimed that L1 children start with SOV and proceed to SVO, while L2 learners start with SVO and learn SOV, something that would be impossible in terms of Universal Grammar; duPlessis, Solin, Travis and White (1987) had shown how a slightly different syntactic analysis accommodated L2 learners within the same UG framework. The closest in spirit to the L1 work is the study by Vainikka and Young-Scholten (1991) of eleven Turkish and Korean learners of German. The early L2 learners had a VP within which they retained the order from their L1s, namely OV, as in:

31.   Oya Zigarette trinken.
      (Oya cigarette drink)

The learners who were slightly further on knew features of the IP, in that they had Verb-raising without agreement, as in:

32.   Ich sehen Schleier.
      (I   see   veil)

which lacks first person agreement on *sehen* but has the Verb correctly in second position. The most advanced group of learners had both full agreement on the Verb and the right order; they were at an AGRP stage where they produced sentences like:

33.　Der kleine　　geht　　Kindergarten.
　　　(the　young one goes to kindergarten)

Thus the functional categories analysis appears to fit L2 acquisition; there seems to be a clear sequence of stages – a 'stagiation' in the Piagetian sense – in the introduction of functional categories: VP → IP → AGRP. Eubank (1992) also analyses L2 German in functional terms but suggests that all the phrases are present from the beginning; lack of agreement, he claims, is due to the learner's initial failure to perceive that the endings of Verbs are indeed inflections rather than part of the Verb itself.

Functional categories have thus opened a new perspective on language acquisition, with repercussions for many topics. In one sense the analysis is still too fluid, with an indefinite number of functional categories and an uncertain hierarchy between them. In general, much of language acquisition is now seen as the acquisition of features of lexical entries. Up to recently the Lexical Parameterization Hypothesis applied to all elements in the lexicon. This has now been restricted just to functional categories via the Functional Parameterization Hypothesis: learning for substantives is reduced to simply matching certain phonological forms to certain universal concepts and their properties, i.e. the word *give* s-selects an Agent, a Theme and a Recipient, no matter which phonological form it is associated with in a given language.

The entries for functional categories include c-selection information about compulsory complements – the head of AGR c-selects a complement TP, the head of TP c-selects a complement VP, and so on. But, if one accepts the Functional Parameterization Hypothesis, 'acquisition of a language reduces to selection of substantives from a given store and fixing of values of parameters that apply to functional elements and to properties of the lexicon as a whole' (Chomsky, 1990, p. 75). Parameters belong to functional categories; each functional head requires the setting of appropriate parameter values – whether AGRP is opaque or not, and whether CP is [±wh]. This is one way of conceptualizing Chomsky's view that 'language acquisition is in essence a matter of determining lexical idiosyncrasies' (Chomsky, 1991c, p. 44).

Missing functional categories analysis

Arguments that early grammars lack functional categories (Radford, etc.)
Up to about 24 months children have only lexical categories and no
  functional categories so that they *inner alia*:
— lack articles (no DPs)
— lack inversion (no CP)
— lack Nominative Case (as this is assigned to the subject after movement to the AGRP)
— lack modals etc. (no IP)
— have SOV order in German (as the Verb cannot move to the non-
  existent CP)

Arguments that early grammars have functional categories (Wexler, etc.)
— German-speaking children move finite Verbs to Verb-second
— French-speaking children move finite Verbs before negative *pas*
— English-speaking children appear to use 3rd person *-s* optionally since
  there is no difference between Verb stem and infinitive in English

---

Alternative Explanations of Children's Null-Subject Sentences

Chapter 3 outlined the research by Hyams (1986) that established that
English children go through a stage when they produce apparent null-
subject sentences such as:

34.   Make a house.

and:

35.   Read bear book.

Children start with a pro-drop setting for English which allows the
empty category *pro* in subject position; they learn with time that English is a non-pro-drop language. Hyams (1986) used an analysis of
pro-drop called the AG/PRO parameter, adapted from Rizzi (1982);
interpreted in the terms being used here, the empty category *pro* is
licensed in subject position by a lexical AGR which can govern it, as

in Italian. A non-lexical AGR cannot govern *pro*, and so yields a non-pro-drop language like English. The children's null-subject sentences have a partial structure that may be represented as:

36.

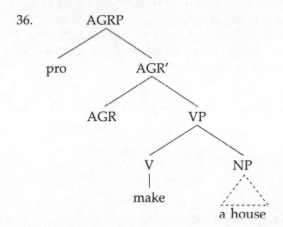

This account explains why *pro* can appear where it does in different languages. We saw in chapter 3 that Hyams (1986) claimed that children's early English was in fact a pro-drop language and so permitted null-subject sentences.

Various difficulties have been found with this account. Radford (1990) pointed out that, although Hyams denied the existence of null-*object* sentences in children's speech, they are in fact far from rare, for example:

37.   Mummy, you wiping.

and:

38.   Me have.

But null objects cannot be handled by the pro-drop analysis provided since AGR does not properly govern the object position. Valian (1989) showed that, though English children indeed have null-subject sentences, they have fewer of them than equivalent Italian children, so they must in some sense know that English needs subjects. Hulk (1987) found that French children did not go through a null-subject stage. Others claimed that lack of subjects might be a matter of performance; Bloom (1990) showed that children's VPs in null-subject sentences were longer than those in sentences with subjects, suggesting the subject was being squeezed out by the length of the VP. Hyams and Wexler (1993), however, retort that the processing account cannot explain why there are more null subjects than null objects; they deny that processing accounts favour linear order nowadays.

Furthermore the Hyams (1986) analysis does not explain how the hearer knows what a null-subject sentence is about, for instance who is referred to in the Chinese sentence:

39. Shuo.
     (speaks)

with the S-structure:

40. *pro* shuo

In other words, how can *pro* be identified with some definite person? Without agreement features such as -*s*, how do children specify who they are talking about? In the original pro-drop work, null subjects were linked to the existence of 'rich' inflections in a language; pro-drop languages such as Italian tend to have complex inflectional morphology so that there is less doubt who the null subject refers to, while non-pro-drop languages such as English tend to have weaker morphology. In the Latin:

41. Amata est.
     (she) was loved

the Verb form *amata* indicates that *pro* refers to something that is both singular and feminine.

Hence the newer account of pro-drop by Rizzi (1986) stressed the importance, not just of licensing *pro*, but also of identifying it. *pro* is licensed by Case Theory, i.e. whether it receives Nominative from AGR; *pro* is identified by the agreement feature that appears on the Verb, i.e. whether the subject is definite or indefinite, singular or plural. But, despite the fact that it has no inflectional morphology, Chinese is a pro-drop language; there is no way that the speaker can unerringly identify the *pro* with some particular person in:

42. *pro* shuo
     (speaks)

as there are no other clues. Huang (1984) suggested that the identification of *pro* relies on discourse factors; if you cannot work out through inflections who is being talked about, look for the topic of conversation. But this seemed to undermine the natural-seeming link between pro-drop and inflections: something else is involved.

Jaeggli and Safir (1989) supply this by introducing a further factor that separates pro-drop languages like Chinese and Italian from non-pro-drop languages like English and French. This factor derives from a comparison of the different morphological forms that Verbs take in the present tense. Assuming a singular/plural contrast and three persons, the six forms of the present tense can be seen in the following paradigm for English *speak*, Spanish *hablar* (speak), Chinese *shuo* (speak) and Irish *labh* (speak).

Paradigms for present tense inflections

	English	Spanish	Chinese	Irish
1st pers. sing.	I speak	hab-lo	shuo	labh-rann
2nd pers. sing.	you speak	habl-as	shuo	labh-rann
3rd pers. sing.	he/she/it speak-s	habl-a	shuo	labh-rann
1st pers. pl.	we speak	habl-amos	shuo	labh-rann
2nd pers. pl.	you speak	habl-àis	shuo	labh-rann
3rd pers. pl.	they speak	habl-an	shuo	labh-rann

Spanish has a different ending for each of the six parts of the paradigm; English has a different ending -*s* only for the third person singular; Chinese has no different endings at all; Irish always has the same present tense ending -*rann*.

What then do Spanish, Chinese and Irish share that English lacks? The claim is that in Spanish etc. *all* the possible inflections are morphologically complex, in Chinese *none*; hence these languages are two extremes, united in being at opposite poles. 'A morphological paradigm is uniform if all its forms are morphologically complex or none of them are' (Hyams, 1992, p. 254). English is in the middle, having some complex morphology but not full present tense morphology. Irish and Chinese are **morphologically uniform**; you know where you are with them in that either all or none of the present tense forms are inflected. English is mixed, i.e. **morphologically non-uniform**, in that you have to know that one of the six forms has an inflection but the other five do not. Pro-drop languages must be uniform; non-pro-drop must be non-uniform. It does not matter if all the forms in the present tense are different from each other; it only matters that all of them are complex. As we saw in Irish, a pro-drop language, each form in the present tense has the same ending *-rann*; but each of them is morphologically complex since it has an additional morpheme *-rann* to indicate present tense. Japanese also has a single present tense form *-ru* without Agreement as in:

43.   Yom-ru.
      (read–Present)
      I/you/he/she/we/they read/s.

Japanese is like Irish in having complex morphology in each present tense form and is therefore pro-drop.

The null subject parameter is then:

Null subjects are permitted in all and only languages with morphologically uniform inflectional paradigms. (Jaeggli and Safir, 1989)

This proposal redefines the pro-drop parameter as a parameter of the IP with two values: [+uniform] with all or no present tense inflections licenses *pro*, and [–uniform] with only some inflections does not license *pro*. The identification of *pro* takes place either through inflections or through the discourse factors of the topic. The new analysis solves the problem of how Spanish and Chinese fall into the same pro-drop group. It does raise the new problem of why German, which has full inflections, is non-pro-drop; Jaeggli and Safir (1989) claim that, while *pro* might well be licensed in German, it could not be identified because the Verb-second movement separates tense and AGR into different nodes; the fact that *pro* is licensed, however, means that expletive subjects may be omitted in German, unlike English, since expletives do not need identifying:

44.   Regnet darausen.
      (*Rains outside)
      It's raining outside.

Hyams (1992, p. 262) claims 'the early grammar is a null-subject grammar in which a null pronominal subject (*pro*) is licensed by morphological uniformity'. Morphological uniformity has been tested against first language acquisition more by reasoning from old data than from new evidence (see, however, Weissenborn, 1992). Some second language acquisition research has tackled the topic more directly. Lakshmanan (1991) looked at three child L2 learners of English, analysing published transcripts. The hypothesis was that, at the stage when children had null subjects, they should lack inflections. She analysed transcripts from the Cancino, Rosansky and Schumann (1978) longitudinal study of Spanish learners of English. This showed that the rapid drop-off in null subjects was not accompanied by a rise in third person -*s* for some ten weeks; hence these two features do not appear to go together. Hilles (1991) looked at six L2 learners from three age-groups, some of them also from the Cancino et al. (1978) study. She concludes that in Marta's development 'the acquisition of pronominal subjects and inflections seems to be intertwined', apparently in contradiction of Lakshmanan (1991). Meisel (1991) found variation between learners in the extent to which null subjects correlated with lack of inflections. Of course none of this precisely proves the point of morphological uniformity, which would mean demonstrating a correlation between the child knowing that the language has all, no, or some inflections in the present tense and the use of null subjects.

The morphological uniformity solution raises as many problems as it solves. Firstly the child has a kind of mental grid for the present tense in which some, all, or none of the cells can be filled in. While the setting is binary, the grid is multiple. The model of language acquisition differs from the one used with other parameter settings (which does not mean that it is necessarily wrong). This is a separate issue from the evidence necessary for setting pro-drop, which might still be the presence or absence of expletive subjects and stressed pronouns. Secondly, why is the morphology of the present tense given such a central role? Why not past tense forms? Gender forms, and so on? The choice of the present tense as the determining aspect of morphology seems arbitrary. For instance, is the six-part paradigm adequate? As well as a singular/plural contrast, many languages have a dual form for two people, as did Old English. Many languages also have different inflections for different genders. The grid for present tense inflections could well be much larger than a six-cell paradigm. Take a full paradigm for the present tense of the Moroccan Arabic Verb *tkəlm* (speak), supplied by Malika Jmila. Moroccan Arabic has distinctions not only for singular and dual, but also for masculine and feminine.

Paradigm for the present tense inflections in Moroccan Arabic

1st person singular	tkəlm-t
2nd person masculine singular	tkəlm-t
2nd person feminine singular	tkəlm-ti
3rd person masculine singular	tkəlm
3rd person feminine singular	tkəlm-at
1st person masc/fem dual	tkəlm-na
2nd person masc/fem dual	tkəlm-tum
3rd person masc/fem dual	tkəlm-u
1st person masc/fem plural	tkəlm-u
2nd person masculine plural	tkəlm-u
2nd person feminine plural	tkəlm-tu
3rd person masc/fem plural	tkəlm-u

Moroccan Arabic fails the requirement for all forms in the six-part paradigm to be complex since the third person masculine singular is the base from *tkəlm*; yet it is clearly morphologically complex in all the other possible eleven forms; it is indeed a pro-drop language. Mühlhäusler and Harré (1990) argue that the restriction to a six-part Verb paradigm is Western centrism. In addition, languages vary in number at least up to the singular/dual/trial/plural distinction of Fijian (Anderson and Keenan, 1985).

What should then be the basis for morphological uniformity? Does the child have a grid with six cells, twelve cells, or what?

So far the presence of *pro* in a grammar has depended upon the properties of I. What happens when there is no I, as the missing functional categories analysis claims for early child language? In one version, the apparent propensity of young children to have null subjects has nothing to do with adult pro-drop. The first null-subject stage is a by-product of the missing functional categories. This still leaves open the question of how the pro-drop setting proper is learnt when it is needed.

Finally, in an approach within the Minimalist Programme, Speas (1994) utilizes the Principle of Economy to suggest that languages vary over whether affixes are generated in the syntax or in the lexicon. If there is either a morpheme in AGR or no AGR, a null subject is possible, hence a pro-drop language; if AGR is already attached to the Verb, it cannot project, hence a non-pro-drop language. Children therefore have to set a parameter about whether inflection is lexical or syntactic; this proposal is neutral about whether children start with AGRP or acquire an AGRP at some point.

Approaches to null-subject sentences in children's language

Morphological uniformity

'Null subjects are permitted in all and only languages with morphologically uniform inflectional paradigms' (Jaeggli and Safir, 1989)
— a language is morphologically uniform if *all*, or *none*, of its present tense forms are morphologically complex, for example Japanese (all complex) and Chinese (none complex)
— a language is morphologically mixed if *some*, but not all, of its present tense forms are morphologically complex, for example English

Missing functional categories analysis of null subjects

— missing subjects are empty NP specifiers within the VP, not *pro*
— missing objects are equally possible
— the true pro-drop parameter only comes into play when the child gets an AGRP into which the subject can be moved

Access to Universal Grammar in Second Language Acquisition

The question of whether L2 learners have access to UG has been perhaps the main topic of research among those interested in applying principles and parameters theory to second language acquisition. The poverty-of-the-stimulus argument led to the conclusion that some L2 learners know things they could not have acquired from the environment. In L1 learning such knowledge is attributed to the inherent properties of the mind – Universal Grammar. In L2 learning this has to be qualified because of the differences in both S_i and S_t, the distinctive initial and terminal states of L2 learning. What could be the role of UG in L2 learning? Cook (1985) put it as a choice between three possibilities. One is that L2 learners start from scratch; they have *direct access* to UG and are uninfluenced by the L1. Or they start from their knowledge of the first language; they have *indirect access* to UG via the L1. Or they do not treat the L2 as a language at all; they have *no access* to UG and learn the L2 without its help. One small terminological pitfall is that, while in the L1 we can distinguish 'learners' from 'speakers', in the L2 people who have learnt an L2 are often still called 'learners'.

Let us spell out these three alternatives and some of the evidence for them.

Direct access to UG

L2 learners may employ the principles of UG and set the parameters without any reference to their L1 values. L2 speakers have parallel competences in L1 and L2 – two instantiations of UG. This metaphor can be put as figure 8.1. The relationship between L1 learning and Universal Grammar leads to L1 competence (S_s); the relationship between L2 learning and Universal Grammar leads to L2 competence (S_t).

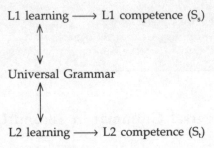

L1 learning ⟶ L1 competence (S_s)

Universal Grammar

L2 learning ⟶ L2 competence (S_t)

Figure 8.1 Direct Access model of L2 learning

If L2 learners have the same access to UG as L1 children, L2 speakers should possess the same linguistic competence as L1 adults. The poverty-of-the-stimulus argument applies to L2 learning in so far as anything that the L2 speaker could not have learnt from the environment must be a property of the human mind.

One way of demonstrating that L2 learners have direct access is to show that they indeed know principles and parameters they could not have learnt. A test of access to UG can be whether L2 learners of English who do not have movement in their L1 display structure-dependency for movement in the L2. White (1989) cites research by Otsu and Naoi (1986) where Japanese learners of English indeed demonstrate a knowledge of structure-dependency. The MUGtest (Cook, in preparation) tested knowledge of several principles and parameters with L2 learners of English from different countries; at present it has been carried out with groups from Hong Kong, Japan, Poland, and Finland, and different groups of native speakers. Chapter 2 described how some languages need the principle of structure-dependency for movement, and some do not. As we saw in chapter 3, groups of Japanese and Chinese learners strongly reject sentences on the MUGtest like:

45. *Is Sam is the cat that brown?

So at least the principle of structure-dependency is known by L2 learners. The status of this as an independent principle of UG is now suspect since it may be a side-effect of the all-encompassing Empty Category Principle (Culicover, 1991). But, even if it is relabelled as something else, knowledge of some aspect of language has been acquired in an L2 that is not learnable from input, that was not part of the learners' L1, and that is unlikely to have been taught by language teachers.

Indirect access to UG

L2 learning might also take the L1 instantiation of the UG steady state S_s as a springboard and utilize the principles and parameters in the same way in the new language as in the first. Figure 8.2 reflects this possibility. L2 learning has access to L1 competence, which was ultimately based on UG. L2 competence will only reflect those parts of UG that are made use of in the L1.

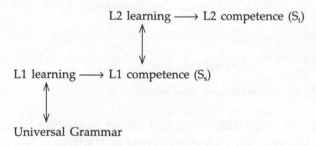

Figure 8.2 Indirect Access model of L2 learning

In indirect access, L2 knowledge is tied into L1 knowledge. For instance, speakers of Japanese would have to learn over time that English needs structure-dependency and subjacency for movement, without making use of UG, since these are not required in their L1; L2 learners would necessarily start from the L1 settings for the parameters, whatever these may be.

The knowledge of parameter settings is thus crucial. Chapter 3 described the finding of White (1986) that Spanish learners at first carry over the pro-drop setting from the L1 to the L2. Zobl (1990) found that Japanese learners at different levels of English produced a very low percentage of null subjects, 2 per cent or less, compared to Spanish learners, despite Japanese being a pro-drop language. Flynn (1987) also found a difference between Spanish and Japanese learners on the head direction parameter. The MUGtest nevertheless found that Japanese teachers of English accepted the sentence *Is French* 39 per cent of the time. While knowledge of L2s also involves knowledge of parameter settings, it is often more complicated than this, with differences between languages that have the same setting. But in this case the evidence goes in favour of indirect access since the L1 setting of parameters seems by and large to be transferred to the L2.

No access to UG

Second languages might also be acquired through non-natural means – other faculties of the mind than language. In the no-access model, L2 competence is distinct from L1 competence and created in a totally different way.

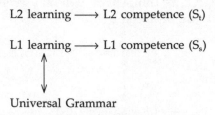

Figure 8.3 No Access model of L2 learning

L2 learning might differ from L1 learning in making no use of UG; a second language can be learnt to some extent from a grammar book or from drills. L2 learning in this case is a parallel process to L1 learning, but without any connection to UG.

Several types of evidence are claimed to demonstrate no access to UG in L2 learning. Clahsen and Muysken (1986) found different sequences of acquisition for L2 and L1 learning of German: L1 learners started with the correct underlying SOV order even if this yielded sentences that were wrong; L2 learners started with the correct surface SVO order even if they were wrong in the underlying structure. The L2 sequence was claimed to demonstrate lack of access to UG: 'by fixing on an initial assumption of SVO order, and then elaborating a series of complicated rules to patch up this hypothesis when confronted with conflicting data, the L2 learners are not only creating a rule system which is far more complicated than the native system, but also one which is not definable in linguistic theory' (Clahsen and Muysken, 1986, p. 116). A second area that has been widely claimed to support no access is subjacency. Bley-Vroman, Felix and Ioup (1988) found that only slightly over half of the L2 subjects they tested knew subjacency in sentences such as:

46.   *What did Sam believe the claim that Mary had bought?

Johnson and Newport (1991) too found that Chinese learners of English scored consistently below natives at subjacency.

General arguments in favour of no access are: the knowledge of the L2 is not so complete (Schachter, 1988; Bley-Vroman, 1989); some L2s are more difficult to learn than others (Schachter, 1988); the L2 gets fossilized (Schachter, 1988); and L2 learners vary in ways that L1 learners do not. The proponents of no access have therefore sought to find explanations for how it is possible to learn an L2 without UG; the typical solution is seen as general problem-solving combined with the knowledge of the L1 (Bley-Vroman, 1989).

One interpretation of no access is that the implications are different for principles and for parameters. The assumption behind access that has been made so far is that principles need to be reinstantiated, parameters to be reset; in direct access these are based on UG, in indirect access on the L1. Clahsen and Muysken (1989), however, propose that principles are available for L2 acquisition via the L1, but parameters cannot be reset: L2 learners carry over from the L1 knowledge of subjacency, the Case Filter, etc.; they cannot reset parameters such as bounding nodes, governing category, etc. A more radical reevaluation of the relative importance of principles and parameters is presented by Tsimpli and Roussou (1991) who likewise claim that parameters are not resettable in L2 learning but go on to assert that principles can be reinterpreted in L2 learning; Greek L2 learners of English discover that English does not allow null subjects by reanalysing subject pronouns as heads of AGRP, as may be done in Greek, but they have more acute problems with *that-trace* as this is a parameter.

Some researchers are then adamant in their belief that there is no access to UG in L2 learning. The problem in choosing between these three models of access is that they might be true for different learners, or for different aspects of language for the same learner; L2 learning depends on an interaction between learner and situation, unlike first language acquisition. Versions of all three have been advocated in language teaching: a translation model of teaching implies indirect access in that the learner creates S_t by relating the L2 constantly to the L1; the communicative approach and the direct method imply direct access since they rely on the target language; techniques of grammatical explanation imply no access and exploit other faculties of the mind. The problem for language teachers is that undoubtedly all of these teaching methods have produced some successful L2 learners; the dispute in language teaching is over the proportion of successes to failures. Hence in a sense all access models are possible.

The view developed in Cook (1994) is that the issue of access is a red herring. The explanatory diagrams used earlier all separated three objects – the processes of learning, the output of linguistic competence, and Universal Grammar; they were variants of one proto-diagram.

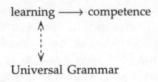

Figure 8.4   Implicit metaphor in access models of L2 learning

The overall metaphor in much of the access research is that learning draws on UG to produce competence.

First let us recall the LAD metaphor in which language input goes into a black box and competence comes out; here UG is not something separate from learning; it *is* the very process through which learning takes place. The access metaphor is wrong in creating two objects, learning and UG, and asking if one has access to the other; if learning is combined with UG into one object, the question of whether UG has access to itself is meaningless. This is not, of course, believed by most L2 researchers; Clahsen and Muysken (1989) for example retain UG as a learning device, but subdivided into two components – transferable principles and non-resettable parameters.

Secondly, chapter 3 described the states metaphor of acquisition in which the initial state S_0 of the mind becomes S_s, the initial L2 state S_i become S_t. It is not that the separate learning component has a product, linguistic competence; it is that the initial state (UG) changes into the steady state: competence = UG + data. There is no division between learning and its product; there is no product of learning other than a changed state of the knowledge in the mind. So the access metaphor reifies three objects – learning, UG, and competence – none of which has any real independent existence. The access question is an artefact of this conceptualization. Any answers to the question of whether L2 learning has access to UG are as meaningless as debating how much calcium unicorns need to develop their horns properly. This is obviously a personal view untypical of the field; to avoid dwelling on it too much, the reader is referred to the discussion in Cook (1993; in preparation), which employs the concept of **multi-competence** – knowledge of more than one language by the same person – as a way out.

Maturation and Universal Grammar

One difficulty with the principles and parameters position in language acquisition is that children do not instantaneously acquire parameter settings as soon as they hear a sentence or two of the language. Instead parameter setting is a process that stretches over years. But, if parameters are triggered by input, why can't children set their values in the first few minutes of hearing their parents' speech? Various possibilities come to mind. One is the other areas of development related to language; perhaps the child has deficient performance processes, a working memory capacity that is constrained, and so on; certainly the child's sentences seem to increase gradually in length and complexity, so that the MLU (Mean Length of Utterance) measure can be successfully used to assess their development for some years. Another possible explanation is properties of the input; perhaps certain structures are more frequent than others or are more salient for the child. But none of these seem strong enough or regular enough to account for the child's gradual acquisition of language through a series of set and uniform stages. Perhaps the explanation is really that all of UG is not available from the start.

Chapter 3 suggested that Universal Grammar might either be present from the beginning of the child's development or might come into being as the child grows. The *continuity hypothesis*, as formulated by Pinker (1984), claims that the principles the child possesses remain the same throughout acquisition; the child is equally subject to UG at all ages; the child's grammars will always conform to UG, even if concealed from us by the shortness of the child's sentences, etc. Weissenborn, Goodluck and Roeper (1992a) divide the concept of continuity in two: the 'strong continuity hypothesis', which claims the child's grammar contains all the principles of UG from the beginning in the form used in the target language; and the 'weak continuity hypothesis' in which the child's grammar conforms to UG but not necessarily to the target language. A *maturational hypothesis* on the other hand claims that certain principles emerge in the mind at particular times. The child's grammar depends on UG so far as the principles that have emerged are concerned but may be radically different in other areas that have not yet come into being. The third possibility would be a true *discontinuity hypothesis*; principles are actually different at different stages; the child's grammar at a particular stage might conform to UG in no wise, and would then have to change totally, as a caterpillar metamorphoses into a butterfly. The continuity hypothesis sees the language faculty as like the heart which is structurally complete from birth; the maturational hypothesis sees it as like the teeth which come into being over time. So children's grammars are either essentially the same in terms of principles and parameters as adult grammars, or have a selection of the same principles and parameters as adults', or have different principles altogether.

The starting point for much discussion of maturation has been Borer and Wexler (1987). Their chief argument relies on the emergence of the passive in children's speech. Chapter 6 showed how the passive consists of movement from a D-structure such as:

47.   *e* opened the door by the butler.

to an S-structure:

48.   The door was opened by the butler.

The *verb + past participle* construction is, however, used in a variety of ways, according to Svartvik (1966), ranging from a passive with complete interchangeability with the active:

49.   He was given this puppy by a farmer in the Welsh hills.

through 'quasi-passives' that may have both passive and adjectival properties such as:

50.   Watson felt compelled to call up Pratt.

all the way to non-agentive passives that have slight connection to the active as in:

51.   A tray on which was tastefully arranged a bowl of turtle soup.

Borer and Wexler (1987) concentrated on the learnability problem of the adjectival construction; this is differentiated from the pure passive in that *very* can be added to it:

52.   He was (very) interested in astrology.

Adjectival passives are treated, roughly speaking, as adjectives formed by adding *-ed* in the lexicon rather than as parts of the Verb involved in syntax. Their lexical entries may differ from those of their verbal homophones; for example the Adjective *interested* requires a following PP with *in* but debars the Agent:

53.   *He was very interested in linguistics by his friend.

Borer and Wexler (1987) claim that children learn adjectival before verbal forms, though both have the same amount of morphological complexity, i.e. end in the passive morpheme *-ed*; they also learn passives without *by* Agents before those with Agents. Typical early passives are:

54.   Tree is broken.

and:

55.   Lamp got kicked.

At the same time as children lack passives, they use wh-questions. What then prevents them from producing verbal passives when they are capable of producing wh-questions, which seem equally complex and equally dependent on movement? Chapter 6 distinguished A-chains that relate one A-position to another, such as NP-movement, from non-A-chains that describe movement from an A-position to a non-A-position, such as wh-movement. Borer and Wexler (1987, p. 149) claim the child does not possess 'the machinery that will enable him/her to assign that θ-role non-locally, using an A-chain'; in other words young children are unable to form A-chains. Consequently they cannot produce the verbal passive and Agent *by*-phrases. They can produce wh-questions because they are able to use non-A-chains. Children cannot use A-chains because this ability is not yet available in their minds; the child's mind has to reach a particular level of maturation to be capable of forming A-chains.

Borer and Wexler (1987) argue in favour of maturation; the child's grammars conform to whatever principles and parameters they possess at a given moment and change as the mental organ of language grows. There has, however, been some dispute over the accuracy of their description of children's passives; Pinker, Lebeaux and Frost (1987) claim that Agent *by*-phrases in fact occur early in children's speech.

Clearly the missing functional categories analysis is ammunition for either maturational or discontinuity accounts. Functional categories differ from lexical categories in many ways, as we saw in the display on page 187: they do not have 'descriptive' content; they do not always have a physical realization in the sentence; they are usually inflections rather than words; they are usually unstressed; they are semantically more complex than lexical categories. If a point of development is reached at 24±4 months at which functional categories come 'on line', as Radford (1990) puts it, any of these might be the reason for their delayed acquisition. First at around 20 months the child acquires the ability to produce lexical structures, i.e. the VP analysis above with the specification of the direction of θ-government; this can be called a 'lexical-thematic' stage (Radford, 1990). Then at around 24 months the child acquires the functional categories IP, CP, DP, etc., complete with their parameters; this is the 'functional-non-thematic' stage (Radford, 1990). This fits in well with the Functional Parameterization Hypothesis in that parameters are acquired en bloc when the functional categories become available, apart from the awkward exception of the parameter for direction of θ-government that affects word order. The child's mind does not possess functional categories till this stage; lexical categories are present from the beginning; functional categories develop at a particular maturational point. Gleitman's discontinuity view was that the child's language metamorphoses from a semantic to a grammatical phase. The missing functional categories analysis brings this within a maturational account by seeing this shift, not as an abrupt change from one type of language organization to another, but as the consequence of the emergence of functional categories in the mind without discarding the earlier organization; it is maturation rather than discontinuity.

As mentioned earlier, there are problems of evidence for these early stages of language acquisition: so much is missing from the child's language that an argument based primarily on absence is hard to sustain. The logical counter-position would be that UG is indeed present in the mind complete with all functional and lexical categories; but something prevents the child from utilizing UG fully, as encountered in the performance explanation of null subjects (Bloom, 1990). An influential work on phonological acquisition (Smith, 1973) claimed that the child's speech could best be described as adult competence with the addition of 'deformation' rules. To maintain a continuity hypothesis, it is necessary to claim that some other aspect of the child prior to 24 months hinders the knowledge of functional categories, perhaps limitations on the performance processes for handing the specialized formal characteristics of functional categories.

The question of maturation has from the early days been associated with Lenneberg's *Critical Period Hypothesis* (CPH) (Lenneberg, 1967). This claims that there is a critical period during which the human mind is able to learn language; before or after this period language cannot be acquired in a natural fashion. The ability to learn language disappears after a particular point in the early teens. UG is no longer available after a particular point of maturation; just as the milk teeth drop out, so UG becomes defunct. The reason for this is variously held to be physical developments such as loss of brain plasticity (Penfield and Roberts, 1959) and the specialization of brain functions to one hemisphere (Lenneberg, 1967), or cognitive development such as the transition to the Piagetan stage of formal operational thinking (Tremaine, 1975; Felix, 1978). The formulation of UG as a system of principles and parameters permits the Critical Period Hypothesis to be phrased in more precise terms, as Ritchie (1983) points out. Clear evidence for the critical period is hard to come by in first language acquisition since after the early teens this typically concerns the regaining of competence destroyed by some physical or mental trauma rather than 'normal' acquisition. Gleitman (1984, p. 578) has nevertheless observed that in deaf people learning American Sign Language 'the character of final knowledge of the manual language is predictable from the age of the learner at first exposure, independent of the number of years the individual subsequently used it'.

So the Critical Period Hypothesis often falls back on L2 learning to bolster its arguments. Lenneberg insisted that the fact that a person over 40 can learn to communicate in a foreign language 'does not trouble our basic assumption that the cerebral organisation for language learning as such has taken place during childhood and since natural languages tend to resemble each other in many fundamental aspects . . . the matrix for language skills is present' (Lenneberg, 1967, p. 176). Interpreted in terms of UG, the CPH claim is that the direct access model is unavailable to older learners, for whom L2 learning depends either on the L1 or on other aspects of the mind. The existing research does not support the popular idea of adult deficiency in L2 learning with any great authority; the weight of the evidence is summed up in Singleton (1989): 'The one interpretation of the evidence which does not appear to run into contradictory data is that in naturalistic situations those whose exposure to a second language begins in childhood in general eventually surpass those whose exposure begins in adulthood, even though the latter usually show some initial advantage over the former.' Nor does the Critical Period Hypothesis succeed in evading the poverty-of-the-stimulus argument. As Chomsky has pointed out, 'while it may be true that "once some language is available, acquisition of others is relatively easy", it nevertheless remains a very serious problem – not significantly different from the problem of explaining first language acquisition – to account for this fact' (Chomsky, 1972a, p. 175). The mere possession of an L1 cannot explain the acquisition of new settings for UG parameters.

The spate of research into the no access position can be readily used as evidence in this argument. It may be not so much that L2 learning is different from first language acquisition, as that L2 learners are often *older* than children acquiring an L1. There are two sub-questions. One is whether the possession of an L1 prevents access to UG; in chronological terms perhaps learning one language prevents another being learnt in the same way. The other is whether access to UG depends upon age. Since much of the L2 research has been done with adults, it is not as yet possible to distinguish these two possibilities clearly. However, part of the research by Johnson and Newport (1991) was aimed at exploring whether access to subjacency varied with age. One type of sentence tested whether L2 learners had access to UG through subjacency violations such as:

56.   *What did the teacher know the fact that Janet liked?

Another type were 'no-inversion' sentences like:

57.   *What the teacher did know that Janet liked?

These were ungrammatical but allegedly did not involve UG violations. They found that the learners' success declined consistently with their age of arrival in the USA for *both* types: 'the changes that occur between childhood and adulthood in language learning seem to affect all aspects of grammar acquisition, including access to UG' (Johnson and Newport, 1991, p. 44). There are some problems with the interpretation of the grammatical foundation of these data (Cook, 1993); for instance it seems odd that the ungrammatical non-UG sentences have *do-support* without anything to support. What seems to be needed is research that directly compares L1 acquisition, L2 acquisition by young children, and L2 acquisition by adults in closely similar circumstances.

Binding Parameters and Acquisition of Binding Theory

Binding Theory was first mentioned in chapter 2, where the basic distinction between anaphors and pronominals was introduced. Chapter 3 gave a brief discussion of some of the findings of work on the acquisition of the Binding Theory, and chapter 7 gave a more detailed account of the role government plays in defining the governing category. This section extends the discussion to consider the ways in which binding phenomena differ cross-linguistically and the implications that this has for the acquisition of the Binding Principles, keeping to the type of account of binding used so far.

One of the major ways in which binding differs between languages concerns the definition of the governing category: some languages allow for a relatively small local domain and others allow it to be as large as the matrix clause. Of course, the result of this is that, in some languages, anaphors can take only local antecedents and in others their antecedents can be some distance away from them. Exactly the opposite applies for pronominals: the larger the governing category, the further away a possible antecedent must be: the pronominal must be free within its governing category.

For example, English allows for a relatively small governing category. We have usually equated this to the smallest clause containing the pronoun. However, the governing category can sometimes be as small as an NP:

58. *Bill read Mary's novel about himself.

Here the reflexive pronoun cannot refer to the subject of the clause that contains it as the NP acts as its governing category (note the sentence would be fine with *himself* replaced with *herself*). The explanation is that the NP contains a possessor element, *Mary's*, and that this acts as the 'subject' of the NP. If the governing category is defined by the presence of a subject, the governing category for English will either be a clause (which always has a subject by the Extended Projection Principle) or an NP with a possessor, whichever is the smallest category containing the pronominal.

However, other languages are not as restrictive as English. For example, Italian allows a reflexive to refer out of an NP with a possessor:

59. Maria$_i$ guardo$_i$ i   ritratti   di sè$_i$ di Mario.
     Maria looked-at the pictures of self of Mario
     Maria looked at Mario's pictures of herself.

Norwegian allows a reflexive to refer out of an infinitival clause:

60. Knut$_i$ ba   Ola korrigere seg$_i$.
     Knut asked Ola to correct self
     Knut asked Ola to correct himself.

Icelandic allows a reflexive to refer out of a subjunctive clause:

61. Jón$_i$ segir að   María elski   sig$_i$.
     John said that Maria loves(subj) self
     John said that Maria loves himself.

Finally, Japanese allows a reflexive to take its antecedent anywhere in the matrix clause, even out of a containing tensed finite clause:

62. John$_i$-wa Sarah-ga Mary-no   zibun$_i$-ni taisuru.
     John-topic Sarah-sub Mary-poss self-dat   towards
     taito-o   hinansita-to   omotte iru
     attitude-acc criticize-comp think
     John thinks that Sarah criticized Mary's attitude towards himself.

Wexler and Manzini (1987) offer an account of this phenomenon with the following parameterized definition of the governing category:

The Governing Category Parameter
β is the governing category for α iff β is the minimal category which contains α and a governor for α and:
(a) a subject; or
(b) an inflection; or
(c) a tense; or
(d) an indicative tense; or
(e) a root tense.

English is associated with value (a) of this parameter as any category with a subject can act as a governing category. Italian takes value (b), as only clauses and not NPs have inflections. Norwegian takes value (c), Icelandic value (d) and Japanese value (e). Actually, as Norwegian does not have subjunctive clauses, it might be argued that the same result would be achieved if Norwegian were associated with value (c) or (d). However, lacking a subjunctive, it makes little sense to claim that the governing category for Norwegian is the minimal indicative clause, so we shall continue to assume that Norwegian selects value (c).

Although we have only demonstrated how this parameter works with anaphors, the same values apply for pronominals as well. To keep the discussion as simple as possible, however, we will restrict our attention to anaphors. The most influential aspect of the Wexler and Manzini (1987) proposal is their learning theory. Concentrating on anaphors, we can see that as each of the governing categories defined by the governing category parameter values from (a) to (e) is potentially bigger than the previous one, they allow for the antecedent of a reflexive to be further and further away from it. Consider the following abstract structure:

63. $[_{S1}\ A\ [_{S2}\ B\ [_{S3}\ C\ [_{S4}\ D\ [_{NP}\ E\ \alpha]]]]]$

where S1 is the root clause, S2 is an indicative finite clause, S3 a subjunctive clause, S4 an infinitival clause, E is the possessor of the NP and α is an anaphor. If this were an English sentence, only E would be available as an antecedent for α as the NP would be the governing category. If this were Italian, both E and D would be possible antecedents as S4 rather than the NP would be the governing category. C, D and E would be possible antecedents in Norwegian, and so on (noting again that as there is no subjunctive in Norwegian, S3 must be taken simply as a finite clause). The important point is that each successive language allows a greater number of possible antecedents for anaphors than the previous ones.

This situation gives rise to a learning problem. One of the things that children must acquire when acquiring the Binding Theory is the value of the governing category parameter to set for their particular language. Suppose that the target language is English. The child might initially suppose that the correct value is (e), which would of course be wrong. But how can the child find out that this is wrong? Recall that chapter 3 suggested that the only sort of data reliably available to the child are positive: negative data in the form of corrections or expansions seem not to be available in a usable form. But it will be impossible for a child who has selected too large a governing category to reverse this decision and choose a smaller one on the basis of positive data alone: every sentence heard will be perfectly compatible with the value chosen; the child will just not hear many sentences that should be grammatical given the selected value.

This is one instance of the **Subset Problem** for language acquisition, the solution being to adopt the Subset Principle, mentioned in chapter 3. This Principle guides the child to try certain parameter values before others. In particular it guides the child to select the most restrictive option available first, and only to reject this when positive data show it to be wrong. Thus, for the governing category parameter, the child will be guided by the Subset Principle to select value (a) first and will move towards value (e) only on presentation of positive data that the lower values are incorrect.

These considerations have a number of implications for the child's acquisition of the Binding Theory. The main issue arising out of research into this area, as reported in chapter 3, is that at an earlier age children seem to perform better with anaphors. Wexler and Chien (1985), for example, report that children of around $6\frac{1}{2}$ years perform at more or less adult levels in using anaphors, but their use of pronominals at the same age stays between 50 and 70 per cent accuracy. Deutsch et al. (1986) report that it is only after anaphors seem to have been mastered that there is much improvement in children's use of pronominals. The question is, why should this be so? There are a number of possibilities. First, some people have believed that children initially misanalyse pronominals as anaphors and therefore they are willing to give a pronominal a too close antecedent (Jakubowicz, 1984; Solan, 1987; and Lust et al., 1989). However, there are reasons to believe that this is not the explanation for children's poor performance with pronominals. Wexler and Manzini (1987) point out that children use unbound pronominals from an early age, which would be unexpected it they thought they were anaphors.

Moreover, as Grimshaw and Rosen (1990) point out, if children thought pronominals were anaphors, this would not explain why they consistently perform at above chance levels with pronominals (even if their performance is less accurate than with anaphors) and their performance with pronominals would be expected to worsen as their performance with anaphors improves, which it does not. The overall conclusion would therefore seem that children know from an early age that anaphors are anaphors and that pronominals are pronominals.

Another possible explanation for the discrepancy in children's performance with anaphors and pronominals is that while Principle A of the Binding Theory is present at an early stage of language development, Principle B develops later (Montalbetti and Wexler, 1985; Wexler and Chien, 1985; and Chien and Wexler, 1987). Again, however, there are problems facing this proposal. If Principle B is not present in the early child grammar, what principle governs the behaviour of pronominals in their language? As we have seen above, it is certainly not Principle A: this would amount to the same as claiming that pronominals are treated as anaphors. Pronominals are also not unrestricted in early child grammars either: they do not use them randomly and, if anything, there is a tendency to treat them in accordance with Principle B, if not entirely accurately. Grimshaw and Rosen (1990) have shown that while children may perform near chance levels at accepting or rejecting sentences which violate Principle B, they actually accept sentences that conform to Principle B 83.3 per cent of the time. If there were no Principle B in the child's grammar, we should expect them to perform randomly with grammatical sentences as well as ungrammatical ones. Again, then, the evidence seems to point in the direction of Principle B being present in the child's grammar from an early stage. Grimshaw and Rosen (1990) argue that it is not lack of knowledge that causes children to perform badly with pronominals, but that this is a consequence of the experiments that have been used to test children's knowledge. For example, a typical task asked a child to report on the accuracy of a statement like *Teddy tickled him*, after watching two puppets act out a situation in which one tickles the other. Grimshaw and Rosen point out that this obviously involves more than the Binding Principles governing the use of pronouns in normal language: there are certain pragmatic principles that, for example, require us to use pronouns only if their referents have been previously fixed in the discourse. We do not tend to say things like *He's a good footballer* without indicating in some way who *he* refers to. So, faced with a situation in which a child hears the sentence *Teddy tickled him*, children are forced into an impossible situation: either they must assume that the adult has violated the pragmatic principle and is using a pronoun without identifying the referent, or that the adult means the referent to be the subject of the sentence, which of course is a binding violation. Given the choice, children seem to opt randomly between these two interpretations of the situation and hence will sometimes appear as though they are not aware of Principle B. In short, Grimshaw and Rosen claim that it is not that children do not know Principle B, but that they are prone to disobey it in certain contexts.

Note that the same is not true of Principle A, as in this case the grammatical and pragmatic principles largely coincide: a sentence which conforms to Principle A also conforms to the pragmatic requirement that the referent be present in the discourse.

For Grimshaw and Rosen, the principles of the Binding Theory are present in the child's grammar from the start. However, their position, while making much sense, still does not account for a number of observations. The fact is that there is development in children's use of anaphors and pronouns, whether this is learning knowledge of grammatical principles or obedience of them. Grimshaw and Rosen have only vague suggestions as to why, as children grow older, they become more prone to disobey the pragmatic principle governing pronoun usage in experimental situations rather than the grammatical one, and they do not mention the development of obedience to Principle A which takes place between the ages of $2\frac{1}{2}$ and $6\frac{1}{2}$. Furthermore, as pointed out in Newson (1990), it seems more than just coincidence that the development in performance with pronominals starts after such development is complete for anaphors. It is claimed in Newson (1990) that children do develop knowledge of certain aspects of Binding Theory, but this does not relate to the categorical status of pronouns, whether they are anaphors or pronominals, nor to the Binding Principles themselves. What children seem to lack is knowledge of what counts as the domain within which anaphors must be bound and pronominals free. In other words, they do not know the correct setting for the Governing Category Parameter. The later development of pronominals can be accounted for if we assume that the learning of pronominals is somehow dependent on that of anaphors. This can be done through the suggestion of a learning mechanism, a Lexical Dependency, which transfers parameter settings learned for certain elements to others; i.e. from anaphors to pronominals. Thus the parameter settings for anaphors must be learned first and then these are transferred to pronominals.

The debate is, of course, far from settled. But the important point to note here is that the grammatical theory has spawned a good deal of actual child language acquisition investigation: a clear indication that there is a growing connection between the two areas.

Second language acquisition research has also been actively involved with binding, as surveyed in Cook (1993, chapter 8). The comprehension experiment in Cook (1990b) compared L2 learners of English who had L1s with different settings for the Governing Category Parameter; this showed a similarity amongst the learners in terms both of difficulty order and of speed of answer depending on the different domains involved in the sentence; but the results did not support the Subset Principle because anaphors had the same pattern of responses as pronominals rather than the reverse. Finer and Broselow (1985) found an intriguing tendency for learners to adopt a setting that was neither their L1 nor their L2, but in between; Thomas (1989), however, found no difference between Spanish and Chinese learners of English with very different L1 settings although both performed well below native levels. In terms of the distinction put forward by Grimshaw and Rosen (1990), most of the second language acquisition research demonstrates that L2 learners of English 'know' the Binding Principles even if they do not fully 'obey' them, another example of UG being available in the L2 but to a lesser extent than in the L1.

Binding Parameters and Acquisition of Binding Theory

The Governing Category Parameter (Wexler and Manzini, 1987)
β is the governing category for α iff β is the minimal category which
   contains α and a governor for α and:
   (a)   a subject; or
   (b)   an inflection; or
   (c)   a tense; or
   (d)   an indicative tense; or
   (e)   a root tense

Accounts of the late development of pronominals

Pronominals as anaphors
Children misanalyse pronominals as anaphors and therefore give them
   too close antecedents.

Missing Principle B
Principle B is missing in early child grammars and hence children are
   unable to comply with it in their use of pronominals.

Disobedience of Principle B
The experimental situation forces children to make a choice between
   disobeying Binding Theory or pragmatic principles: they randomly
   opt for one of these strategies.

Lexical Dependencies
Children know Binding Principles and the categorization of pronouns
   from an early stage, but cannot set the Governing Category Parameter
   for pronominals until after this has been done for anaphors because
   a learning mechanism makes pronominals dependent on anaphors for
   their parameter settings.

The areas covered in this chapter represent a sample of those that are being investigated in contemporary research. The interested reader can pursue these and others in books such as Atkinson (1992) and collections such as Weissenborn et al. (1992b), Goodluck and Rochemont (1992), and Meisel (1990). Clearly they demonstrate that principles and parameters theory and language acquisition have made firm contact. The UG model of language acquisition is no longer based on the poverty-of-the-stimulus argument alone but on a wealth of factual information about children. The problems, as always, are that the theory of syntax changes so rapidly it is hard to keep the acquisition research in touch, and that the methodology of competence research using performance data is never fully settled. But, to come back to a theme in this book, much of the excitement of principles and parameters theory lies in this continuous tension between the pure theories of syntax and the messy facts of language acquisition, previously achieved perhaps only in the heyday of systemic grammar (Halliday, 1975).

9

A Sketch of the Minimalist Programme

This chapter will discuss the following topics:

— Why minimalism?
— A brief sketch of the minimalist framework
— How minimal can the Minimalist Programme get?
— Getting rid of D- and S-structure
— Getting rid of government
— Getting rid of X-bar.

This final chapter sketches some of the main aspects of Chomsky's most recent work to date, called the Minimalist Programme. The intention is to give the reader an insight into where the theory is going now, rather than a complete presentation. Needless to say, it avoids many of the technicalities that Chomsky himself addresses as well as much of the detail. This chapter starts by examining the reasons why the Minimalist Programme has been developed and moves on to an overall outline of how it works. Then a little more flesh is added to these bones by discussing some of the differences between the minimalist framework and 1980s theory.

Since the Minimalist Programme is very much work in progress, sources on it are not as yet easily available, apart from the original papers on which we have drawn here, namely Chomsky (1993; 1995b) and Lasnik (1993). In addition, Chomsky and Lasnik (1993) forms an important documentation of the transition between the earlier perspective and Minimalism. Readers will also find some of the issues are briefly introduced in the second edition of Liliane Haegeman's *Introduction to Government and Binding Theory* (1994); a useful account is provided in Marantz (1995). Readers should be on their guard that the Minimalist Programme is substantially different from any of the general accounts yet in print, even textbooks such as Ouhalla (1994).

We have termed the approach presented so far in this book 'principles and parameters theory'. The majority of the innovations in the Minimalist Programme do not depart from the basic concept of principles and parameters, only from the particular version of these proposed by Chomsky (1981a) and its subsequent development. So, as both approaches can be called principles and parameters theory with equal justification, a new term is needed for the earlier work; we will revive the term GB (Government and Binding) theory here as a convenient label for the earlier principles and parameters theory from, say, Chomsky (1981a) to Chomsky (1986b) – despite Chomsky's dislike of the term.

Why Minimalism?

Despite its radically different analyses, the Minimalist Programme is a progression rather than a complete U-turn. The overall aim continues the tradition of making statements about human language that are as simple and general as possible; 'From the early 1960s its [generative grammar] central objective was to abstract general principles from the complex rule systems devised for particular languages, leaving rules that are simple, constrained in their operation by these UG principles' (Chomsky, 1995b, p. 388). The minimalist framework continues this drive for simplification. In particular it draws on concepts from Chomsky's late 1980s papers, such as Full Interpretation and Economy of representation and derivation, which have already been discussed (see chapter 5 in particular). To recap, the principle of Full Interpretation claims that there are no redundant elements in the structure of the sentence: each element plays some role, whether semantic, syntactic, or phonological, and must be interpreted in some way. The Principle of Economy is a more general requirement that all representations and processes used to derive them be as economical as possible.

It is fairly easy to see how the Principle of Economy leads to minimalism: if the linguistic system needs to be as economical as possible, in terms of both how it represents and generates structures, clearly the smallest possible set of devices to account for language phenomena should be used – the defining characteristic of the Minimalist Programme. Economy of representation requires that representations of syntactic structure contain no more than the required elements (the principle of Full Interpretation may be a consequence of this condition).

But what elements *are* necessary? In Chomsky's earliest writing on this issue (Chomsky, 1991c), it was assumed that the answer to the question was elements that you could expect to find at any level of linguistic representation: 'we can also perceive at least the outlines of certain still more general principles, which we might think of as "guide-lines" . . . Some of these guidelines have a kind of "least effort" flavour to them, in the sense that they legislate against "superfluous elements" ' (Chomsky, 1991c, p. 418). That is to say, it was a general requirement with no implication about the number of levels involved.

In the grammar presented throughout this book, the linguistic system has been assumed to use two external interface levels, which are interpreted by the semantic and phonetic components, LF and PF, and an internal level that represents basic lexical information, D-structure. These three levels are connected by a single level of representation: S-structure. These combine to form the well-known (upside-down) T-model, redrawn here slightly from the figure in chapter 2 (page 47):

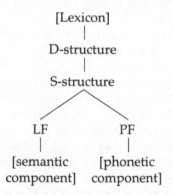

The Minimalist Programme questions whether all these levels of representation are really necessary. In Chomsky's most recent writing to date (1993, 1995b) it is argued that, since language is a mapping between sound and meaning, the only absolutely necessary representations are at the interfaces of the meaning and sound components of the linguistic system where language connects, on the one hand to the physical world of sounds, on the other to the mental world of cognition, as we saw in chapter 2. 'UG . . . must specify the properties of SDs [structural descriptions] and of the symbolic representations that enter into them. In particular, it must specify the interface levels, the elements that constitute these levels and the computations by which they are constructed. A particularly simple design for language would take the (conceptually necessary) interface levels to be the only levels' (Chomsky, 1993, p. 3).

So, in the minimalist famework, only LF and PF are really necessary and there is the possibility of doing away with D-structure and S-structure. Of course there must still be a lexicon and a 'computational system' which forms LF and PF representations from lexical information. 'The I-language consists of a computational procedure and a Lexicon' (Chomsky, 1995a, p. 15). Hence the ideal minimalist design would be something like:

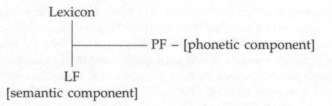

where the lines represent the computations that form the LF and PF representations, drawing from the lexicon.

The Minimalist Programme is also in part a reaction to some of the problems that have plagued GB theory. One problem that the GB perspective could only solve by fairly unconvincing stipulation is the definition of A- and A-bar-positions, as given in chapter 5. Under the early assumptions of GB theory, this distinction was unproblematic: an A-position was a potential θ-position, that is to say a position to which θ-roles may be assigned, such as complement of V; an A-bar-position such as specifier of CP could not have a θ-role assigned to it. In *Barriers* syntax the A-positions were the object (sister to a head) and the subject (specifier of the inflectional nodes). However, once the subject is seen to originate within the VP – as is typical of late GB theory and as has been adopted throughout this book – there are two subject positions: one is the original specifier position inside the VP and the other is the specifier position of AGRP, to which most subjects move. Both of these are required to be defined as A-positions since they are both subject positions, but this raises the problem of distinguishing A-from A-bar-positions: the specifier of AGRP is no more a potential θ-position than is the specifier of CP, yet the former is an A-position and the latter is an A-bar-position. Furthermore, the specifiers of both AGRP and CP have other things in common: they are both landing sites for various XP-movements and they are both specifiers of functional heads; and so on. So any attempt to group together the subject specifiers of AGRP and VP in opposition to the specifier of CP (as is attempted in Chomsky and Lasnik, 1993) comes over as stipulative and counter-intuitive.

But so much of GB theory rests on the A- and A-bar distinction that it cannot be discarded without radical change to the structure of the theory itself. For example one distinction between movement to A- and A-bar-positions is that the former leaves behind a trace that is an anaphor and the latter a trace that is an r-expression; A-positions do not interfere with A-bar movement, and vice versa, according to the principles of Relativized Minimality; and so on. Furthermore, the distinction is important for Binding Theory where the distinction between A-binding (binding from A-positions) and A-bar-binding (binding from A-bar-positions) accounts for why empty r-expressions (e.g. wh-traces) can be bound by some element (the moved wh-element) while overt r-expressions (e.g. names) cannot be bound by anything, as we saw in chapter 7.

Developments in some areas of the GB theory therefore caused tensions for other areas which had long been taken as crucial to the whole theory. Something had to give: the result was that in the Minimalist Programme, the A- and A-bar-positions are no longer taken to be basic, their effects stemming from more fundamental principles concerning how the computational system works.

A second GB problem is the concept of government, which, despite having considerable empirical motivation, is none the less an 'arbitrary syntactic relation' (Lasnik, 1993, p. 3). Moreover there are many different notions of government, some working better than others for certain phenomena; unfortunately, no version is perfect for all purposes. The one presented in chapter 7 (p. 240) was as follows:

Government
α governs β if and only if
   (1) α is a governor (e.g. N, V, P, A, etc.)
   (2) α and β mutually c-command each other
   (3) if α governs β, then α governs the specifier of β

This was chosen mainly because of its relative simplicity, but it allows too wide a range of relationships for it to be considered perfect. For example, under this version, a Verb is allowed to govern the specifier of its CP complement and therefore to assign Case to a wh-element in this position, which would mean that the chain formed by the moved wh-element would receive at least *two* Cases as the original trace of a wh-element sits in a Case-marked position. Whether or not this is a true problem depends on how we set the theory up, of course. But it seems reasonable to start with the assumption that each chain is assigned only a single Case.

A more serious problem is that, under these assumptions, AGR governs, and therefore can assign Case to, the specifier of TP. If this is so, there needs to be an explanation why the subject moves into the specifier of AGRP to receive Nominative Case instead of staying in the specifier of TP. Whatever solution we give to this problem takes us further away from pure explanation as it clears up a problem caused by an imperfect definition of government rather than by the nature of grammar itself: ideally, the answer might be expected to lie in the definition of government rather than in patching it up with yet more stipulations.

The minimalist solution to the problem is to abandon government as a fundamental notion of the theory. Of course, given that so much of GB theory is based on the notion of government, this is a radical move. Again, the argument is that the effects of government can be reduced to more fundamental relations, as we see shortly.

Other developments within GB theory itself also paved the way for the development of the Minimalist Programme. One recurrent theme (seen in chapter 6 above) since the work of Pollock (1989) has been the distinction between languages that raise Verbs to the inflectional nodes, such as French, and those that seem unable to move main Verbs out of the VP, such as English. In the latter case, there is the problem of how Verbs which do not move get their inflections, the usual solution being that, at least at some level of representation, the inflectional elements themselves lower onto the Verb (p. 215 above). This idea, however, is unwelcome since it would be the only type of movement that shifts an element to a position *lower* in the tree rather than raising it higher. Furthermore, it expressly goes against the Empty Category Principle, which says that the trace of a moved element must be properly governed. Moving a head to a lower position in a tree means, if anything, the trace will govern the moved head rather than the other way round.

There have been various solutions to this problem, most of them of an unconvincing stipulative kind. However, Chomsky and Lasnik (1993) manage to do away with the assumption that the inflections lower in English, and so the problem of how to circumnavigate the ECP disappears. The solution is to assume that Verbs are given their inflectional properties (and forms) in the lexicon; an already 'inflected' Verb is inserted into its base position in the VP and so does not have to move anywhere to become inflected. The inflectional nodes, instead of adding inflections to a bare Verb, perform the function of **checking** that the inserted Verb has the appropriate features when it moves into them. For example, in a sentence such as:

1.   Juliet loves Romeo.

the Verb would be inserted into the VP as a present tense third person singular Verb *loves*. It first moves to the T position to check that it has the right tense, and then to the AGR position to check that it has the right agreement features. If the checking procedure is satisfied, a grammatical sentence results. If, for example, the wrong Verb is inserted (e.g. *love* rather than *loves*), checking will not be satisfied and the sentence will be ungrammatical:

2.   *Juliet love Romeo.

To sum up, inflections originate in the lexicon and are checked against the positions to which they move.

So, if the Verb already has its inflectional form in its original position, the movement of the Verb to check its features can take place covertly (i.e. at LF) without any consequences for the form the Verb takes. The difference between French-type languages and English-type languages is that the former raise Verbs *overtly* in the syntax while the latter raise Verbs *covertly* at LF. Of course, it is another matter to *explain* this difference, but at least this account does away with the unwanted assumption that inflections can lower in certain languages. We will see in later sections that one principle that plays a large part in explaining the different Verb movement properties of French and English states that movement operations should be delayed for as long as possible. This principle is called **Procrastinate**. So in English, where the Verb is not raised until LF, we can see that Verb movement accords with Procrastinate. French Verb movement on the other hand operates earlier and so does not fit in with Procrastinate. There must be some other feature of French that forces Verb movement to take place earlier than it does in English. These issues will be developed later. Moreover, this analysis has other appealing qualities, such as accounting for how a number of inflections can be expressed by a single morpheme, for example -*s*, rather than many morphemes, and for other more complex morphological phenomena, such as the changing vowel of the stem in certain irregular English Verbs (*take–took*, etc.). These are not problematic if they are formed in the lexicon rather than being added as the Verb form moves to the inflectional nodes.

The important point about this analysis is not so much that it solves a tricky problem, but that it allows us to assume that some movements actually take place later at LF rather than occurring at S-structure. As we will see, this analysis can be extended to other cases, diminishing the role of S-structure almost to nothing. This paves the way for the Minimalist Programme to reduce the levels of structural representation to the bare minimum, LF and PF, and it demonstrates once more how the Minimalist Programme develops directly out of the GB approach.

Steps towards Minimalism

1. Some notions developed within GB have a distinct 'minimalist flavour' and hence suggest a programme of research in which the grammar is restricted to the bare minimum.
   e.g. Principles of Economy and Full Interpretation
2. Some developments in GB caused tensions within the framework that suggest abandoning them as unsustainable.
   e.g. the notions A- and non-A-position are difficult to maintain under the assumption of a VP-internal subject.
3. Attempts to solve certain problems within GB led to assumptions that enable simplification of the grammar.
   e.g. adopting a 'checking' theory of Verb movement as a way of solving theory-internal problems to do with 'affix lowering' enables simpler views on other issues such as word order and Case assignment (see next section).

A Brief Sketch of the Minimalist Framework

So the theory attempts to reduce the grammar to its minimum, reconstructing the effects of the grammatical mechanisms that it abandons on the basis of more fundamental, and therefore more explanatory, considerations. What remains are the bare essentials that necessarily have to be assumed: given that languages have meaning and form, it is not possible to dispense with the interface between the grammar and semantics (LF) or with that between the grammar and phonetics (PF). Furthermore, there has to be some syntactic mechanism that forms the structures that appear at the interface levels, i.e. a computational system of some kind. Finally, there will be considerations of what constitutes a legitimate object at each representational level, which possibly have their foundations in the interpretative components themselves. Ideally the grammar should consist of only the bare minimum.

The first question to address is: how are the structures that constitute LF and PF representations formed? The process must start from the lexicon as lexical elements will, on the whole, determine the content of any legitimate expression in a language. Chomsky (1995b) supposes that we start by selecting a set of lexical items from which the structural description (SD) is to be built. This set of lexical items is called a **Numeration**; the ultimate SD formed will only be grammatical if each element from the Numeration is used the required number of times, that is to say items cannot be left in the Numeration unused if a grammatical sentence is to result. For example, suppose the Numeration consists of the three elements {Juliet, loves, Romeo} (for simplicity we ignore here the question of whether functional elements such as tense and agreement are also included in the Numeration or whether they are added by the computational system). As we saw, Verbs are formed in the lexicon together with all their features, which must be checked at some point in the derivation. The computational system builds structures by selecting elements from the Numeration and combining them in the relevant ways. For the moment let us suppose that this process forms structures that conform to the X-bar principles. The process may take the Verb and form a VP structure consisting of just the Verb, as in:

3.

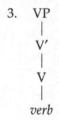

Then it may take a Noun and form an NP structure from this:

4.

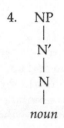

It may combine these two trees in the relevant way with the NP as the object of the VP:

5.

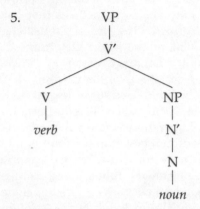

And so on until the Numeration has used up all the lexical choices it made. The computational system can form as many separate trees as it likes, but at some point in the derivation it must combine these trees in appropriate ways to form a single tree, otherwise a single SD has not been formed and the result will be ungrammatical.

Now let us turn to the end results of the computations, which must be two fully formed structural representations, one at LF and one at PF. The fact that there are two of these means that the computations must split at a point known as **Spell-Out**, after which the computational system proceeds to form two independent representations with quite different properties:

6.

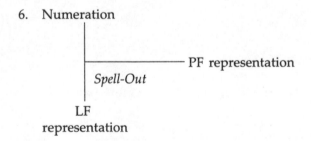

Spell-Out is an operation that takes a partially formed SD which contains all phonetic and semantic information from the lexicon and splits these so that on the one hand there is a representation consisting of just phonetic information and on the other there is a representation consisting of everything that is left. The minimal assumption is that

Spell-Out can divide up the information in an SD in any way it wants to. However, we would not wish to let the wrong sort of information into either representation. Suppose then that there are conditions on what counts as proper objects at each of the interface levels.

Specifically, semantic information is not allowed to appear at PF and phonetic information is not allowed to appear at LF. A derivation **converges** at each of the interface levels if such conditions are met, otherwise it **crashes**. For an SD to be grammatical, it must converge at both LF and PF. So a PF representation that contains semantic information crashes, causing the SD to be ungrammatical; an LF representation that contains phonetic information crashes, again causing the SD to be ungrammatical. In this way, Spell-Out is confined to splitting the derivation in the appropriate way.

This idea can also be extended to grammatical features, which presumably are also irrelevant to both the semantic and the phonetic interpretations of a structure. How are these eliminated before they arrive at LF or PF? This is the function of the **checking** procedure that happens, for example, when a Verb moves to the inflectional nodes. 'Checking' the grammatical features actually cancels them out so that they do not survive into the interface representations. This must be slightly more complicated, as we see later.

The interface conditions become even more general, and thus more explanatory, if they are taken to instantiate the Principle of Full Interpretation: each representation at LF and PF can only contain elements which are interpreted at these levels with no superfluous elements allowed. Hence, if a piece of phonetic or semantic information ends up in the wrong representation, Full Interpretation is violated and the derivation crashes. To summarize in Chomsky's words, 'We say that a computation (derivation) *converges* at one of the interface levels if it forms an interpretable representation in this sense, and *converges* if it converges at both interface levels, PF and LF; otherwise it *crashes*' (Chomsky, 1995b, p. 390).

A further question is when Spell-Out should take place. Again, this will be answered by the general conditions on interface representations (Full Interpretation). If Spell-Out happens too early, say before all the lexical elements of the Numeration have been included, and these are introduced at some post-Spell-Out point, either in the branch that leads to LF or the one that leads to PF, there will either be an element at LF which still has its phonetic information or there will be an element at PF which still has its semantic information: if lexical items are inserted after Spell-Out, Spell-Out cannot split the relevant information into the correct level of representation for those lexical items. Again the derivation will crash. Furthermore, if Spell-Out happens before the computational system has combined all the sub-trees that it is creating, again the result is an uninterpretable representation at PF, presuming that after Spell-Out the computational path to PF involves only operations relevant for the phonetic component: i.e. no major syntactic processes occur between Spell-Out and the fully formed PF. If Spell-Out happens too late, there will be a conflict with the principle of Procrastinate, mentioned earlier: Procrastinate states that, unless forced to do otherwise, all movements must be delayed for as long as possible, i.e. until after Spell-Out. Spell-Out must therefore apply at a point which will enable movement to happen after it.

Relating the interface conditions to Full Interpretation in this general way also enables us to say more about what constitutes a legitimate object at each level. For example, the only legitimate objects allowed at LF are those that can be given a semantic interpretation: anything that cannot will cause the derivation to crash. Chomsky (1993) supposes that what can be interpreted at LF are 'legitimate' chains: 'At LF, we assume each legitimate object to be a chain $CH = (\alpha_i, \ldots, \alpha_n)$: at least (perhaps at most) with CH a head, an argument, a modifier, or an operator-variable construction' (Chomsky, 1993, p. 27).

Numerations, Spell-Out and Convergence

Numeration: a set of elements selected from the lexicon which is the starting point of the structure building process.

Spell-Out: the point in the derivation of a structure at which phonetically relevant information is separated from all other information. In this way two structures, an LF and a PF, are formed from a single Numeration.

Convergence: LF and PF representations must contain information of the relevant sort (semantic and phonetic respectively) in order to satisfy the Principle of Full Interpretation. If a representation at LF or PF conforms to Full Interpretation, it **converges** at that level. A whole derivation converges if it converges at both LF and PF. If not, it **crashes** and the structure is ungrammatical.

Finally let us see how the computational process forms structures out of this. One important difference between minimalism and GB is that, in the former, structures are built up piecemeal. In GB, D-structure was presented as a complete structure and not much was said about the internal process of how it was formed: it was an ' "all-at-once" operation' (Chomsky, 1993, p. 21). However, in getting rid of D- and S-structure, minimalism places more emphasis on the internal workings of the structure formation process. We have already said that part of this process involves building individual trees for lexical items (perhaps conforming to the X-bar requirements) and then combining these at some point to form a larger tree. How and when they are combined will have repercussions on the eventual SD formed; hence the process will ultimately be constrained by the convergence requirement at the interface levels. Chomsky calls the process of combining lexical items and partial trees **Merge** – 'an operation that forms larger units out of those already constructed' (Chomsky, 1995b, p. 396).

The Minimalist Programme is transformational and so a movement operation is part of the computational system. As well as actually building trees, the computational system also moves elements about in the trees. This may indeed be part of the tree formation process as elements may be moved into structural positions created by the process itself. For example, consider the position where the AGR system has just been added to a partially formed tree with the subject still inside the VP, presented here in a simplified tree:

7.

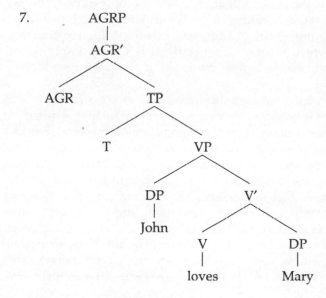

As it stands here, AGRP has no specifier position. So, for the subject *John* to move into AGR, the specifier position will need to be created and then the subject moved into it, forming the tree:

8.

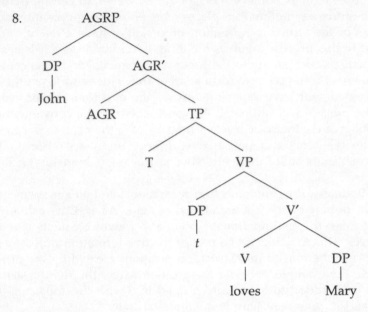

This device of adding specifier position is in fact found in many of the trees in chapter 6. We see later that, in his most recent work, Chomsky has proposed a radical reformulation which simplifies the structure down to its bare minimum. But for now this illustration will suffice. The operation which moves elements about is called simply **Move**. The tree building process is thus made up of two basic operations – Merge and Move.

A final point about the computational system concerns how it is constrained. Obviously the convergence condition at the interface levels offers some constraint on the computational process. But this does not seem to be enough. As is well known, movement is not an unconstrained operation; in particular movement needs to be kept local. Following the basic observation of Relativized Minimality, Chomsky proposes that movements are constrained by a **Minimal Link Condition** that only accepts movement into the nearest relevant position: 'α must make the "shortest move" . . .' (Chomsky, 1995b, p. 401). There are two other major constraints on the Move operation, one which delays movement for as long as possible i.e. '**Procrastinate**', and one, called '**Greed**', which allows movement of an element only if it satisfies some property of the moved element – movement cannot be made to satisfy the properties of an element that becomes related to the moved element by the movement process: 'Move raises α to a position β only if morphological properties of α itself would not otherwise be satisfied in the derivation' (Chomsky, 1995b, p. 400). How these constraints work and their purpose will become apparent as we proceed. However, their general effect is to cause a derivation to crash if they are not adhered to.

Structure Building

Merge: the combinatorial process which forms structures from elements in the Numeration and other partially built structures.

Move: the movement process which also plays a role in structure building – e.g. a specifier position will be created as part of the process of moving an element into it.

The Minimal Link Condition: a constraint on Move which prevents elements moving further than the nearest relevant position.

Procrastinate: a general constraint on the computation which says delay doing anything until it needs to be done.

Greed: another general constraint on the computation which says that processes only affect an element to satisfy the requirements of that element – e.g. to check the features of a Verb, the Verb will have to move to AGR and T and these cannot move to the Verb.

To summarize, the computation system starts off with a Numeration of the lexical items from which the SD is to be formed. Then, by the operations of Merge and Move, SDs are built up piecemeal, with the Move operation being constrained by the Minimal Link Condition, Procrastinate and Greed. Hence the whole system is in a sense 'driven' by the lexical items and their morphology; 'operations are driven by morphological necessity: certain features must be checked in the checking domain of the head, or the derivation will crash' (Chomsky, 1993, p. 32). This process proceeds to a point at which the derivation splits into phonetically relevant and semantically relevant information: Spell-Out. From here two separate representations are formed. The computational system continues to form structures after Spell-Out, but, if the end points of these operations do not conform to a Full Interpretation condition, the derivation crashes. If these conditions are met at both LF and PF, the derivation converges. We can represent this in the following diagram:

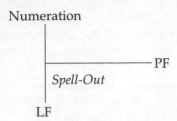

In this diagram, the lines represent the workings of the computational system: Full Interpretation is applied to both interface representations, but of course differently according to whether semantic or phonetic information is being interpreted.

How Minimal Can the Minimalist Programme Get?

So far we have outlined the basic aims of the Minimalist Programme and given general hints as to how a minimalist grammar might work, summed up in Chomsky's description of the minimalist design as 'a theory of language that takes a linguistic expression to be nothing other than a formal object that satisfies the interface conditions in the optimal way' (Chomsky, 1993, p. 5). However, given that the whole programme depends on the ability to reduce certain elements of the grammar to more basic elements and relations, the most important question is whether such reduction is possible. After all, the Minimalist Programme is intent on ridding the grammar of some basic elements that have underpinned most assumptions in this field since the early 1980s, such as government, or even as far back as the early 1960s, such as D- and S-structure. This final section looks at specific areas to see what getting rid of these notions implies.

Getting Rid of D- and S-structure

The main problem to be tackled if we wish to reduce the notions of D- and S-structure to more fundamental considerations is how to capture the empirical consequences that originally motivated them. For example, it is often argued that certain modules of the grammar 'apply' at D- or S-structure and from this certain empirical consequences follow. But, if there is no D- or S-structure, these sorts of argument cannot be maintained and the empirical observations will have to be captured in some other way.

One thing that is often claimed to apply at D-structure is θ-theory, in particular the θ-Criterion. Already in later versions of GB theory the θ-Criterion had been more or less replaced by the Principle of Full Interpretation. Still, we might want to push things a little at this point and to ask specifically how the Minimalist Programme intends to capture the effects of the θ-Criterion and in particular how we ensure that the arguments that accompany the Verb correspond to those determined by the s-selection properties of that Verb stated in the lexical entry. Chomsky's (1993) solution to this depends on an assumption concerning the structure of sentences that plays an important role in many arguments from the minimalist perspective. In chapter 5 we briefly mentioned the possibility of there being two agreement elements, one for the subject (AGR_sP) and one for the object (AGR_oP). The Minimalist Programme explicitly adopts this assumption. Thus, ignoring the possibility of a plethora of other functional categories, the basic clause structure assumed is:

9.

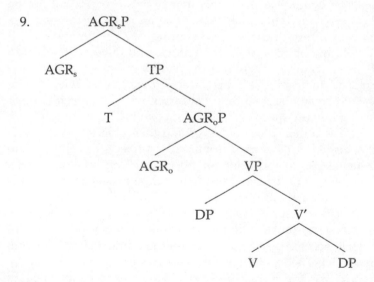

AGR_s and AGR_o are not really different things; both of them are instances of nominal features that 'agree' with certain nominal elements.

What they agree with depends on which elements move into their specifiers, triggering specifier–head agreement. Without going into the technicalities, it turns out that the only valid solution for movement in this situation is for the subject to move to the top AGRP (hence it is denoted AGR_sP), and the object to move to the lower AGRP (hence AGR_oP). The reason is that, if the subject were to move to AGR_oP, the movement of the object into AGR_sP would violate the Minimal Link Condition and cause the derivation to crash. AGR_s is then associated with the subject and AGR_o is associated with the object.

The Extended Projection Principle states that there must be a subject and, as a consequence (perhaps as a cause), AGR_s is obligatory. However, there is no such compulsory requirement on the presence of objects and hence AGR_o may be optional. So, when there is an object, there will be an AGR_0 and, when there is no object, there will be no AGR_o. Turning now to Verbs, recall that Verbs are assumed to be inserted from the lexicon complete with all their features, which need to be checked off at some stage in the derivation to avoid these grammatical features surviving to the interface levels. Checking is done by the Verb moving to the relevant element. So, for example, a Verb which has tense features moves to the T position and checks these features off. Now, presumably, a transitive Verb will have object agreement features as well as subject agreement features, even if in languages such as English the object agreement features will not be reflected phonetically. Thus, there has to be an AGR_o in the sentence for the transitive Verb to check these features off. The derivation will crash if a Verb has object agreement features and there is no AGR_o to check off these features. Therefore the Verb's object agreement features force there to be an AGR_o and the appearance of an AGR_o in turn forces there to be an object so that this can move to its specifier position and enter into the specifier–head relationship. This guarantees the co-occurrence of certain types of Verbs and their objects: a Verb with an object specified in its entry automatically projects the appropriate phrase which leads to the need for an object. This solution works without postulating D-structure and hence allows us to get rid of this level of representation entirely.

What about S-structure? Here the problems are greater as more things have been assumed to apply at this level and hence there are more things to accommodate elsewhere in the minimalist framework. For instance, Case Theory and Binding Theory were supposed to apply at S-structure. For the S-structureless version to work, we need to show that the effects that these modules deal with can be handled at the interface levels, thus making S-structure superfluous. Let us take

Case Theory first. This was assumed to apply at S-structure because it has implications for both LF and PF representations. Recall that one way to view the Case Filter is to assume that there is a 'visibility' condition such that if a DP is not Case-marked it will not be visible for θ-marking (page 230 above). Therefore Case Theory must apply at or before LF. Also, although the relationship is not straightforward, abstract Case is linked to morphological Case. Morphological Case is obviously a PF phenomenon and so Case Theory must apply at or before PF. Putting these two conclusions together, we can see that Case Theory cannot apply at *either* LF *or* PF as it has implications for both of these. Therefore, it must apply before *both*, i.e. at S-structure (it does not apply at D-structure because DPs are allowed to appear in Case-less positions at this level, as long as they move to be Case-marked by S-structure).

How, then, can we counter these arguments that some other level of representation besides LF and PF is necessary? Here again, Chomsky turns to the notion of 'checking'. If Verbs are inserted in the VP along with their verbal features, such as tense and agreement, etc., why can the same not be true of DPs? If we suppose that DPs have Case features in their original positions, but have to move to the specifier position of some AGRP to check these features, movement to this specifier position can happen either before or after Spell-Out without any implications for the phonetic form of the DP. If this is so, Case-marking is reduced to Case-checking and this obviously does not need S-structure in order to take place: 'elements enter the computational system with their Case features already indicated, these being checked only at the LF level. Any apparent S-structure requirement for Case would have to be satisfied in some other way' (Chomsky and Lasnik, 1993, p. 539).

Case Theory

In the Minimalist Programme, Case Theory essentially involves checking the Case features of DPs inserted from the lexicon. DPs move to the specifier position of an AGRP to check their Case features. This movement can be done overtly, before Spell-Out, or covertly, after Spell-Out. There is no need to suppose S-structure under these assumptions.

Turning now to Binding Theory, the arguments that motivate putting this at S-structure include the following observations. Firstly, Binding Theory applies after D-structure because elements can move to positions where they enter into a binding relationship in their S-structure positions that does not hold for their D-structure positions. Consider the following example:

10.   the men$_i$ seem to each other t_i to be intelligent

Here the subject of the main clause is raised into this position from the lower clause and the D-structure representation is:

11.   *e* seem to each other the men to be intelligent

In this position the lower clause subject *the men* cannot bind the reciprocal pronoun *each other* which, being an anaphor, must be bound and hence, if raising does not take place, we get an ungrammaticality:

12.   *it seems to each other that the men are intelligent

Because the situation can be rescued by movement, the Binding Principles must apply *after* the movement takes place: i.e. not at D-structure.

The reason why it is supposed that Binding Theory applies at S-structure and not, for example, at LF, is that typical LF movements (i.e. covert movements) do not have the ability to 'rescue' binding violations. For example, consider the following sentence:

13.   John asked which picture of himself$_i$ Mary liked t_i

Here the main subject is allowed to bind a reflexive pronoun which originates in the lower clause because the DP that contains the reflexive overtly moves out of the clause. Again, if the movement were not to take place, an ungrammaticality would follow:

14.   *John said that Mary liked that picture of himself.

Now, consider the following example:

15.   John asked who liked which picture of himself.

Obviously, the reflexive cannot be bound by *John* in this sentence. It is usually assumed that in such cases of multiple wh-questions the wh-element which remains *in situ* (e.g. *which picture of himself*) never-theless moves at LF. But this movement obviously does not make the main clause subject available as an antecedent and therefore we conclude that the binding conditions must apply before the covert movement takes place. Again, then, we are forced to accept that Binding Theory takes place at S-structure, thus motivating the assumption of this level of representation.

The way out of this problem involves introducing another set of phenomena. Consider the following problematic case:

16.   Which picture of himself$_i$ did Mary say John liked t_i

Here the subject of the lower clause *John* is obviously the antecedent of the reflexive *himself* in the wh-phrase, despite the fact that this has been moved to a position from which it would not seem to be able to be bound by this element. The standard solution is to assume that the sentence gets 'reconstructed' at LF. What this means is that every part of the wh-phrase that is not itself 'wh' (i.e. everything that gets carried along with the wh-element as it moves) gets put back in its original position, forming an LF representation such as:

17.   which x Mary said that John liked x picture of himself

Here, *John* can bind the reflexive and hence the structure is rescued from the Binding Principles.

But two things follow from this argument. Firstly, structures of the above kind are legitimate LF representations; secondly, despite what was argued before, Binding Theory *can* take place at LF. So we now have contradictory evidence: covert movement suggests that binding cannot take place at LF and reconstruction suggests that Binding Theory must take place at LF. The solution to this dilemma lies in the obser-vation that the structure given above is a legitimate LF representation. Consider the covert movement case again. We said that because the following is ungrammatical:

18.   *John$_i$ asked who liked which pictures of himself$_i$

the covert movement of the wh-phrase *in situ* cannot rescue the bind-ing violation. But the assumption here is that the relevant LF repres-entation is something like the S-structure representation with overt movement, i.e.:

19.   John asked which picture of himself$_i$ who$_j$ t_j liked t_i

As this is 'covert' movement, who knows what the LF representation looks like? We already have evidence that structures of this kind are reconstructed, putting back the non-wh-material into its original position. So it is at least a possibility that the LF representation looks like:

20.   John asked which$_i$ who$_j$ t_j liked t_i pictures of himself

This structure agrees with the observation that the main clause subject cannot be the antecedent of the reflexive and is also compatible with the assumption that binding conditions hold at LF. Assuming these things therefore enables us to drop the assumption that binding must take place at S-structure and hence allows us to assume that S-structure is not necessary and can be done away with in accordance with the Minimalist Programme.

Binding Theory

In the Minimalist Programme, the Binding Theory applies at LF. At LF only 'wh-material' is in wh-positions. As a consequence, non-wh-material which is overtly moved along with a wh-element is **reconstructed** back into its original position and only wh-elements undergo covert movement to wh-positions at LF. These assumptions overcome a number of well-known problems for the claim that binding takes place at LF, such as why LF movement does not allow a reflexive pronoun to be bound by an element in a higher clause. E.g.
John asked who likes which picture of himself.
has the LF form:
John asked [which x, who likes x picture of himself]
and not:
John asked [which picture of himself, who likes *t*]
as was previously thought.

To summarize, it is possible, under a certain set of assumptions, to reject arguments that D- and S-structure are necessary parts of the grammar and to capture phenomena that were thought to hold at these levels by mechanisms holding at the interface levels; 'all conditions are interface conditions; a linguistic expression is the optimal realization of such interface conditions' (Chomsky, 1993, p. 26). Chomsky (1993) argues that the new picture formed under minimalist assumptions is not only conceptually better, but is also empirically more adequate, as under these assumptions many problems that arose in the GB framework are given satisfactory solutions.

Getting Rid of Government

Government is another fundamental concept of the GB framework to fall foul of the minimalist doctrine. Basically the idea is that all structural relations should be limited to a small number of very basic relations, specifically those that fall directly out of the X-bar framework such as head–complement and specifier–head relations. But government plays a substantial part in nearly all of the modules of the GB approach. This again entails reinterpreting each relevant phenomenon in terms of these more basic structural relations. This section considers this programme in relation to a limited number of phenomena, namely Case Theory, the distribution of PRO, and the ECP.

We have already indicated how the notion of government might be replaced in Case Theory by the specifier–head relationship (page 202). Recall from the previous section that the Minimalist Programme replaces Case-marking with the notion of Case-checking. According to Chomsky (1993), the features of an element can be checked in the 'checking domain' of the relevant head, which informally can be taken to be any position related to the head which is not the complement (i.e. adjunct or specifier). Thus, a DP which is inserted into a structure along with its Case features must move to the relevant position to have these features checked. The relevant position, as was already mentioned, is the specifier of an AGRP. This fundamentally differs from the assumptions of GB theory, where Nominative Case was assigned to the specifier of AGRP, but Accusative Case was assigned by Verbs to their objects (page 225 above). Lasnik (1993) points out the uniformity of the minimalist assumptions: both Nominative and Accusative Case are assigned under a very similar set of circumstances. So, while a subject will move to the specifier of AGRP and a tensed (auxiliary) Verb will move to AGR, as is normally assumed, an object will move to the specifier of AGR_oP and the Verb will move to AGR_o itself. Thus we have one general structural configuration under which structural Case is assigned (checked):

21.

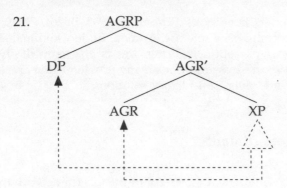

If finite T and Verbs, when combined with an AGR element, license Case checking – Nominative for T and Accusative for V – the parallel is complete: in both cases the combination of some verbal element with an AGR licenses Case-checking and in both cases the checking is done in the specifier position of AGRP.

In fact, the generalization can be extended even further to cover cases of Exceptional Case Marking. ECM structures involve an infinitival subject receiving Accusative Case, presumably from the governing Verb in the higher clause. However, under the minimalist assumptions this involves the subject of the lower clause raising to the specifier of the AGR_o of the higher clause:

22.

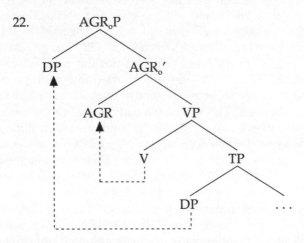

The details of this need to be expanded to explain why the surface word order of English is SVO and not SOV: if both the subject and the object move to the specifier of an AGRP then both will obviously precede the Verb. The answer is that, while the subject moves to the specifier of AGR$_s$P before Spell-Out, and hence the movement is overt, the object movement takes place after Spell-Out and hence is covert. Why is there this difference? Firstly, Chomsky (1993) notes that object movement is more in line with the principle of Procrastinate, which requires movement to be as late as possible (i.e. after Spell-Out), whereas the subject movement does not accord with this principle. Consequently something must force the subject to move in English. Languages differ in this respect; for example, one analysis of languages which have VSO word order, such as Welsh, is that the Verb is raised out of the VP to the inflection nodes before Spell-Out, but that both the object and the subject stay inside the VP until after Spell-Out. VSO languages therefore differ from SVO languages, such as English, in that the latter must also move the subject before Spell-Out.

Chomsky puts the difference down to the checking features, distinguishing '**strong**' features from '**weak**' features, the difference being that strong features cannot survive at PF without causing the derivation to crash, whereas weak ones are invisible at PF and so will not cause a crash, even if they appear. Specifically, Chomsky assumes that the DP-features of T are strong in English; thus a DP will have to raise to the specifier of AGR$_s$ (the position to which T raises) before Spell-Out so that they will not appear at PF. In VSO languages, the DP-features of T are weak and so the subject does not have to raise and therefore, by the principle of Procrastinate, will not raise until LF. The same is true of the object in English: as this does not have to raise before Spell-Out, it will not do so. Finally, DPs must move to the specifier of AGRP, rather than anything moving to the DPs to check their Case features, by the principle of Greed: movement is allowed only to satisfy the features of the element being moved and not the element being moved to. Overall, then, the Minimalist Programme adopts a very uniform Case Theory and one which has positive consequences for accounting for certain word order differences.

Essentially the same analysis accounts for the difference in Verb movement properties in English and French. Recall that we mentioned that English accords with Procrastinate in not allowing its Verbs to move before Spell-Out whereas French must overtly move its Verbs, i.e. before Spell-Out. This difference can be put down to one between the weak verbal features of English which can survive at PF as they are invisible, and the strong verbal features of French which must be checked off before Spell-Out. So French Verbs *must* move before Spell-Out otherwise there will be violation of Procrastinate. Finally, Greed ensures that in all cases it will be the Verb that moves to get its features checked off, rather than the inflections that move.

Word Order and Verb Movement

The notion of feature checking enables a particularly simple theory of word order and Verb movement. All languages move Verbs to the inflectional nodes and DPs to the specifier of some AGRP. Languages differ in *when* these movements take place: before or after Spell-Out. Procrastinate suggests that all movements take place after Spell-Out, but the need to check grammatical features before PF will force movement to take place before Spell-Out. What decides which of these conflicting considerations wins out is whether the grammatical features are **strong** or **weak**: weak features can appear at PF without problem and so Procrastinate can be adhered to when these are involved. Strong features must be checked before Spell-Out. Thus, whether Verbs and DPs move overtly depends on whether their features are strong or weak.

In GB theory, the distribution of PRO was determined by the principle:

PRO must not be governed.

and so government plays an obvious part in accounting for certain facts about control structures. But, if government is done away with, these facts must be made to follow from other considerations. Chomsky and Lasnik (1993) discuss the possibility of reducing the distribution of PRO to considerations of Case Theory. While similar ideas have been attempted in the past (e.g. Manzini, 1983), it is by no means straightforward to say that the distribution of PRO is determined by a principle such as, for example:

PRO must not be Case-marked.

One reason for this is that there are positions in which PRO cannot appear even though they are not Case-marked. For instance, the object of a passive Verb is not a Case-marked position (hence objects move to subject position in passives), yet PRO is still prevented from appearing in such a position:

23.   *it was killed PRO

Obviously, the principle that PRO cannot be governed works better here, as although this position is not Case-marked, it is none the less still governed.

Chomsky and Lasnik adopt a different perspective. They suggest that PRO is like other DPs in that it must receive Case but, unlike any other DP, this must be a special sort of Case, namely **Null Case**, associated with a non-finite T. PRO must move to the specifier position of the inflectional nodes containing a non-finite T in order for its Case features to be checked in the usual way. But this will only be possible from a non-Case-marked position as other 'Case-marked' positions will signal the appearance of an AGR element which will not be able to check the relevant Case. Furthermore, a finite T will not be able to check the Case features of PRO as it will not have the appropriate Case to check: finite T has Nominative Case. This theory, then, accounts satisfactorily for the distribution of PRO without recourse to the notion of government: the only structural relation needed is specifier–head agreement in order to check PRO's Case features. This is in addition a more uniform theory as PRO is not exceptional in being able to avoid the Case Filter.

> **Control**
>
> The distribution of PRO is determined by Case Theory rather than government. PRO has **Null** Case features which can only be checked in the specifier of a non-finite TP.

Finally, we turn to the Empty Category Principle. Chomsky (1993) does not give a particularly technical account of how the ECP can be reduced to minimalist considerations and so we will concentrate here only on the intuitive content of his proposals. One of the clearest statements concerning the ECP comes from Rizzi's (1990) work on Relativized Minimality (see chapter 7). The basic observation is that elements of a particular kind – heads, arguments and non-arguments – cannot move across c-commanding positions of their own kind.

Rizzi's Relativized Minimality is, however, stated in terms of the ECP and hence couched in terms of government. Chomsky (1993) observes that the effect of Relativized Minimality is to require that movement be over the shortest possible distance; 'it is clear that in all the "bad" cases, some element has failed to make "the shortest move"... . the moved element has "skipped" a position it could have reached by a shorter move, had that position not been filled' (Chomsky, 1993, pp. 14–15). This appears to be another instantiation of a Principle of Economy: short moves are more economical than longer ones. Hence, given the foundation of the Minimalist Programme on economy, the Minimal Link Condition seems to fit well. Obviously, there is more to be said on this issue, but this would lead us into some rather technical and as yet insufficiently worked out areas.

Getting Rid of X-bar

This final section outlines Chomsky's most recent, and perhaps most radical, proposals to date for how the Minimalist Programme should handle basic phrase structure. Up to this point we have been assuming that the principles which govern the construction of structural descriptions, i.e. Merge and Move, are constrained by the X-bar principles: these operations cannot form structures which do not conform to the sorts of patterns that the X-bar framework allows. X-bar theory was taken as fundamental in Chomsky (1993), the first minimalist paper: 'UG must provide means to present an array of items from the lexicon in a form accessible to the computational system. We may take this form to be some version of X-bar Theory. The concepts of X-bar Theory are therefore fundamental' (p. 6).

However, this means that the X-bar principles exist separately from the operations that form and constrain structural descriptions. An even more minimalist perspective might expect these restrictions to follow from properties of the tree building processes themselves. If this can be achieved, X-bar theory would be superfluous as a separate module of the grammar and could be got rid of. Clearly this is a radical departure, not only because X-bar theory has been part of Chomskyan grammar since the 1970s, but also because the majority of other generative theories such as GPSG accept some version of X-bar theory; so it has seemed for some time that the X-bar principles are unchallengeable. However, theoretical linguistics constantly holds every assumption up for scrutiny: challenging X-bar theory in this way is part of the process of developing new perspectives from which old assumptions can be re-evaluated.

The method by which Chomsky proposes to make X-bar theory redundant is, as one would expect, rather technical, and so here we will aim to convey only the general idea. The Merge operation takes elements from the Numeration – the set of selected lexical elements in the sentence – and combines them to form trees. What is the basic operation of combination? The minimal assumption is that the combination of two elements forms a set consisting of these two elements, thus combining the lexical elements *the* and *dog* forms the set {the, dog}. However, this is obviously too minimal as it misses the important observation that combined sets of lexical items have special features which they take primarily from one of their members: in other words, each 'phrase' has a 'head' that determines the properties of that 'phrase'. Thus, what is formed by the combination of two elements has to also include information about which of the two provides the properties for the combined set. Suppose we allow the choice of the head to be free, subject to the satisfaction of the lexical properties of the elements involved, then in our example, assuming the DP hypothesis, the selection of the determiner as the head will satisfy its lexical property of having a nominal complement. Chomsky proposes to represent this extra information again through the set notation: the combination of two elements forms a binary set, one member of which is the **label** of the set and the other is the set of the two elements combined. If we take the label to be identical with the chosen head of the phrase, we arrive at a representation such as: {the, {the, dog}}. Here the first element of the larger set is the label, indicating that it is a DP as its label *the* is a determiner, and the second member {the dog} is made up of the two constituents; 'we keep to the assumption that the head determines the label' (Chomsky, 1995b, p. 398).

In terms of tree diagrams, this produces a much simplified structure. Our example yields the following structure:

24.

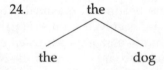

Obviously, we have to take this in the manner that it is intended and try to ignore the limitations of orthographic systems. Using *the* as the category label does not mean that this constituent is to be represented by the word *the*. It is better to look at the elements in these trees as sets of lexical features which are, for simplicity, represented by the orthographic forms – 'the', 'dog', etc. The phonetic form of an element is clearly one part of this set of features. But this is presumably only relevant at PF: by the time the representation reaches its final PF form after Spell-Out, all the structural information will have been stripped away, leaving just the phonological forms of elements at the bottom of the tree. Thus, in the tree given above, the label 'the' is a set of lexical features, irrelevantly including the phonetic form, but more importantly including semantic and syntactic information which tells us that the set has the properties of a definite determiner (phrase). Looked at in this way, this is not as radical as would at first appear. In fact, Chomsky (1995b) rarely uses this form of representation for tree structures, preferring to use the standard X-bar representations as an 'informal' way of encoding the results of the combinatorial computations. It is important to note, however, that these results follow directly from the operation that forms the structures and are not separately constrained by an X-bar module.

But this is only combining two words together: what happens after that? The structures which are formed by the combinatorial operation Merge are also available as elements that can be 'Merged' with others: the main difference being that, when deciding what is going to be the label for the newly formed binary set, it is the label of the existing set that is considered. For instance, if we want to Merge the two elements *feed* and {the, {the, dog} }, we shall have to decide which is going to be the label of the new set. Clearly, lexical properties determine that the Verb will be the head, and hence the new structure will be {feed, {feed, {the, {the, dog} } } }. At this point it can be easily seen that this way of representing the derivation is not going to be very helpful: it is far too unwieldy, even at this stage. For this reason we will not make use of the set notation in what follows but will continue to use tree diagrams as these are far more transparent.

But how are the basic observations of X-bar theory captured by this method? Since the early days of GB theory it has been observed that the only active elements in a derivation are heads and maximal projections: these are the only elements that are involved with syntactic processes such as movement and these are the elements which enter into semantic relations, denoting predicates and arguments. If the X' category exists at all, and there is empirical evidence for this, it should be a derived category rather than a basic one: i.e. it should appear by the operations of the computational system rather than being inserted as an element in its own right. Chomksy (1995b) achieves this by making the natural assumption that a maximal projection of any element is the furthest that that element is projected. In terms of the operation Merge, 'projection' is simply which element gets selected as the label for the combined set of elements. If an element does not project at all, as is the case for *dog* in our example:

25.

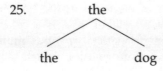

then this element is both a head and a maximal projection simultaneously: it is not only a head (because it is a lexical item that does not
project) but also a maximal projection (because it has no further projections). In our example, the lexical item *the* is just a pure head as it
does project; its maximal projection is the label 'the'. So where does
the X' category fit in?

This requires a slightly more complicated example. Take the situation where Merge adds a subject to the VP:

26.

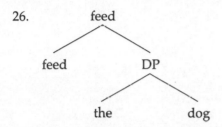

Assuming the VP-internal subject hypothesis, the label 'feed' will again
be chosen as the new label of the new set, forming:

27.

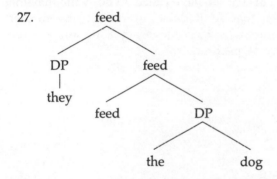

When the object was added to *feed*, the label 'feed' was the maximal
projection of this Verb. As this label is then further projected, it is no
longer a maximal projection but the new label is. If the projecting label
is neither a maximal projection nor a head, it must be something else,
i.e. an X'. Thus in this way, X's are derived as elements which are
neither maximal projections nor heads, though at some stage in the
derivation they may have been a maximal projection.

A similar account can be given for the structures formed by the
Move operation. Suppose that we extend our example to make it a
full clause, rather than just a VP. At some point in the derivation,
before Spell-Out in English, the subject will need to move out of the

VP into AGRP. Prior to that movement, the structure can be represented informally, in more familiar terms, as:

28.

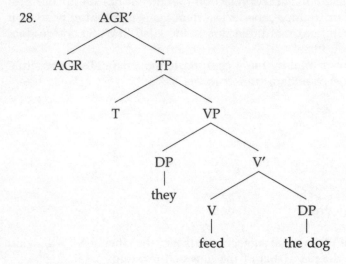

At this stage, the element that we have called AGR' is the maximal projection of AGR, given that AGR does not project any further. However, when the VP-internal subject moves, creating a new structure, AGR' will no longer be maximal:

29.

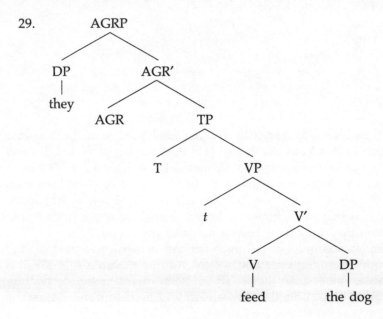

Again the X' category, AGR', is not inserted as an element, but is derived as an X' element because it is neither maximal nor lexical.

To summarize this section, the minimalist assumptions make X-bar theory an unwanted extra as a separate module of the grammar. This is especially so when it is interpreted as an external constraint on computational processes that build structures: it would be more in line with minimalist ideas if X-bar structures were to fall out from the structure building processes themselves. Taking a very simple theory in which the operation Merge combines any two elements and selects one as the projecting head, we build into the process the major features of X-bar theory and hence X-bar as a separate module can be jettisoned from the grammar. The major difference between the structures formed by the new theory and by X-bar theory is that maximal projections are simply the furthest that an element projects; hence it is possible for an element to have the multiple status of being both a head and a maximal projection at one and the same time. One small piece of empirical evidence in favour of the new theory pointed out by Chomsky is the behaviour of pronoun clitics in Romance languages, such as the following French example:

30. Jean le lit.
     John it reads.
     (John reads it)

The clitic behaves like a head in that it attaches to another head (the Verb), but it also acts as a full phrase in that it is an argument having a θ-role. So there are examples of apparently ambiguous elements which are difficult to accommodate under the stricter assumptions of X-bar theory.

X-bar

X-bar theory is not a module of the Minimalist grammar, but X-bar structures follow directly from the structure building processes. These combine two elements, words or phrases, and select one as the **label**. Maximal projections are simply the furthest an element 'projects' and thus some elements can be words and maximal projections simultaneously. X' categories are those projections which are neither words nor maximal.

This section has briefly sketched Chomsky's 'Bare Phrase Structure' proposals (Chomsky, 1995b), leaving out such important points as adjunction and the abolition of word order effects in favour of a universal (specifier–) head–complement order. This should suffice for the reader who wants to know the basic properties of the system. For more detail the reader is directed towards Chomsky's own work.

Conclusion

This chapter has set out an informal sketch of the Minimalist Programme to give the reader some idea of Chomsky's latest work to date. As can be seen, the thrust of the Programme is to reduce the grammar down to its bare essentials, with no more stipulation than absolutely necessary. Everything is cut out but the interface levels and the minimum of operations. If successful, the Minimalist Programme will achieve high standards of explanation, with most phenomena accounted for by a very small number of assumptions about the structure of the grammar, most of which are necessary for any grammar. Clearly it is early days yet; it remains to be seen how successful the Minimalist Programme will be in pursuing its goal. As Chomsky puts it, 'We are left with hard and challenging questions, of a new order of depth, and prospects for a theory of language with properties that are quite surprising' (Chomsky, 1995b, p. 434). One thing is apparent: given the influence that each successive Chomskyan model has had on the field since 1957, these developments will not be easily ignored.

Principles, Parameters and Operations: Quick Reference List

This first gives the chapter in which the notion is introduced, then any later chapter in which it is revised or rejected, together with appropriate definitions. A brief indication is given of whether the term is roughly associated with early principles and parameters theory, i.e. Government/Binding Theory (GB), or the *Barriers* period (B), or with the Minimalist Programme (MP). The entries are in alphabetical order; this occasionally distorts the name, for example the Economy Principle as given here is usually known as the Principle of Economy.

	Chapter	*Theory*
• **AGR$_o$P Parameter**: in languages like English V cannot cross AGR$_o$P; in French it can	6	B
• **Barriers**	7	B

γ is a Blocking Category for β if and only if γ is not L-marked and γ dominates β

γ is a barrier for β if and only if:
(1) γ is a Blocking Category for β, $\gamma \neq$ IP;
(2) γ dominates a Blocking Category for β, or
(3) γ immediately dominates the governor of β

	Chapter	*Theory*
• **Binding Principles:**	2	GB

A.   An anaphor is bound in a local domain
B.   A pronominal is free in a local domain
C.   A referring expression is free.

	Chapter	*Theory*
• **Case Adjacency Principle**: some languages such as English require Case assigners to be adjacent to the NP that receives Case; others, such as French, have no such requirement	6	GB

	Chapter	Theory
• **Full Interpretation:** 'every element of PF and LF, taken to be the interface of syntax with systems of language use, must receive an appropriate interpretation – must be licensed in the sense indicated.' (Chomsky, 1986a, p. 98)	5	MP
• **Functional Parameterization Hypothesis:** only functional categories have grammatical features such as number, person etc., and only functional categories have parameters	5	B
• **Government:** A syntactic relationship between a governor and an element that is governed. α governs β if and only if (1) α is a governor (e.g. N, V, P, A, etc.) (2) α and β mutually c-command each other (3) if α governs β, then α governs the specifier of β	2 7	GB GB
• **Head Movement Constraint (HMC):** a zero-level category can only move to a position that governs its maximal projection	6	B
• **Head Parameter:** a particular language consistently has the heads on the same side of the complements in all its phrases, whether head-first or head-last	1	GB
• **Lexical Parameterization Hypothesis:** parameterization is essentially lexical	2	B
• **Merge:** 'an operation that forms larger units out of those already constructed' (Chomsky, 1995b, p. 396)	9	MP
• **Minimal Link Condition:** 'α must make the "shortest move"' (Chomsky, 1995b, p. 401)	9	MP
• **Minimality Condition:** nodes become barriers for an element if they immediately dominate the nearest governor of that element	7	B
• **Movement:** a relationship linking the two levels of structural representation:	2	G

— D-structure where basic argument structure is
directly represented
— S-structure, an intermediate level of
representation where certain elements may
have been displaced
— LF, where logical relations such as scope are
directly represented

- **Move α:** where α stands for any category.   6   GB
'The movement operation (henceforth Move α)
is an invariant principle of computation, stating
that a category can be moved to a target
position' (Chomsky and Lasnik, 1993, p. 522).

- **Null Subject Parameter:** 'Null subjects are   8   B
permitted in all and only languages with
morphologically uniform inflectional paradigms'
(Jaeggli and Safir, 1989)

- **Principle of Proper Government:** lexical   2   GB
categories govern properly, non-lexical do not

- **Principle of Subjacency:** no movement can   7   GB
move an element over more than one bounding
node at a time (bounding nodes = S (AGRP)
and NP (DP) in English)

- **Pro-drop Parameter**
whether a language allows null subjects or not
— depends on whether INFL is a proper
governor   2   GB
— depends on morphological uniformity   8   B
— depends on whether affixes are generated in   8   MP
the syntax or in the lexicon

- **Procrastinate:** movement operations should be   9   MP
delayed as long as possible

- **Projection Principle:**   1   GB
'lexical structure must be represented
categorially at every syntactic level'
(Chomsky, 1986a, p. 84)
'Representations at each syntactic level   5   GB
(i.e. LF, D- and S-structure) are projected

from the lexicon, in that they observe the
subcategorisation properties of lexical items'
(Chomsky, 1981a, p. 29)

• **Relativized Minimality** An element will minimally govern its trace if there is no other 'typical potential governor' that is closer to the trace.	7	B
• **Spec/Head Agreement** Agreement between the head of a phrase X and the element which occupies the specifier of that phrase	6	B
• **Spell-Out:** The point in the derivation of a structure at which the phonological information is split off from semantic information, the former going to PF, the latter to LF	9	MP
• **Structure-Dependency Principle** 'all known formal operations in the grammar of English, or of any other language, are structure-dependent' (Chomsky, 1971, p. 30)	1	pre-GB
• **θ-Criterion:** constrains θ-assignment by making certain no element gets more than one θ-role and every θ-role is assigned.	2	GB
'Each argument bears one and only one θ-role, and each θ-role is assigned to one and only one argument' (Chomsky, 1981a, p. 36) Replaced by Full Interpretation	5	GB
• **Wh-Criterion:** All [+Wh] complementizers must contain a [+Wh] element	6	GB
• **X-Bar Principles** — a phrase always contains a head of the same type	4	GB

X" ⟶ specifier X'
— a two-bar category consists of a head that is
   a single-bar, a specifier position, and a
   possible adjunct

X' $\longrightarrow$ X complements
— a single-bar category contains a head with no
   bars and possible complements

X' $\longrightarrow$ X' adjunct
— a single-bar category can also contain a further
   single-bar category and an adjunct

References

Abney, S. P. (1987), *The English Noun Phrase in Its Sentential Aspect*. Ph.D. Thesis, MIT.

Anderson, J. R. (1983), *The Architecture of Cognition*. Cambridge, Mass.: Harvard University Press.

Anderson, S. R. and Keenan, E. L. (1985), Deixis. In T. Shopen (ed.), *Language Typology and Syntactic Description, Volume III*. Cambridge: Cambridge University Press, 259–308.

Aoun, J., Hornstein, N. and Sportiche, D. (1981), Some aspects of wide scope quantification. *Journal of Linguistic Research*, 1, 69–95.

Aoun, J. and Sportiche, D. (1983), On the formal theory of government. *The Linguistic Review*, 2, 211–36.

Atkinson, M. (1992), *Children's Syntax*. Oxford: Blackwell.

Bach, E. (1962), The order of elements in a transformational grammar of German. *Language*, 38, 263–9.

Baker, C. L. (1979), Syntactic theory and the projection problem. *Linguistic Inquiry*, 10/4, 533–81.

Baker, C. L. (1991), The syntax of English *not*: the limits of core grammar. *Linguistic Inquiry*, 22, 387–429.

Belletti, A. (1990), *Generalised Verb Movement*. Turin: Rosenberg and Sellier.

Bellugi, U. and Brown, R. (eds) (1964), *The Acquisition of Language*. Monographs of the Society for Research in Child Development, 29, 92.

Berwick, R. C. (1985), *The Acquisition of Syntactic Knowledge*. Cambridge, Mass.: MIT Press.

Berwick, R. C., and Weinberg, A. S. (1984), *The Grammatical Basis of Linguistic Performance*. Cambridge, Mass.: MIT Press.

Bierwisch, M. (1963), *Grammatik des Deutschen Verbs*. Berlin: Akademie Verlag.

Bley-Vroman, R. W. (1989), The logical problem of second language learning. In S. Gass and J. Schachter (eds), *Linguistic Perspectives on Second Language Acquisition*. Cambridge: Cambridge University Press.

Bley-Vroman, R. W., Felix, S. and Ioup, G. L. (1988), The accessibility of Universal Grammar in adult language learning. *Second Language Research*, 4/1, 1–32.

Bloom, P. (1990), Subjectless sentences in child language. *Linguistic Inquiry*, 21/4, 491–504.

Bloomfield, L. (1933), *Language*. New York: Holt.

Bonet, E. (1990), Subjects in Catalan. In L. C.-S. Cheng and H. Dermidash (eds), *MIT Working Papers in Linguistics*, B. MIT, Cambridge, Mass.

Borer, H. and Wexler, K. (1987), The maturation of syntax. In T. Roeper and E. Williams (eds), *Parameter Setting*. Dordrecht: Reidel, 123–72.

Bosewitz, R. (1987), *Penguin Students' Grammar of English*. Harmondsworth: Penguin.

Botha, R. P. (1989), *Challenging Chomsky: The Generative Garden Game*. Oxford: Blackwell.

Bouchard, D. (1984), *On the Content of Empty Categories*. Dordrecht: Foris.

Braine, M. D. S. (1971), On two types of models of the internalisation of grammars. In D. I. Slobin (ed.), *The Ontogenesis of Grammar*. New York: Academic Press, 153–86.

Brody, M. (1993), θ-theory and arguments. *Linguistic Inquiry*, 24/1, 1–24.

Brown, R. (1973), *A First Language: The Early Stages*. London: Allen and Unwin.

Brown, R. and Hanlon, C. (1970), Derivational complexity and the order of acquisition in child speech. In J. R. Hayes (ed.), *Cognition and the Development of Language*. New York: Wiley.

Bruner, J. (1983), *Child's Talk*. Oxford: Oxford University Press.

Burling, R. (1981), Social constraints on adult language learning. In H. Winitz (ed.), *Native Language and Foreign Language Acquisition*. New York: New York Academy of Sciences, 279–90.

Cancino, H., Rosansky, E. and Schumann, J. (1978), The acquisition of English negative and interrogatives by native Spanish speakers. In E. Hatch (ed.), *Second Language Acquisition*. Rowley, Mass.: Newbury House.

Carroll, S. and Swain, M. (1993), Explicit and implicit negative feedback: an empirical study of the learning of linguistic generalisations. *Studies in Second Language Acquisition*, 15/3, 357–86.

Cazden, C. R. (1972), *Child Language and Education*. New York: Holt, Rinehart, and Winston.

Chien, Y.-C. and Wexler, K. (1987), Children's acquisition of the locality condition on reflexives and pronouns. MS, University of California.

Chomsky, N. (1957), *Syntactic Structures*. The Hague: Mouton.

Chomsky, N. (1959), Review of B. F. Skinner *Verbal Behavior*. *Language*, 35, 26–58.

Chomsky, N. (1964), *Current Issues in Linguistic Theory*. The Hague: Mouton.

Chomsky, N. (1965), *Aspects of the Theory of Syntax*. Cambridge, Mass.: MIT Press.

Chomsky, N. (1969), Linguistics and philosophy. In S. Hook (ed.), *Language and Philosophy*. New York: New York University Press.

Chomsky, N. (1970), Remarks on nominalisation. In R. Jacobs and E. Rosenbaum (eds), *Readings in English Transformational Grammar*. Waltham, Mass.: Ginn and Co.

Chomsky, N. (1971), *Problems of Knowledge and Freedom*. New York: Pantheon.

Chomsky, N. (1972a), *Language and Mind*, enlarged edition. New York: Harcourt Brace Jovanovich.

Chomsky, N. (1972b), Some empirical issues in the theory of transformational grammar. In S. Peters (ed.), *Goals of Linguistic Theory*. New Jersey: Prentice-Hall, 63–130.

Chomsky, N. (1973), Conditions on transformations. In S. R. Anderson and R. Kiparsky (eds), *A Festschrift for Morris Halle*. New York: Holt, Rinehart and Winston.

Chomsky, N. (1976), *Reflections on Language*. London: Temple Smith.

Chomsky, N. (1979), *Language and Responsibility*. Brighton: Harvester Press.

Chomsky, N. (1980a), *Rules and Representations*. Oxford: Basil Blackwell.

Chomsky, N. (1980b), On cognitive structures and their development. In M. Piattelli-Palmarini (ed.), *Language and Learning: The Debate between Jean Piaget and Noam Chomsky*. London: Routledge & Kegan Paul.

Chomsky, N. (1981a), *Lectures on Government and Binding*. Dordrecht: Foris.

Chomsky, N. (1981b), Principles and parameters in syntactic theory. In N. Hornstein and D. Lightfoot (eds), *Explanations in Linguistics*. London: Longman.

Chomsky, N. (1982a), *Some Concepts and Consequences of the Theory of Government and Binding*. Cambridge, Mass.: MIT Press.

Chomsky, N. (1982b), On the representation of form and function. In J. Mehler, E. C. T. Walker and M. F. Garrett (eds), *Perspective on Mental Representation: Experimental and Theoretical Studies of Cognitive Processes and Capacities*. Hillsdale: Erlbaum.

Chomsky, N. (1982c), *The Generative Enterprise: A Discussion with Riny Huybregts and Henk van Riemsdijk*. Dordrecht: Foris.

Chomsky, N. (1986a), *Knowledge of Language: Its Nature, Origin and Use*. New York: Praeger.

Chomsky, N. (1986b), *Barriers*. Cambridge, Mass.: MIT Press.

Chomsky, N. (1987), Transformational Grammar: past, present, and future. In *Studies in English Language and Literature*. Kyoto University, 33–80.

Chomsky, N. (1988), *Language and Problems of Knowledge: The Managua Lectures*. Cambridge, Mass.: MIT Press.

Chomsky, N. (1990), Language and mind. In D. H. Mellor (ed.), *Ways of Communicating*. Cambridge: Cambridge University Press, 56–80.

Chomsky, N. (1991a) Linguistics and adjacent fields: a personal view. In A. Kasher (ed.), *The Chomskyan Turn*. Oxford: Blackwell, 5–23.

Chomsky, N. (1991b), Linguistics and cognitive science: problems and mysteries. In A. Kasher (ed.), *The Chomskyan Turn*. Oxford: Blackwell, 26–53.

Chomsky, N. (1991c), Some notes on economy of derivation and representation. In R. Freidin (ed.), *Principles and Parameters in Comparative Grammar*. Cambridge, Mass.: MIT Press, 417–545; preliminary draft in *MIT Working Papers in Linguistics* (1989), 10, 43–74.

Chomsky, N. (1993), A minimalist program for linguistic theory. In K. Hale and S. J. Keyser (eds), *The View from Building 20*. Cambridge, Mass.: MIT

Press, 1–52; preliminary version in *MIT Occasional Papers in Linguistics* (1992), No. 1.

Chomsky, N. (1995a), Language and nature. *Mind*, 104, 413, 1–62.

Chomsky, N. (1995b), Bare phrase structure. In G. Webelhuth (ed.), *Government and Binding Theory and the Minimalist Programme*. Oxford: Blackwell, 383–440; preliminary version in *MIT Occasional Papers in Linguisitics* (1994), No. 5.

Chomsky, N. and Halle, M. (1968), *The Sound Pattern of English*. New York: Harper and Row.

Chomsky, N. and Lasnik, H. (1977), Filters and control. *Linguistic Inquiry*, 8, 425–504.

Chomsky, N. and Lasnik, H. (1993), Principles and parameters theory. In J. Jacobs, A. von Stechow, W. Sternefeld and T. Vennemann (eds), *Syntax: An International Handbook of Contemporary Research*. Berlin: de Gruyter, 506–69.

Clahsen, H. and Muysken, P. (1986), The availability of universal grammar to adult and child learners – a study of the acquisition of German word order. *Second Language Research*, 2/2, 93–119.

Clahsen, H. and Muysken, P. (1989), The UG paradox in L2 acquisition. *Second Language Research*, 5, 1–29.

Clark, H. H., and Clark, E. V. (1977), *Psychology and Language*. New York: Harcourt Brace Jovanovich.

Cobbett, W. (1819), *A Grammar of the English Language*; reprinted by Oxford University Press, 1984.

Cook, V. J. (1985), Chomsky's Universal Grammar and second language learning. *Applied Linguistics*, 6, 1–18.

Cook, V. J. (1990a), Observational evidence and the UG theory of language acquisition. In I. Roca (ed.), *Logical Issues in Language Acquisition*. Dordrecht: Foris, 33–46.

Cook, V. J. (1990b), Timed comprehension of binding in advanced L2 learners of English. *Language Learning*, 42/4, 557–91.

Cook, V. J. (1991), The poverty-of-the-stimulus argument and multi-competence. *Second Language Research*, 7/2, 103–17.

Cook, V. J. (1993), *Linguistics and Second Language Acquisition*. Basingstoke: Macmillan.

Cook, V. J. (1994), UG and the metaphor of access. In N. Ellis (ed.), *Implicit Learning of Language*. London: Academic Press.

Cook, V. J. (in prep.), *Multi-competence*.

Cromer, R. F. (1987), Language growth with experience without feedback. *Journal of Psycholinguistic Research*. 16/3, 223–31.

Crystal, D. (1991), *A Dictionary of Linguistics and Phonetics*, 3rd edition. Oxford: Blackwell.

Culicover, P. W. (1991), Innate knowledge and linguistic principles. *Behavioral and Brain Sciences*, 14/4, 615–16.

Denison, D. (1994), *English Historical Syntax*. Harlow: Longman.

Deprez, V. and Pierce, A. (1993), Negation and functional categories in early grammar. *Linguistic Inquiry*, 24/1, 25–67.

Deutsch, W., Koster, C. and Koster, J. (1986), What can we learn from children's errors in understanding anaphora? *Linguistics*, 24, 203–25.

de Villiers, J. (1992), On the acquisition of functional categories: a general commentary. In J. M. Meisel (ed.), *The Acquisition of Verb Placement*. Dordrecht: Kluwer, 423–44.

duPlessis, J., Solin, D., Travis, L. and White, L. (1987), UG or not UG, that is the question: a reply to Clahsen and Muysken'. *Second Language Research*, 3/1, 56–75.

Eubank, L. (1992), Verb movement, agreement, and tense in L2 acquisition. In J. M. Meisel (ed.), *The Acquisition of Verb Placement*. Dordrecht: Kluwer, 109–38.

Felix, S. W. (1978), Some differences between first and second language acquisition. In N. Waterson and C. Snow (eds), *The Development of Communication*. New York: Wiley.

Finer, D. (1987), Comments on Solan. In T. Roeper and E. Williams (eds), *Parameters and Linguistic Theory*. Dordrecht: Reidel, 211–20.

Finer, D. and Broselow, E. (1985), Second language acquisition of reflexive binding. *North East Linguistics Society*, 16.

Flynn, S. (1987), *A Parameter-Setting Model of L2 Acquisition*. Dordrecht: Reidel.

Fodor, J. A. (1981), Some notes on what linguistics is about. In N. Block (ed.), *Readings in the Philosophy of Psychology*. London: Methuen, 197–207.

Fodor, J. A. (1983), *The Modularity of Mind*. Cambridge, Mass.: MIT Press.

Freidin, R. (1978), Cyclicity and the theory of grammar. *Linguistic Inquiry*, 9, 519–49.

Freidin, R. (1991), Linguistic theory and language acquisition: a note on structure-dependence. *Behavioral and Brain Sciences*, 14/4, 618–19.

Fukui, N. (1986), *A Theory of Category Projection and its Applications*. Ph.D. Thesis, MIT.

Gardner, B. T., and Gardner, D. A. (1971), Two way communication with an infant chimpanzee. In A. Schrier and F. Stollwitz (eds), *Behavior of Non-Human Primates: vol. 4*. New York: Academic Press.

Garnham, A. (1985), *Psycholinguistics: Central Topics*. London: Methuen.

Gazdar, G. (1987), Generative Grammar. In J. Lyons, R. Coates, M. Deuchar and G. Gazdar (eds), *New Horizons in Linguistics 2*. Harmondsworth: Penguin.

Gazdar, G., Klein, E., Pullum, G. and Sag, I. (1985), *Generalised Phrase Structure Grammar*. Oxford: Basil Blackwell.

Gleitman, L. (1982), Maturational determinants of language growth. *Cognition*, 10, 103–14.

Gleitman, L. (1984), Biological predispositions to learn language. In P. Marler and H. Terrace (eds), *The Biology of Learning*. New York: Springer.

Gold, E. M. (1967), Language identification in the limit. *Information and Control*, 10, 447–74.

Goodluck, H. (1986), Language acquisition and linguistic theory. In P. Fletcher and M. Garman (eds), *Language Acquisition: Studies in First Language Development*. Cambridge. Cambridge University Press, 49–68.

Goodluck, H. (1991), *Language Acquisition: A Linguistic Introduction*. Oxford: Blackwell.

Goodluck, H. and Rochemont, M. (eds) (1992), *Island Constraints*. Dordrecht: Kluwer.

Gopnik, M. and Crago, M. B. (1991), Familial aggregation of a developmental language disorder. *Cognition*, 39, 1–50.

Gould, S. J. (1993), *Eight Little Piggies*. London: Jonathan Cape.

Grimshaw, J. (1979), Complementation selection and the lexicon. *Linguistic Inquiry*, 10, 279–326.

Grimshaw, J. and Rosen, S. T. (1990), Knowledge and obedience: the developmental status of the Binding Theory. *Linguistic Inquiry*, 21, 187–222.

Grodzinsky, Y. and Reinhart, T. T. (1993), The innateness of binding and coreference. *Linguistic Inquiry*, 24/1, 69–101.

Haegeman, L. (1990), Non-overt subjects in diary contexts. In J. Mascaró and M. Nespor (eds), *Grammar in Progress*. Dordrecht: Foris, 167–74.

Haegeman, L. (1994), *Introduction to Government and Binding Theory*, 2nd edition. Oxford: Blackwell.

Haider, H. (1986), V-Second in German. In H. Haider and M. Prinzhorn (eds), *Verb Second Phenomena in Germanic Languages*. Dordrecht: Foris.

Halliday, M. A. K. (1975), *Learning How to Mean*. London: Edward Arnold.

Harris, M. and Coltheart, M. (1986), *Language Processing in Children and Adults*. London: Routledge and Kegan Paul.

Haynes, J. H. (1971), *Morris Minor 1000 Owners Workshop Manual*. Sparkford: Haynes Publications.

Hilles, S. (1991), Access to Universal Grammar in Second Language Acquisition. In L. Eubank (ed.), *Point Counterpoint: Universal Grammar in the Second Language*. Amsterdam: Benjamins, 305–38.

Hirsh-Pasek, K., Treiman, R. and Schneiderman, M. (1984), Brown and Hanlon revisited: mothers' sensitivity to ungrammatical forms. *Journal of Child Language*, 11/1, 81–8.

Horrocks, G. (1987), *Generative Grammar*. Harlow: Longman.

Horvath, J. (1985), *FOCUS in the Theory of Grammar and the Syntax of Hungarian*. Dordrecht: Foris.

Howe, C. (1981), *Acquiring Language in a Conversational Context*. London: Academic Press.

Huang, C.-T. J. (1984), On the distribution and reference of empty pronouns. *Linguistic Inquiry*, 15, 531–74.

Hulk, A. (1987), L'acquisition du français et le parametre pro-drop. In B. Kampers-Manhe and Co Vet (eds), *Etudes de linguistique française offertes à Robert de Dardel*. Amsterdam: Editions Rodopi.

Hyams, N. (1986), *Language Acquisition and the Theory of Parameters*. Dordrecht: Reidel.

Hyams, N. (1989), The null subject parameter in language acquisition. In O. Jaeggli and K. J. Safir (eds), *The Null Subject Parameter*. Dordrecht: Kluwer, 215–38.

Hyams, N. (1992), A reanalysis of null subjects in child language. In

J. Weissenborn, H. Goodluck and T. Roeper (eds), *Theoretical Issues in Language Acquisition*. Hillsdale: Erlbaum, 269–300.

Hyams, N. and Wexler, K. (1993), On the grammatical basis of null subjects in child language. *Linguistic Inquiry*, 24/3, 421–59.

Hymes, D. (1972), Competence and performance in linguistic theory. In R. Huxley and E. Ingram (eds), *Language Acquisition: Models and Methods*. New York: Academic Press.

Iatridou, S. (1990), About AGR(P). *Linguistic Inquiry*, 21, 551–77.

Jaeggli, O. (1986), Passive. *Linguistic Inquiry*, 17, 587–622.

Jaeggli, O. and Safir, K. J. (1989), The null subject parameter and parametric theory. In O. Jaeggli and K. J. Safir (eds), *The Null Subject Parameter*. Dordrecht: Kluwer, 1–44.

Jakubowicz, C. (1984), On markedness and binding principles. *North East Linguistics Society*, 14.

Johnson, J. S. and Newport, E. L. (1991), Critical period effects on universal properties of language: the status of subjacency in a second language. *Cognition*, 39, 215–58.

Joseph, B. D. and Smirniotopoulos, J. C. (1993), The morphology of the modern Greek verb as morphology and not syntax. *Linguistic Inquiry*, 24/2, 388–98.

Kasher, A. (ed.) (1991), *The Chomskyan Turn*. Oxford: Blackwell.

Keenan, E. L., and Comrie, B. (1977), Noun phrase accessibility and universal grammar. *Linguistic Inquiry*, 8, 63–99.

Kenstowicz, M. (1994), *Phonology in Generative Grammar*. Oxford: Blackwell.

King, E. S. (1980), *Speak Malay!* Kuala Lumpur: Eastern Universities Press, Malaysia.

É. Kiss, K. (1987) *Configurationality in Hungarian*. Studies in Natural Language and Linguistic Theory. Dordrecht: Reidel.

Klima, E. S. and Bellugi, U. (1966), Syntactic regularities in the speech of children. In J. Lyons and R. J. Wales (eds), *Psycholinguistics Papers*. Edinburgh: Edinburgh University Press.

Koopman, H. (1984), *The Syntax of Verbs*. Dordrecht: Foris.

Koopman, H. and Sportiche, D. (1991), The position of subjects. *Lingua*, 85, 211–58.

Kubo, M. (1989), Wh-movement in Japanese NPs. In I. Laka and A. Mahajan (eds), *MIT Working Papers in Linguistics*, 10, *Functional Heads and Clause Structure*. MIT, Cambridge, Mass.

Kuroda, S.-Y. (1988), Whether we agree or not: a comparative syntax of English and Japanese. In W. Poser (ed.), *Papers on the Second International Workshop on Japanese Syntax*. CSLI, Stanford University, California.

Lakshmanan, U. (1991), Morphological uniformity and null subjects in child second language acquisition. In L. Eubank (ed.), *Point Counterpoint: Universal Grammar in the Second Language*. Amsterdam: Benjamins, 389–410.

Langacker, R. (1966), On pronominalisation and the chain of command. In D. Reibel and S. Schane (eds.), *Modern Studies in English*. New Jersey: Prentice-Hall.

Lasnik, H. (1993), Case and expletives: notes towards a parametric account. *Linguistic Inquiry*, 23, 381–405.

Lasnik, H. and Saito, M. (1984), On the nature of proper government. *Linguistic Inquiry*, 15, 235–89.

Lenneberg, E. H. (1967), *Biological Foundations of Language*. New York: Wiley.

Liceras, J. M. (1989), On some properties of the 'pro-drop' parameter: looking for missing subjects in non-native Spanish. In S. M. Gass and J. Schachter (eds), *Linguistic Perspectives on Second Language Acquisition*. Cambridge: Cambridge University Press, 109–33.

Lightfoot, D. (1982), *The Language Lottery: Toward a Biology of Grammars*. Cambridge, Mass.: MIT Press.

Lightfoot, D. (1989), The child's trigger experience: degree-0 learnability. *Behavioral and Brain Sciences*, 12/2, 321–34.

Lightfoot, D. (1991), *How to Set Parameters: Arguments from Language Change*. Cambridge, Mass.: MIT Press.

Lightfoot, D. and Hornstein, N. (eds) (1994), *Verb Movement*. Cambridge: Cambridge University Press.

Lovelace, E. (1985), *The Dragon Can't Dance*. London: Longman.

Lust, B., Loveland, K. and Kornet, R. (1980), The development of anaphora in the first language: syntactic and pragmatic constraints. *Linguistic Analysis*, 6/4, 359–92.

Lust, B., Mazuka, R., Martahardjone, G. and Yoon, J. M. (1989), On parameter setting in first language acquisition: the case of the Binding Theory. Paper presented at GLOW, Utrecht.

Malinowski, B. (1923), The problem of meaning in primitive languages. In C. K. Ogden and I. A. Richards (eds), *The Meaning of Meaning*. London: Routledge & Kegan Paul.

Manzini, M. R. (1983), On control and control theory. *Linguistic Inquiry*, 14, 421–46.

Marantz, A. (1995), The Minimalist Programme. In G. Webelhuth (ed.), *Government and Binding Theory and the Minimalist Programme*. Oxford: Blackwell, 351–84.

McCabe, C. (1986), *The Face on the Cutting-Room Floor*. Harmondsworth: Penguin.

McCawley, J. D. (1992), A note on auxiliary verbs and language acquisition. *Journal of Linguistics*, 28/2, 445–52.

McDaniel, D. and Cairns, H. S. (1990), The child as informant: eliciting linguistic intuitions from young children. *Journal of Psycholinguistic Research*, 19/5, 331–44.

McLelland, J. L., Rumelhart, D. E. and the PDP Research Group (1986), *Parallel Distributed Processing: Volume 2. Psychological and Biological Models*. Cambridge, Mass.: MIT Press.

McNeill, D. (1966), Developmental psycholinguistics. In F. Smith and G. A. Miller (eds), *The Genesis of Language: A Psycholinguistic Approach*. Cambridge, Mass.: MIT Press.

Meisel, J. M. (1990), INFL-ection: subjects and subject–verb agreement. In

J. M. Meisel (ed.), *Two First Languages: Early Grammatical Development in Bilingual Children*. Dordrecht: Foris, 237–300.

Meisel, J. M. (1991), Principles of Universal Grammar and strategies of language learning: some similarities and differences between first and second language acquisition. In L. Eubank (ed.), *Point Counterpoint: Universal Grammar in the Second Language*. Amsterdam: Benjamins, 231–76.

Meisel, J. M. (ed.) (1992), *The Acquisition of Verb Placement*. Dordrecht: Kluwer.

Meisel, J. M., and Müller, N. (1992), Finiteness and verb placement in early child grammars. In J. M. Meisel (ed.), *The Acquisition of Verb Placement*. Dordrecht: Kluwer, 109–38.

Montalbetti, M. and Wexler, K. (1985), Binding is linking. *Proceedings of the Western Conference on Formal Linguistics*, 4, 225–45

Morgan, J. L. (1986), *From Simple Input to Complex Grammar*. Cambridge, Mass.: MIT Press.

Mühlhäusler, P. and Harré, R. (1990), *Pronouns and People: The Linguistic Construction of Social and Personal Identity*. Oxford: Blackwell.

Nelson, K. E., Carskaddon, G. and Bonvillain, J. D. (1973), Syntactic acquisition: impact of experimental variation in adult verbal interaction with the child. *Child Development*, 44, 497–504.

Neville, H., Nichol, J. L., Barss, A., Forster, K. I. and Garrett, M. F. (1991), Syntactically based sentence processing classes: evidence from event-related brain potentials. *Journal of Cognitive Neuroscience*, 3/2, 151–65.

Newmeyer, F. J. (1994), Parametric variation and pragmatics: the case of preposition stranding. Paper presented at First International Linguistics Conference, University of Sidi Mohamed Ben Abdellah, Fes, March.

Newport, E. L. (1976), Motherese: the speech of mothers to young children. In N. Castellan, D. Pisoni and G. Potts (eds), *Cognitive Theory: Vol 2*. Hillsdale: Erlbaum.

Newson, M. (1990), Dependencies in the lexical setting of parameters: a solution to the undergeneralisation problem. In I. Roca (ed.), *Logical Issues in Language Acquisition*. Dordrecht: Foris.

Newson, M. (1991), Negative phrases: further considerations. Paper presented at the LAGB meeting, York University.

Ochs, E. and Schieffelin, B. (1984), Language acquisition and socialisation: three developmental stories and their implications. In R. Shweder and R. Levine (eds), *Culture and Its Acquisition*. New York: Cambridge University Press.

Otsu, Y. and Naoi, K. (1986), Structure-dependence in L2 acquisition. Paper presented at JACET, Keio University, Tokyo, September. Cited in White (1989).

Ouhalla, J. (1991), *Functional Categories and Parametric Variation*. London: Routledge.

Ouhalla, J. (1994), *Introducing Transformational Grammar*. London: Edward Arnold.

Paivio, A. and Begg, I. (1981), *Psychology of Language*. New York: Prentice-Hall.

Paley, W. (1802), *Natural Theology*. London: E. Paulder.

Patterson, F. G. (1981), Innovative uses of language by a gorilla: a case study. In K. Nelson (ed.), *Children's Language: Vol. 2.* New York: Gardner.

Penfield, W. G. and Roberts, L. (1959), *Speech and Brain Mechanisms.* New Jersey: Princeton University Press.

Pesetsky, D. (1982), *Paths and Categories.* Ph.D. Thesis, MIT.

Piaget, J. (1980), The psychogenesis of knowledge and its epistemological significance. In M. Piattelli-Palmarini (ed.), *Language and Learning.* London: Routledge and Kegan Paul.

Piattelli-Palmarini, M. (1980) (ed.), *Language and Learning: The Debate between Jean Piaget and Noam Chomsky.* London: Routledge and Kegan Paul.

Piercy, Marge (1979), *Woman on the Edge of Time.* London: Woman's Press Ltd.

Pinker, S. (1984), *Language Learnability and Language Development.* Cambridge, Mass.: Harvard University Press.

Pinker, S., Lebeaux, D. and Frost, L. (1987), Productivity and constraints in the acquisition of the passive. *Cognition,* 26, 195–267.

Platt, C. B. and McWhinney, B. (1983), Error assimilation as a mechanism in language learning. *Journal of Child Language,* 10, 104–14.

Pollard, C. and Sag, I. A. (1994), *Head-driven Phrase Structure Grammar.* Stanford: Stanford University Press.

Pollock, J.-Y. (1989), Verb movement, universal grammar, and the structure of IP. *Linguistic Inquiry,* 20, 365–424.

Priestley, J. (1761), *The Rudiments of English Grammar.* London: R. Griffiths.

Radford, A. (1986), Small children's small clauses. *Bangor Research Papers in Linguistics,* 1, 1–38.

Radford, A. (1990), *Syntactic Theory and the Acquisition of English Syntax.* Oxford: Blackwell.

Reinhart, T. (1976), The Syntactic Domain of Anaphora. Ph.D. Thesis, MIT.

Ritchie, W. C. (1983), Universal Grammar and Second Language Acquisition. In D. Rogers and J. A. Sloboda (eds), *The Acquisition of Symbolic Skills.* New York: Plenum Press.

Rizzi, L. (1982), *Issues in Italian Syntax.* Dordrecht: Foris.

Rizzi, L. (1986), Null objects in Italian and the theory of *pro. Linguistic Inquiry,* 17, 501–57.

Rizzi, L. (1990), *Relativised Minimality.* Cambridge, Mass.: MIT Press.

Rizzi, L. (1991), Residual verb second and the Wh-criterion. *Technical Reports in Formal and Computational Linguistics.* Faculty of Letters, University of Geneva.

Rizzi, L. (1994), Early null subjects and root null subjects. In T. Hoekstra and B. F. Schwartz (eds), *Language Acquisition Studies in Generative Grammar.* Amsterdam: Benjamins, 151–76.

Roca, I. (1994), *Generative Phonology.* London: Routledge.

Roeper, T. and Williams, E. (eds) (1987), *Parameter Setting.* Dordrecht: Reidel.

Rose, S. (1992), *The Making of Memory.* London: Bantam.

Ross, J. R. (1967), *Constraints on Variables in Syntax,* Ph.D. Thesis, MIT.

Rumbaugh, D. M. (ed.) (1977), *Language Learning by a Chimpanzee: The Lana Project.* New York: Academic Press.

Rumelhart, D. E. and McLelland, J. L. (1986), On learning the past tenses of English verbs. In J. L. McLelland, D. E. Rumelhart and the PDP Research Group. *Parallel Distributed Processing: Vol. 2: Psychological and Biological Models*. Cambridge, Mass.: MIT Press, 216–71.

Salkie, R. (1990), *The Chomsky Update*. London: Unwin Hyman.

Sartre, J.-P. (1957), *Being and Nothingness*. London: Methuen (trans. Hazel Barnes).

Schachter, J. (1988), Second Language Acquisition and its relationship to Universal Grammar. *Applied Linguistics*, 9/3, 219–35.

Sharpe, T. (1982), *Vintage Stuff*. London: Secker and Warburg.

Singleton, D. (1989), *Language Acquisition: The Age Factor*. Clevedon: Multilingual Matters.

Skinner, B. F. (1957), *Verbal Behavior*. New York: Appleton-Century-Crofts.

Smith, N. (1973), *The Acquisition of Phonology: A Case Study*. Cambridge: Cambridge University Press.

Solan, L. (1987), Parameter setting and the development of pronouns and reflexives. In T. Roeper and E. Williams (eds), *Parameters and Linguistic Theory*. Dordrecht: Reidel, 189–210.

Speas, M. (1994), Null arguments in a theory of economy of projection. *North East Linguistics Society*, 24, 179–208.

Spencer, A. (1992), Object agreement in Chukchee. In A. Radford (ed.), *Functional Categories: Their Nature and Acquisition*. Occasional Papers No. 33, Department of Language and Linguistics, University of Essex.

Stowell, T. (1981), *Origins of Phrase Structure*, Ph.D. Thesis, MIT.

Svartvik, J. (1966), *On Voice in the English Verb*. The Hague: Mouton.

Thiersch, C. L. (1978), *Topics in German Syntax*. Ph.D. Thesis, MIT.

Thomas, M. (1989), The interpretation of English reflexive pronouns by non-native speakers. *Studies in Second Language Acquisition*, 11, 3.

Tomlin, R. S. (1986), *Basic Word Order: Functional Principles*. London: Croom Helm.

Towell, R. and Hawkins, R. (1994), *Approaches to Second Language Acquisition*. Clevedon: Multilingual Matters.

Travis, L. (1984), Parameters and Effects of Word Order Variation. Ph.D. Thesis, MIT.

Tremaine, R. V. (1975), Piagetan equilibration processes in syntax learning. In D. P. Dato (ed.), *Psycholinguistics: Theory and Applications*. Washington, D.C.: Georgetown University Round Table.

Tsimpli, I.-M. and Roussou, A. (1991), Parameter-resetting in L2. *UCL Working Papers in Linguistics*, 3, 149–89.

Vainikka, A. and Young-Scholten, M. (1991), Verb raising in Second Language Acquisition: the early stages. *Theories des Lexikons*, 4, Düsseldorf University.

Valian, V. (1989), Children's production of subjects: competence, performance, and the null subject parameter. *Papers and Reports on Child Language Development*, 28, 156–63.

van Gelderen, E. (1993), *The Rise of Functional Categories*. Amsterdam: Benjamins.

van Riemsdijk, H. and Williams, E. (1986), *Introduction to the Theory of Grammar*. Cambridge, Mass.: MIT Press.

Vikner, S. (1995), *Verb Movement and Expletive Subjects in the Germanic Languages*. New York: Oxford University Press.

Wallman, J. (1992), *Aping Language*. Cambridge: Cambridge University Press.

Weissenborn, J. (1992), Null subjects in early grammars: implications for parameter-setting theories. In J. Weissenborn et al. (eds), *Theoretical Issues in Language Acquisition*. Hillsdale: Erlbaum, 269–300.

Weissenborn, J., Goodluck, H. and Roeper, T. (1992a) Introduction. In J. Weissenborn et al. (eds), *Theoretical Issues in Language Acquisition*. Hillsdale: Erlbaum, 1–23.

Weissenborn, J., Goodluck, H. and Roeper, T. (1992b) (eds), *Theoretical Issues in Language Acquisition*. Hillsdale: Erlbaum.

Wells, C. G. (1985), *Language Development in the Pre-school Years*. Cambridge: Cambridge University Press.

Wexler, K. (1994), Finiteness and head movement in early child language. In D. Lightfoot and N. Hornstein (eds), *Verb Movement*. Cambridge: Cambridge University Press, 305–50.

Wexler, K. and Chien, Y.-C. (1985), The development of lexical anaphors and pronouns. *Papers and Reports on Child Language Development*, 24. Stanford: Stanford University Press.

Wexler, K. and Culicover, P. W. (1980), *Formal Principles of Language Acquisition*. Cambridge, Mass.: MIT Press.

Wexler, P. and Manzini, R. (1987), Parameters and learnability in Binding Theory. In T. Roeper and E. Williams (eds), *Parameter Setting*. Dordrecht: Reidel, 41–76.

White, L. (1986), Implications of parametric variation for adult second language acquisition: an investigation of the pro-drop parameter. In V. J. Cook (ed.), *Experimental Approaches to Second Language Acquisition*. Oxford: Pergamon.

White, L. (1989), *Universal Grammar and Second Language Acquisition*. Amsterdam: Benjamins.

White, L. (1992), Adverb placement in second language acquisition: the effects of positive and negative evidence in the classroom. *Second Language Research*, 7, 2, 133–61.

Zobl, H. (1990), Evidence for parameter-sensitive acquisition: a contribution to the domain-specific versus central processes debate. *Second Language Research*, 6/1, 1–38.

Index